VIOLETA TRECIOKAITE

BLACKMAIL

Violeta Treciokaite "Blackmail"

You can also order this book at the address:

Jurate Somerville
224304 E 421 PR SE
Kennewick, WA 99337
(509) 582-6403
Eagleview1@live.com

Cover page is created by using an image at http://freebigpictures.com

Printed in the United States of America

ISBN: 978-0-692-02097-5
Library of Congress Control Number :   2014933713

Following the Molotov-Ribbentrop Pact of 1939, the Soviet Army entered eastern Poland as well as military bases in the Baltic states, which were granted after U.S.S.R. had threatened the three countries with military invasion. In June 1940, the Red Army occupied all of the territory of Estonia, Latvia, and Lithuania, and the Red Army installed new, pro-Soviet governments in all three countries. Following rigged elections, in which only pro-communist candidates were allowed to run, the newly "elected" parliaments of the three countries formally applied to "join" the Soviet Union in August 1940 and were incorporated into it as the Estonian Soviet Socialist Republic, the Latvian Soviet Socialist Republic, and the Lithuanian Soviet Socialist Republic.

Repressions, executions, and mass deportations followed after that in the Baltics. Deportations were used as a part of the Soviet Union's attempts, along with instituting the Russian Language as the only working language and other such tactics, at sovietization of its occupied territories. The Soviet government deported more than 200,000 people from the Baltic states in 1940-1953 to remote, inhospitable areas of the Soviet Union. In addition, at least 75,000 were sent to Gulag. 10% of the entire adult Baltic population was deported or sent to labor camps.

The forced collectivization of agriculture began in 1947, and was completed after the mass deportation in March 1949. Private farms were confiscated, and farmers were made to join the collective farms. In all three countries, Baltic partisans, known colloquially as the Forest Brothers, Latvian national partisans, and Lithuanian partisans, waged unsuccessful guerrilla warfare against the Soviet occupation for the next eight years in a bid to regain their nations' independence. Although the armed resistance was defeated, the population remained anti-Soviet...

CONTENTS

DEPORTATION

Vilnius, March 1946

Today probably more than ever during the past few years, Bronius Adomaitis awoke after a good night's sleep. Lately anxiety had been chasing him during most days, never allowing him to relax. Being constantly tortured by the same thoughts, most men can get used to almost anything. This had happened to Adomaitis; he had become used to the ill-fated events in his life just like other ordinary people in similar situations.

Many families had become used to the new government order imposed on them. Such was the regime of the Soviet government. Every day innocent people were being persecuted. It had been happening for a period of a few years now, causing people to fear what the future might bring to their families and to the whole county of Lithuania. People living under such conditions were accustomed not so much to their fears as to the fact that they had been destroyed morally.

Feeling a little depressed upon returning home from work the night before, Adomaitis had gone to bed early and slept without waking up once. This particular morning, he felt well rested and in fairy cheerful mood. After a modest breakfast, he left for work.

Deep in his heart, he had to admit that his job had not been making him happy lately. The reason for that was fear. Quite a few of his co-workers in Bronius' same department had not returned to their homes after their workday was over. People did not really know what had happened to them. They all simply felt that they probably had become the victims of Red Army executioners.

Every day Bronius's workday started at nine in the morning. He left his flat on this particular day earlier than usual. Although he never was early for work, this time some imperceptible power drove him out of his flat an entire half an hour earlier than normal.

As soon as he stepped outside, the pleasant but still cool spring air welcomed him. The large oblong courtyard paving stones were covered with heavy dew because of the fluctuations in temperature. He walked slowly accompanied by wonderful, bright spring sunbeams.

One could say it was a nice day like none had been thus far. It had been a couple of weeks since the warm season started, and the trees cheerfully had been broken into leaf after the first rainstorm. People gladly welcomed the spring. This season of the year brought life and hope to most human beings.

It was no wonder that Adomaitis also was full of energy as he walked briskly along the pavement. In fact, he was in such a good mood that he could barely feel the ground beneath his feet. He kept going with his chest thrust forward. He was filled with pleasant feelings. He never suspected anything bad might be lurking down the road for him over the course of this beautiful, sunny day.

When he arrived at his office, he politely greeted the staff as usual, shook hands with his closest colleagues, and exchanged a few words with them about the weather.

He sat down at his desk and started working on the same tasks he had to perform every single day. Being pretty occupied with his work, he did not notice when a whole hour had passed by. He probably would have even missed his lunch today. This had already happened a few times before, when he became deeply involved with his tasks. The secretary walked in suddenly and broke his concentration.

She said, "Director asked you to come and see him."

Adomaitis cast a puzzled glance at her. He did not have enough time to come to his senses in order to inquire as to why he was being called to the director's office. One more second passed and the secretary was gone leaving him scratching his head. A whole torrent of questions suddenly flooded his mind.

"What does Director want from me?" he asked himself.

After all, Director had never before invited him personally and, not to mention, so formally through his secretary. Usually the supervisor notified Bronius Adomaitis about anything that needed to be done at work. Now, suddenly, he was being called to see the director himself. For some reason, Adomaitis started feeling a slight fear creeping into his heart. What could he have done at that moment? Certainly, he could not leave the top person of the factory waiting for him in vain. One way or another, soon he would find out everything for himself.

Disturbing thoughts flashed through his mind while he climbed the stairs. They danced in his head while he hopelessly tried to remember any act of misconduct. He kept asking himself if maybe he had been late to work or made some mistake filling out documents. Maybe he had leaked some careless words. Because of the latter, quite a few of his former associates had been interrogated at the NKVD (People's Commissariat of Internal Affairs) building.

Soon he was at the director's office door, when the latest idea rushed into his head. At this particular moment, there was really no time to hesitate. Adomaitis heard footsteps behind him on the stairway. They prompted him to knock with a trembling hand on the tall wooden door. He did not expect to hear a welcoming, "Come in" since he knew that it was impossible to hear anything through the heavy door. Therefore, he gathered himself to open it bravely.

Adomaitis walked inside and quite firmly said, "Sir, you asked me to come and see you?"

"Yes, yes, come closer, please. There is somebody here who wants to talk to you," Director said.

Director, with his head slightly tilted to the right, pointed with his eyes at the stranger in the room. Adomaitis now noticed a small but rather full-bodied man with a face like an owl sunken deeply into an armchair. Adomaitis also noticed his immediate supervisor standing by the window. The supervisor cast a couple of somewhat indifferent glances at Bronius Adomaitis, which disturbed his composure.

Bronius thought, "What does this midget want from me? I wonder what his intentions are. Probably not good. There must be more to this situation than meets the eye."

Everybody around Bronius was acting very official. He wondered, moreover, why his supervisor had not come right to Adomaitis as he usually did. Why had not he presented the matter personally and without beating around the bush, so Adomaitis would be prepared?

"Mr. Adomaitis, have you ever worked as an activist?" the little man in the armchair came straight to the point.

"There the dog lies buried," thought Adomaitis. "Maybe some imprudent words have slipped out of my mouth. Is it why this short man with a bird's face has come here and is ready to start some kind of moral extortion?"

"Yes, I have, perhaps a couple of times," he responded to the question.

"Great! That tells me you are familiar with this type of work."

"What does this owl mean? It feels like he is interrogating me," Adomaitis thought. He responded, "I hardly have any experience doing this kind of activity. I only helped the staff at the University with the election preparations a couple of times."

"Well, I think it is good enough," Mr. Owl-face continued. "I'm looking for people exactly like you who are familiar with moving other people to action. We are going to send you on a business trip. Here is the voucher. You need to sign it in order to receive the travel allowance."

Director stretched out a clean piece of paper to Adomaitis.

"How long will I have to be gone?" Bronius asked.

"We don't know yet. However, you can have the advance money today. I will inform you about the duration of this trip later."

"I don't know how much money I will need since it's unclear yet how many days I will be away from work."

"Take more money, you'll need it. It can't hurt if, at the end of your trip, there is some left."

For a moment, Adomaitis felt puzzled not knowing how much money to ask for. He remembered when he had gone on a business trip previously, and he hadn't known how much to ask for then, too. The accountant at work had refused to give him the amount he had asked for. Therefore, he was hesitant to name a specific amount. What if he asked for too much? He knew he might not get it. In addition, if he requested too little, it might not be enough to pay for his living costs while gone.

"Okay, I will sign the voucher. I'm just not sure how much to ask for."

"Ask for as much as you want," suggested Director.

Thinking the conversation was over, Adomaitis rose from his chair and headed toward the door, but the "owl-man" stopped him.

"We're not finished here," he said. "You need to fill out an application." For some reason, Adomaitis started sensing the familiar feeling of anxiety slowly creeping up his throat. He sat back down in front of Director and quickly scribbled on the paper in front of him the amount of five hundred rubles. He was certain they would not give him so much money. However, as soon as he put his signature on the voucher and application, Director affixed a seal to it and called their accountant and cashier to come to his office.

The money was immediately paid right then in the Director's office. At that moment, Adomaitis was amazed at the swift movement of the office administration. He recalled his earlier business trips. Then it was not as easy to get the assigned money since the cashier had to go to the bank in order to get the money, which had taken her the whole day. Sometimes one day was not enough to get ready for a work trip, and Adomaitis had to keep running around the building knocking on the doors of different staff members getting signatures until every requirement was met and every little detail was arranged. Nevertheless, today, without even leaving Director's office, everything was taken care of efficiently and quickly.

In addition, two more candidates were found to go along with him on this business trip. Adomaitis continued to be amazed when the other peoples' trips were organized right there, too, with no one leaving the room. When all the documents were in order, the little man rose out of an armchair and announced, "Now we can go."

"I should notify my family and my landlady about the trip, and, if you don't mind, I would also like to take some food with me," said Adomaitis.

"For now, follow me, please, and I will let you swing by your homes later."

Soon, they came to the Executive Committee Building, which was crammed full of people. People were crowded everywhere in the corridors and on the stairs. With great difficulty, Adomaitis, his two co-workers, and the man they were following forced their bodies through the crowd of people and found themselves in a big room that was also filled with people.

In the corner of the room, a little underling was sitting at a low, small table. A long line of people stretched in front of him. The underling was leaning low over the table registering everyone's names into a journal. The three new walk-inns were told to go to the end of the line. As soon as their names were put on the list, the little officer rose up from the table, disappeared, and never returned.

Another underling came in and rather imperiously ordered everyone to stay where they were. In a loud, distinct voice, he announced his name and asked people to remain in their places in the room so that he would not have search for anyone. He told them that soon they all would need to leave the building.

Less than half an hour later, another "master" appeared. Without even introducing himself, he commanded loudly, "Let's go, everyone!"

Adomaitis and his small group of people forced their way through the crowd, left the room, and descended to the second floor. Soon, they found themselves on the sidewalk where a few trucks were waiting on the street. Two of the trucks were filled with people sitting almost on top of each other on benches. They looked just like Adomaitis felt - confused and scared. Bronius Adomaitis realized his two partners and he would also soon be sitting in the back of a truck.

Without hesitation, he walked back inside the building and approached one of the officers asking if he might be allowed to go home and pick up some things to take with him. That was not fated to happen, however. The officer just bawled the order again and even accused him of planning sabotage. Adomaitis did not dare to resort to asking for help from the infuriated Russian officers who acted like dogs just broken off their chains.

Upon finding himself in the back of one of the trucks, Adomaitis sat quietly like everyone else. Apparently, the other passengers had also been warned not to leave or speak, because no one uttered a word. All of them sat like some kind of prisoners with their heads down, all quiet and deep in grievous thoughts. Their faces reflected deep concern that apparently was stirred up because of the unknown awaiting them.

Soon four more trucks were filled with more men. An extra officer was assigned to each truck. Every officer occupied the place next to the driver. About an hour later, all the trucks drove off and began slowly climbing up steep Basanavicius Street. After passing the Russian Orthodox Church and just before reaching the building with white columns, the trucks stopped at the end of yet another relatively long queue of lorries.

The Russian officers had ordered the passengers to stay in the trucks. People sat silently and, without questioning, obeyed the order.

Soon ten additional trucks full of men were lined up behind the lorry that Bronius was in. Finally, at noon, the convoy of lorries took off and, at sixty kilometers per hour, started their journey down Red Army Boulevard.

After the trucks had turned onto Gardinas Highway and were just passing the village of Kazbejai, an elderly man knocked on the wall of the truck cab asking the driver to stop the truck. He told the driver that he lived in this village and that his house was only few meters away from the road. He begged the driver to let him quickly run into his house in order to get some food and, at the same time, let his family know that he was going away so that they would not be looking for him.

The driver did not stop the truck. Instead, the officer sitting next to the driver shouted for the old man to shut up.

For a few hours, the convoy with the trucks trundled down the highway, and nobody knew where and for what purpose they were going, but each person sitting in the lorries has carried a foreboding of an evil and fear in their hearts and minds.

The trip was not an easy one. Everybody was badly jolted while being driven at a high speed on a road that had become very rough because of being traveled on by countless lorries, tanks, and cars during World War II. It seemed to Adomaitis that his guts had been shaken down because not only his loins hurt but all his intestines hurt as well. It felt as if his insides were turning, twisting, and cramping.

Moreover, the huge clouds of dust raised by the great number of vehicles trundling the dirty road made breathing difficult, in addition to the fact that it already was an unbearably stifling hot day.

People in the trucks felt like prisoners and slaves who had been collected from their workplaces and taken to places unknown.

The trucks lumbered past Pirciupis. Before Valkininkai, the convoy turned from the highway to the left and stopped in a large forested area where machines were arranged in rows for a military procedure.

People finally were allowed to get out of the trucks and shake off the dust. With sighs of relief, they set down under the trees to rest. Some of men found it more comfortable to lie down on the grass. One Russian officer walked by and told them not to go off into the forest.

Most of the men had extremely dry palates due to the nasty dust, which made them extremely thirsty. However, there was no water anywhere near and no one was allowed to go in search of it. Officers kept walking by and quickly turned back even those who had to relieve themselves, forcing them to carry on their private affairs in the presence of all.

After about an hour, the order was given for everyone to get back into the trucks. Soon, the vehicles one by one left Rudininkai Forest and started rolling quickly down the highway. The people were again jolted back and forth, but no one paid any attention.

Finally, the convoy crossed into the second Varena town. Everyone was released from the trucks and allowed to roam around the city for a half an hour. After that, in compliance with their orders, they were to come straight back to the NKVD Building. They had been allowed to leave so that the men could buy some food to eat.

Indeed, upon receiving permission to go to town, many poured into Varena looking for the grocery store. Adomaitis and his new companions were quick in finding the bakery where some people were already waiting in line. As soon as they purchased few loaves of bread, they found close to hundred of the other men had lined up behind them.

The bakery was small and was unable to provide enough bread for such an influx of people. It was no wonder that many of the men were left just as hungry walking back to the NKVD Building as they had been to begin with.

They approached a large fenced area featuring a tall brick wall with several rows of a barbed wire on the top. The huge metal doors of the gate were wide open with two soldiers standing on guard. The men could freely come inside, but they were not allowed to leave. Those wishing to get back outside the gate were harshly poked with bayonets positioned on the soldiers' rifles.

Adomaitis felt satiated after eating almost half of a loaf of bread. He began to make himself familiar with his surroundings. There were people of diverse backgrounds among the civilians and the military staff. There were people of various nationalities present as well. He heard many different languages spoken, including Lithuanian, Russian, Polish, Belorussian, and Yiddish.

The soldiers walking around were all armed. However, Adomaitis could also see a rifle hanging here and there on the shoulders of some civilian men as well. Added to all of the chaos were two armored trucks sitting in the middle of the big yard.

When it got close to evening, everyone was handed a weapon. They each received a rifle along with forty bullets. The bullets were not in iron rings but were loose.

Adomaitis had to wait in a long line to get his rifle. He had no desire to have a weapon because he had not wanted to get involved in any of the propaganda affairs in the first place. At the very last moment, however, he changed his mind. He saw that the men who refused to take a weapon were isolated with guards monitoring them. However, those who took the guns were seated back into the trucks.

Two generals, Macijauskas and Karvelis, went up to the group that had refused to take weapons. They wanted to know why the men would not comply with the order to be armed.

The bravest one of men started talking, "I am a teacher. Therefore, my profession requires implanting trust in people and not promoting violence. You are literally forcing me to take a gun against my free will when I don't even have the slightest idea how to use it. How can I convince people doing anything, while I'm holding a gun in my hands? I can't show up in a village looking like that! What would I say to the locals anyway? I refuse to do it! I consider myself a person of high moral values, and I choose, by my own free will, to act but not be forced to do something with guns. Everybody knows me in the area and they expect me to be a good example."

"Take him to the Military Procurator," General Macijauskas commanded the officer standing nearby.

The officer in the midst of all the people observing this scene walked up to the teacher and took him away.

Upon seeing this, Adomaitis lost all his desire to criticize Russian officers about anything. He meekly took the riffle and stuffed his pockets up to the top with the bullets. Soon, he was once again sitting in the back of a truck ready to go wherever they sent him.

The colonnade of four trucks left the NKVD fenced territory and soon was flying along the highway raising big clouds of dust. The fiery ball of the sun was already hanging over the western horizon when they passed the town of Perloja. However, Bronius could not bring himself to enjoy the beautiful sunset. Instead, he blankly gazed at the bushes streaking past on the sides of the road.

The officers in the cabs of the trucks were growing restless. The land of an enslaved nation was apparently burning under their feet. Soon, the column of trucks reduced their speed and, before the bushes ended, came to a halt.

All the military officers jumped out of the trucks and started walking ahead on foot with their guns pointing forward, ready for any surprises. When they got satisfied that there was no resistance to their journey, they boarded the trucks and ordered the drivers to continue.

The sun was already hidden behind the clouds and the sky growing dark when they drove into the town of Merkine. There were already some trucks full of men who had apparently arrived before them.

The officer in charge of each truck warned the passengers not to scatter themselves around in order to make it easy to find them if it became necessary.

A dark whitish veil of mist, growing slowly, had already enclosed the town. Nevertheless, the Merkine farmers' market was still crowded with people. All of them were armed. They kept pushing each other from one place to the other not knowing where to take shelter or what to do next.

Adomaitis acted like the others. He was marking time and making no headway. He went near a large building, the Department of the Executive Committee. There were so many people around the building, and Adomaitis had considerable trouble getting inside.

A large kerosene lamp was burning lighting up a large portion of the huge room already packed with people. Some just sat dozing on the floor with their backs against a wall, while others stood resting on their riffles. Several other men were sitting on the tables.

Most of those in the room talked quite loudly and resentment was in the air. They wanted to hear the truth concerning why they had been taken from their work and their families and brought here. Even without any explanations, they all knew in their hearts that the evil Russian government was to blame for their distressful situation. They found themselves crammed into this strange place like some kind of animals.

Adomaitis was able to find an empty place by the wall and sat down on the floor. He was so exhausted that he soon began to doze while leaning upon his gun. Bronius was not able, however, to get much sleep. A loud noise coming from the crowd soon woke him. He rubbed his eyes and began looking around concernedly, while trying to find out what was happening. Bronius assumed that some officials had shown up while he was asleep because he heard people expressing all kinds of concerns.

Mostly, people were asking for the food. They were angry because they had not eaten since the early morning. Others in the group were insisting on shelter in order to get some rest. An official was trying to explain something to the unhappy crowd, but Adomaitis did not want to hear it. He left the room and soon found himself outside.

The weather was still warm, and there was quiet in the yard now. He sat down on the ground, pulled out his remaining piece of bread, and started chewing on it. He quickly ate it all and resumed his nap.

Soon, the night sank into the darkness, and midnight had arrived. Once again, people started bustling inside the building. Someone woke Adomaitis up from his troubled sleep.

He heard a stranger whispering in the dark, "Get up, we must leave now."

Bronius rubbed his sleepy eyes, got up with difficulty, and mixed in with the flow of people slowly walking in one direction in the early morning darkness. When they reached a large building, another crowd of people was already waiting by the brick fence. The black metal gate was closed. No one was allowed to go inside. When someone came too close to the gate, the guards gave a harsh warning to leave.

People in the crowd were guessing how long they would have to stand there. No one dared to resist, they simply stood there waiting quietly and humbly.

At last, those gates of "hell" opened widely. The group carefully walked through and found themselves in a spacious courtyard. The silhouettes of armored trucks with small caliber cannons could still be seen through the thick veil of darkness.

The crowd was led into a big hall. There, a few kerosene lamps were brightly burning and lighting the premises well. At the very end of the room, there was a long table where several uniformed officers and a few civilians had their heads together quietly discussing something.

Somehow, all the people managed to crush themselves into the hall. The first-comers sat down on chairs or lined up themselves along the walls of the room. The majority of the people, however, were left standing since there was no room left to sit.

Once the uproar stopped, one of the civilians at the table began talking to the crowd. People listened quietly, but they could understand neither the essence nor the purpose of the speech. The speaker kept circling around while trying to explain something and never got down to the point he was trying to make.

Bronius Adomaitis, just like everyone else, tried to understand the message this civilian was trying to convey. Bronius even made an effort to memorize some of the words he heard. His mind struggled to understand their meaning and uncover the logic behind everything that was being spoken. He did not succeed, though, and there was no one to ask for an explanation.

The speaker spoke further while constantly glancing at his pocket watch. It looked as if he was impatiently waiting for someone important to arrive. Even some of the people in the crowd began looking toward the door. No one, however, appeared in the doorway, and nothing substantial has been said. The speaker kept repeating the words "Soviet authorities" and vaguely talked about some mystical danger from some unknown, invisible enemy. The speaker concluded that the enemy must be defeated and eliminated all together. He then urged everyone to be especially vigilant even though he had never revealed who the enemies were, and what measures would have to be taken in order to eliminate them.

Adomaitis had stood in one spot still not able to catch the meaning of the message. He scratched his head in an attempt to comprehend why all these men were gathered in this place at night and in such a hurry.

As soon as the ancient wall clock struck two o'clock in the morning, the lengthy speech ended. However, the meeting was far from over, as another officer began another speech.

This time the speaker immediately came to the essence of the matter. He spoke in a relatively concise manner using short and clear sentences. He was very straightforward and told people why they were being troubled. He even repeated some of his sentences a few times for emphasis. The officer explained that the relocation of these men was necessary in connection with the many people hiding in the forests, who had been undermining the Soviet regime in various ways.

The speaker called the local men hiding in the forests "the woodmen". He said that the new Russian government had ordered all families and individuals having a personal relationship with the woodmen to be evicted from their homes. In other words, these people had to be exiled from the Soviet Republic of Lithuania so that they could not help the woodmen in the future. According to him, the men's presence should also serve to aid in catching and suppressing the remaining rebels who had been hiding in the nearby forests.

All the men were notified that they were to be separated into crews at various designated locations at about four o'clock in the morning. Their job then was to go to the woods and search for the local hideouts there. They would also be responsible for arresting woodmen and bringing them to the NKVD regardless of their age or sex.

Everybody in the room also was ordered to shoot if someone tried to stop the siege. If it happened to be an adult male, they were to shoot without warning; if it happened to be a woman or a child younger than ten years old, they were to yell out, "Stop!" once. If the command to stop was not obeyed then they were to shoot them as well.

Those arrested were allowed to take up to a thousand kilograms of food and other supplies and clothes for their whole family. Butchering animals was strictly prohibited. If the refugees had some meat, grain, flour, or other food, they were allowed to take it as long as it did not exceed the thousand kilogram limit. In addition, they were allowed to take chickens if they had been already killed. All the rest of their movable assets had to be carefully registered, forfeited, and submitted to the executive committee.

At the end of the meeting, a few civilians were selected from the crowd of people. Each of them had to join a Russian officer and soldier. Finally, the speaker announced the end of the meeting.

Now it was very clear to everybody the disgraceful mission they were here to carry out. For a moment, there was a dead silence in the air. No one, however, dared to oppose the evil, since it would have only been useless attempt and nothing decent could have been achieved. In addition, they would only bring harm to themselves and their families. Therefore, no one could bring himself to disobey the order.

Finally, everybody was told to vacate the building. Adomaitis, with the other two men sent from his work, had to find their new groups in order to start carrying out this horrible mission.

Bronius found himself in the yard looking for the Russian officer and soldier he was to work with. While working his way through the crowd, he was not able to find them anywhere. It turned out that they found him first.

Suddenly, they sprang up as if out of the ground right in front of Bronius. Much to Adomaitis's surprise, the two men he had worked with introduced themselves as a Russian army senior lieutenant and a common Russian soldier.

The officer did not speak much; he just introduced himself by his surname and added that he was a chief. Therefore, both Bronius and the soldier were to carry out his instructions. He reiterated the words of the orator regarding their mission and advised them concerning what they needed to do in order to obey the government rules. At that point, the three men walked out of the courtyard surrounded by the tall brick wall on top of which several lines of barbed wire were growing into the sky.

Soon they found themselves in the street at the end of which was a long wooden bridge across the Nemunas River. The water below the bridge was flowing quietly. A holy, undisturbed tranquility enveloped everything around them with a robe of darkness. The three men walked over the bridge to the other side of the river.

They climbed a small hill and stood there for a while listening to the sounds of the night. Everything was so quiet around them, that they even started feeling uncomfortable standing in this remote place. The whole atmosphere was ripe with fear.

The little crew of three moved down the hill and slowly walked along the bottom of it stopping from time to time. Now and then, a frightened bird would wing skyward as if from under their feet.

The officer became frightened, stopped suddenly, and listened closely. Then he spat on the ground and resumed walking further. Adomaitis mechanically followed a little behind the two soldiers, his mind not troubled with any thoughts of danger.

Finally, they reached a lonely farmstead bordering the nearby forest. It appeared as if the house among the tall trees was hiding from the eyes of the passersby. The mysterious forest was still asleep on both sides of the home, stretching far to the north and west. As they got closer to this small farmstead, the officer ordered them to turn left. Thus, the three men, after making a little curve, found themselves at the northern side of the forest, where they came to a halt.

The officer gave instructions to shoot without warning if anyone tried to run from the home. At the same time, he strictly told them to keep it as quiet as possible.

Lying on the ground close to each other in a battle position, they fixed their eyes on the lonely homestead waiting expectantly for someone to come out.

Bronius was reluctant to participate in this operation, but he had no say, so he lay down with the other two men hiding behind a pine tree. He had his rifle in his hands; it was loaded with five cartridges. In addition to that, his pockets were full of spare ammunition.

Bronius thought that even if someone tried to escape from this farmhouse, he would not be the first to shoot unless he really had no other choice. Then his intent would be to aim over the head of the runaway.

It made him furious that Russian invaders had already spread in all directions of the territory. Using all kinds of cruel repression and deportation, they tried to beat down Lithuanian residents, forcing them to fight against even their native brothers and sisters.

Fortunately, no bullets were fired. They did not have to lie there for long, lying on the ground like common thieves or robbers waiting for a victim they had never seen before. As soon as the horizon in the east brightened a little bit, their tension and fear decreased significantly. They knew that now it would just get brighter and lighter as morning dawned. Precisely at that time, the farmhouse door opened with a quiet squeak disturbing the silence.

A man, dressed only in a shirt, appeared in the doorway. The Russian officer aimed his gun but did not fire. The man slowly walked around the corner of the house and started urinating there. Undoubtedly, that was why he had gotten out of bed at such an early hour. Meanwhile, the officer started moving closer to the homestead, running from one tree to another and keeping himself hidden.

The farmer was already headed back to his house, when the officer's loud scream, "Freeze!" in Russian broke the silence.

Stunned, the man turned around but apparently, he could not tell where this voice was coming from, as he kept looking in every direction.

The officer shouted again, "Hands up! Stand still!"

The man raised his hands high above his head and stood frozen, facing the wall of his house. Then the officer, pointing his gun forward, approached the farmer and stopped a few steps away.

For a few minutes, the officer talked to the man, but Adomaitis could not hear what he was saying. Soon, he saw the man's raised hands drop down to his sides. Then he walked toward the entrance of the house at gunpoint with the officer following.

The two disappeared in the doorway. Even though the door remained wide open, dead silence reigned inside the house. Soon a light came on at one end of the house. Time passed slowly. It seemed as though a great deal of time had elapsed since the eastern side of the sky started lighting up. Nevertheless, no one was seen at the front door. Close to half an hour later, the dark silhouette of the officer came outside. He waved at Adomaitis and the soldier to come closer.

When the two of them entered the house, they saw that the whole family was up. The first thing that struck Bronius was the extremely poor surroundings. There was no typical flooring but only a dirt floor, and the air in the room was very stuffy and stagnant. It intertwined with the smell of some kind of acidity. After having recently left the fragrant pine forest where the air had been saturated with the scent of the trees' resin and everything around smelled so pleasant, the odors in the house literally took Bronius's breath away making him want to throw up.

The walls and the ceiling in the room were blackened with age. A small crooked table stood in one corner of the room with several black and white pictures of saints hanging on the wall above it. They also had turned black, just like the ceiling and the walls. The poor lighting in the room did not make things better, either. Even after looking at the pictures at close proximity, it was nearly impossible to discern what was depicted in them.

A couple of long wooden benches were standing in the corner on both sides of the table along the walls. On one of the benches by the wall with the photographs, a little row of small children was sitting dressed in rags. They looked to be anywhere from two to eight years of age; the smallest child sat in the lap of the oldest.

Not far away from the children, two women were standing. One was a little elderly woman and the other appeared to be about thirty years of age with an already withered face. The later was holding her head in her hands as if she was totally lost and did not know what to do next. She looked so pitiful. She had aged before her time because of her difficult state of life.

Upon entering the room, the Russian officer soon started searching behind the inglenook. He thoroughly read every single piece of paper found in the house. As soon as he was familiarized with the documents, he started throwing them onto the dirt floor. The Russian soldier helped him by poking into all the remaining corners and rooms in the house. Only Adomaitis, during all this time, was unaware of what he was to do. Therefore, he just stood numbly with his hands holding the barrel of his gun. Time from time he glanced at the frightened children and the two confused women.

After the search was finally over, the officer ordered Adomaitis to list all the items of confiscated property belonging to the family. The homemaker was asked to get her children ready to leave. The women, stumbling here and there, began gathering some of their household items and clothing for the little ones. The younger woman was so upset that things just kept falling out of her hands. Despite that, she struggled to collect the most necessary items.

The Russian officer did not pay much attention to the feelings of the family members. Obviously, he did not care whether the children would have any food to eat or if they went hungry.

Suddenly, the children's mother abruptly disturbed the prevailing tension in the room. As if caught by an invisible force, she ran into the kitchen corner and seized a large carving knife from the kitchen shelf. Immediately, she ran at the children, her face distorted with horror. The knife in her hand missed to going into the smallest child's tiny body because Bronius grabbed her by the wrist and took the knife from her. The officer interfered, too, by ordering her to sit on the bench and remain there. For a while, all the little children, like some chicks, grasping at their mother's long heavy skirt while lamenting something difficult to understand. An outsider could only react with pain in his heart after listening to it all.

As soon as the woman calmed down and her children stopped crying, the officer urged her to continue getting ready to leave their home. This time, as well, it was as if some sleeping panther had awakened in her body as soon as she approached the kitchen cabinet. She, in a bound, jumped to the cabinet, grabbed the knife, and, with one slash, tore the ragged shirt on her gaunt body. As soon as the knife in her hand rose again, the officer jumped on her and took it away so she would not be able to stick it into her own bony chest. The children, shrieking like slaughtered sucking pigs, rushed again to their mother where she was kneeling on the clay floor.

This time the officer grabbed woman by her hair, dragged her across the room, and planted her firmly on the bench in the corner. He also asked the soldier to stand guard her. He was bound to make certain she could not make another move. This time, even though she started begging them to let her get the children ready for their departure, the soldier was unrelenting. He made her sit on the bench, occasionally striking her with his fist.

The grandmother, looking calm, but barely able to drag herself around, was hauling ragged clothing and blankets from all the corners of the house. She then put them into bundles. She noiselessly muttered prayers under her breath, occasionally moaning as though some inner pain was tormenting her.

Adomaitis's heart was breaking while witnessing the terrible scene taking place in this grim cottage. He was witnessing some his own countrymen being brutally terrorized by the vicious invaders who had been trampling the small, peaceful nation on the Baltic Sea by desecrating its customs and traditions and treating its people disgracefully. The saddest thing of all was that he was unable to do anything to stop it, even more so now, that he had become one of the occupiers, despite being forced to carry out their crimes against humanity.

Ready for anything, Adomaitis without thinking about the consequences told the Russian officer, "Lieutenant, maybe we could use a couple of neighbors from adjacent homestead. They might come in handy helping Grandma pour grain into sacks gathering the family's clothes. You can see that Grandma can hardly drag herself along. It would be a disaster to let them be on their way with this entire flock of little kids and no food."

"And how do you know that there are some neighbors available next door?" asked the officer while casting an angry glance at Adomaitis.

"I am not sure, but one of us could certainly walk over and find out."

The officer said nothing to Adomaitis but ordered the soldier to walk to the house next door to see if he could get some help.

Soon the soldier returned with two men who were ordered to pour the rye grain into bags out of the barrel standing behind the inglenook in the corner. Less than an hour later, everything was ready. The grain was packed into the bags and the family's belongings were tied into bundles.

Daylight had grown fast outside although the sky looked gloomy. It even appeared as if it was about to start raining. The air was heavy; however, not a drop of rain had fallen from the low hanging clouds.

First, they brought all the meager belongings out into the yard and loaded everything into a one-horse cart that had been confiscated from the neighbors.

The officer was already going to give an order to get the children and women into the cart when Bronius Adomaitis asked, "Maybe we should feed the kids before leaving?"

The officer had just then released the mother of the children, accompanied by the Russian soldier. She was allowed to milk their family cow for the last time. Adomaitis followed them to the barn since he was instructed to draw a list of the confiscated animals.

When they opened the barn, the woman stepped inside first and began quietly milking the cow. The soldier stood in the doorway watching the long streams of milk loudly hit the bottom of the metal pail. He looked frightened as if he feared that someone might walk in at any minute and strangle him right on the spot. Adomaitis also stood nearby watching the woman whose trembling hands milked her cow for last time. With one hand, she pulled cow's teats while she held the bucked by its rim with the other. Only about half of the milk was hitting the pail while the other half splashed out onto her skirt or fell on the hay-strewn ground where she was kneeling.

Adomaitis looked around and immediately noticed a few chickens sitting on a ladder in the corner of the cow-house. It was only then he remembered that deportees were allowed to take their chickens with them if they had already been butchered.

Therefore, he brought himself to offer in a quavering voice, "Hostess, you are allowed to take the chickens with you, too. They will come in handy during the trip. I don't think you should leave them here. But you must kill them first."

The woman with a trembling, barely audible voice mumbled, "Who will butcher them? I can't do it myself; I don't have any strength left."

Adomaitis shoved his hand into his pocket and clasped his pocketknife. However, he did not take it out. He thought back to good times when he, while still studying in high school, used to visit his parents' house for summer vacation. His grandmother always wanted to treat him with a bowl of tasty homemade chicken noodle soup.

Snatching a rooster, she used to say, "Grandson, cut the cock's head off, so he won't wake me up so early and let me have some rest."

Several times Bronius had taken an ax in his hands and laid the rooster's head onto the stump in the woodshed. The ax, however, had never risen over the bird's head. Instead, he had always dropped it in the corner full of wood chips and set the chicken free saying, "Granny, we'd better let the cock crow. Why should he become a victim upon my arrival?"

His grandmother never gave in to him, though. She used to seize the bird and cut its head off herself. When that happened, Bronius used to disappear and hide somewhere in the orchard behind the dense cherry trees. This way, neither his eyes saw nor his ears heard his grandma plucking the bird. He also would not come anywhere near while she was preparing the bird by the inglenook in the kitchen.

He usually liked to sit near his grandma and listen to her stories about the memories of family's distant past. He, too, had the opportunity to share with his grandma some of his stories about life in Vilnius, the capital city of Lithuania.

Bronius liked to tell her everything about his school life, how much fear he had to endure during exams at school and lots more.

Bronius always had to eat the very first pancake that his granny cooked in her big, heavy, black cast iron frying pan. For some reason the first pancake used to be less palatable than all the pancakes fried after that. He used to cut away small pieces of bacon with a knife, wrapping them into the pancakes and gobbling one after another so fast that at times he had to wait until she had baked another batch.

Bronius's thoughts returned to the farmstead. Soon, the picture of chickens with their feathers already plucked away again took over his mind. He understood that the time had come when would be necessary to help this poor family to get their food supply ready for the trip. It would not be easy to lift his hand to kill those chickens, though. This time, however, it would be necessary to do just that.

He looked at the chickens while his hand squeezed the knife in the pocket, but there was no way he could bring himself to pull it out. At that moment, before his eyes, emerged an image of the four small, ragged children and their pale, little faces. Bronius's heart began racing when he took a step toward the chickens in the corner. It felt like salvation when he turned around and saw the solder still standing in the doorway.

"Brother, can you kill those chickens?" asked him Adomaitis in Russian.

"Easy…"

"Let's give them to this woman, so that she can feed her kids during their long trip," Bronius uttered in Russian with a tremor in his voice.

The soldier did not need to be asked a second time. He walked to the corner of the barn and grabbed the first chicken that he came across by the neck. The frightened bird started flapping his wings and began to make noise. Adomaitis opened his pocketknife and stretched to hand it the soldier.

"Take my knife."

"I don't need it."

Moreover, the soldier did not even have to work for long; he just pressed the bird between his legs and tore the live chicken's head off in a ringing motion with his bare hands! Then he threw the bloody body of the bird out the opened barn door. The chicken fell on the ground not too far from Adomaitis, still flogging its wings, rolling topsy-turvy, and spraying the soil with its blood. The headless chicken was still moving when another beheaded chicken was tossed down on the grass. It too thrashed its wings on the ground and jumped like some kind of horrible toy.

Adomaitis stood in shock and stared, his eyes widen open with horror at the bird's tragedy, not fully aware of what had just happened in front of him. Shortly after, six more headless chickens were lying, their feathers splattered with blood at Adomaitis's feet. A few of them stretched out their wings for the last time and their legs curled under them in the agony of death.

After the woman finished milking the cow, she walked out with the bucket in her hand. Bronius, feeling like a murderer, sneaked out of the barn behind her. In the house, she passed the milk through a sieve, and divided it by pouring into five cups. She gathered the children at the table and sat the two year old in her lap. She also handed a cup of milk to the grandmother. Then she began feeding the baby.

One of the neighbors walked inside of the room and said, "Have some bread, too. Bread always fills you up."

"I don't think there is any bread left," answered the barely audible voice of the mother.

"Yes, there is," the neighbor said opening the cupboard door widely for her to see. He took out a large loaf of bread, sliced it himself, and placed it on the table in front of them.

For the last time today, this family was having their breakfast under their own roof and in their native land. The poverty in this home was so obvious; there was nothing but the milk to give to the children to eat. Despite that, no one family member wanted to leave the home. This was where they had been born, had grown up, got married. Some family members had even grown old there. While living in this house, they still had a glimmer of hope that life somehow might take a better turn. No one wanted to part with this small patch of land, either. It was soaked with their tears and sweat.

As the cart with the whole family in it rolled out of the yard, the women wept loudly and wrung their hands. Watching their mother crying so desperately, the little ones also started screaming at the top of their lungs, huddled close to her like chicks to a brood-hen.

The cart, harnessed with one old horse, was slowly swinging along the bumpy, narrow forest road. Together with the family in the cart were the two neighbors who had helped. Upon reaching the edge of the woods, they got out. One of the men offered to take the smallest girl with him. She looked about two years old. The Russian officer, however, threatened the neighbor with arrest and jail time in Merkine. The two men turned and walked away at fast pace.

As soon as the cart started moving forward again, the woman began singing a holy church song,

"Mary, Mary, Purest Lily,
You shine high in the heavens.
Alleviate the slavery.
Help the humanity,

Save it from the dangerous enemy…"

No one joined in the singing, but no one forbade her to sing either. The children stopped crying.

It started to drizzle slowly and soon began raining harder and harder. It was raining cats and dogs by the time they reached the Nemunas River.

The mother of the children continued singing her song verse after verse. She ceased chanting only when they drove onto the bridge since the wooden wheels of the cart rumbled loudly hitting the pavement of the bridge.

When they entered Merkine town, she resumed her singing,

"Let's fall on our knees,

And ask the Almighty…"

Thus chanting, the crew entered the NKVD courtyard.

Adomaitis and the soldier returned to the homestead so that they could gather the confiscated items from the family's home.

Just before entering the farmyard, however, he and the soldier noticed several men rooting around the grounds surrounding the house. Adomaitis felt very uncomfortable. Nevertheless, he could do nothing about the whole situation. After all, he had been forced to go against his own people. He did not dare enter the yard first, and he only jogged after the soldier with his eyes cast down.

In this manner, without making eye contact with anyone, he found himself at the farmhouse feeling like some of criminal. Bronius removed the forms from his pockets. He started making the list of whatever was left in the house.

The soldier kept dragging all kinds of troughs, barrels, benches, and other household items, which did not seem to have much value. Adomaitis made a detailed list of every single item.

Finally, it was time to list the table where he had laid his paper forms and pencils. This piece of furniture, if it could even be called that, was so crooked and damaged by insects that it was barely standing on its four squeaky legs. White particles of dust spread over the sides as someone had accidentally moved it.

After completing his list, Adomaitis got up to exit the hut.

The soldier came up to him and pulled a metal shaver wrapped in a shred of newspaper from his overcoat pocket. He showed it to Adomaitis while smiling innocently, "Don't list this; I want to keep it for myself."

Adomaitis carefully inspected the razor and wrapped it again in the paper. Not uttering a word, he returned the razor to the soldier. Content, the soldier followed him to the yard.

Adomaitis ordered the soldier to remove the cow from the barn. He led it out with lightening speed, and the cow stood tied to the fence.

Adomaitis opened another stall in the barn, where, without any break, a hungry piglet was squealing. As soon as he slightly opened the little gate, the piglet poked his little muzzle out. Adomaitis had to close the gate quickly. He found the soldier and asked him to get a crate for the pig. The soldier, as quick as a bullet, swept to the house and dragged a buggy, which he found there, to the barn. Bronius waited for him by the open barn door.

Adomaitis did not want anybody from the village seeing him participating in the shameful activity of emptying the contents of a household. Therefore, he went into the farmhouse and started handing things to the soldier through an open window. The soldier waited on the other side of the house wall loading everything into the buggy.

After their work was finished, Adomaitis pulled a handkerchief from his pocket. Wiping the sweat from his forehead, he walked back into the yard.

Both Adomaitis and the soldier went to the barn in order to tie up the piglet, but it escaped right through their hands. The pair of men chased the mangy piglet into the forest and through the plowed field until they were completely exhausted.

However, the filthy creature, as if intentionally, kept slipping out of their hands. It seemed as though they were out of luck and would not be able to drive it into a pen. After all their work, they thought they had lost the little villain in the forest.

If one had taken a detached view, it was bitterly funny watching these two officials with firearms in their hands, running after the scrawny little pig in an open field. Sometimes it seemed they had managed to get pretty close to the piglet when it got their scent and rushed away just like a bird right under their feet. Again, they brandished their guns and took off again running breathlessly after the little bastard.

Bronius was relieved thinking that the chase was over. Nevertheless, the soldier urged him to continue searching. They decided that one of them would look on the side of the forest that ran next the field and the other would look on the opposite side.

After a short walk, Adomaitis spotted the piglet peacefully nuzzling some roots sticking out of the soil between some trees. At first, Bronius hesitated, not knowing what to do. He did not want to make a fool of himself any longer by chasing the little thing. Therefore, he drove the damned pig deeper and further into the forest and slowly walked back to the homestead.

Soon the soldier, having found nothing for his pains, also returned to the farmyard. Both young men were tired and wet through from the rain. In addition, both of them were afraid of the other. Neither man wanted the other to report about releasing government-owned property. At the same time, neither had any willingness to continue running around the field or the forest.

Having finally recovered his breath, Adomaitis walked up to the cart and cast a long glance at the pile of worthless property. For a moment, he thought that the items in the cart were so insignificant that there was ultimately no reason to transport it to the Executive Committee. Furthermore, he knew that he would be delighted to voluntarily throw everything away, except that no one had given him the right to do so. With the cow tied to the carriage, they left the farmyard accompanied by the resentful glares of the few people gathered around.

When they arrived at the Russian authorities, Adomaitis was ordered to throw all the junk into a large mow. After turning in the property list he had made, he finally felt free. He was very tired because he had not slept well and had had almost nothing in his stomach since the previous morning.

Bronius found himself a dry and warm room in the Building of the Executive Committee. All he wanted was to fall into a corner and take a nap. However, he knew his hunger would have not let him sleep even for a minute. His growling stomach, like a fierce dog, kept reminding him about its need to be fed. His constant hunger, along with a substantial amount of noise around the building, made him aware that he would not find enough quiet to sleep either.

Therefore, he left the building and went to the local town farmers' market in hopes of finding some food to purchase. There, carriages loaded with diverse goods drove by constantly. He could see polished wardrobes, large mirrors, chests and other household furnishings passing by. Some trucks were heaped with ramshackle furniture. Nevertheless, Bronius did not see trash like the one they had brought this same day from the farmstead.

He no longer wanted to look at the items that people had obtained over the years by toiling hard to earn the money to buy them just to have them confiscated by the Russian government. All these household goods, wet from the rain, were going to be moved straight into barns that had also been taken from local people. Within a few months, it all would become unfit for any use.

Bronius wanted to have some peace. Passed the NKVD Building, he saw a full yard of people. Some were sitting on the ground and some were squatting in the rain shielding themselves with a variety of rags. Even the children, in little groups, were sitting directly on the soil with their tiny bodies covered with old blankets and sacks.

No one seemed bothered by seeing this grim sight. It seemed that nobody cared that people were hungry, drenched by the rain, and freezing cold. No one even bothered to bring to the little ones a cup of hot water.

Now Bronius noticed the victims he and the soldier brought to this enclosure. The mother with the grandmother and four children, all numb because of the cold, were sitting on the ground soaking wet from the constant drizzling rain. Adomaitis approached the gate. He wanted to take a closer look at these unfortunates, the poor people abandoned by Fate.

At that moment, from behind the gate he heard a harsh, angry command in Russian, "Remove yourself from here!"

Adomaitis did not dare resist, as he was well aware that very little was needed before he found himself among those unlucky ones. Without saying anything, he quickly turned away and started walking rapidly in the opposite direction.

Soon, he passed the bridge. When he got to the other side of the river, he sat down on its high bank and fixed an interminable gaze on the water whorls. The fine rain kept coming down.

Who knows how long he would have sat there if not for the rain and hunger that had tormented him. He probably could have tolerated the rain, but the feeling of hunger was eating him from the inside and had not left him alone even for a short moment. Bronius wanted to eat so badly that he had become weak and dizzy. He had to put some food inside his stomach soon. He tried to decide how to act at this point. Whom should he contact? There was no old government, and the new one at the NKVD had shut itself off by not allowing any outsiders to come near.

Adomaitis, driven by hunger and with the rifle still on his shoulder, went to the nearest homestead in search of something to eat. However, his efforts were in vain. No one would give him a piece of bread when he offered to pay for it. Greatly disappointed and not knowing what to do, he returned to the Executive Committee Building that was now crowded with hungry people like him. All they wanted was food.

The people in the crowd became so enraged that they began threatening to do harm. Soon several men were selected to talk to Russian authorities at the NKVD, the only institution that currently existed in this chaos.

The small delegation was not allowed to walk inside to talk to the government officials. They, however, insisted that they be let inside to talk to a chief or that a chief himself might come outside to talk to them. At last, after much long negotiation, they were admitted. As soon as the delegation entered the chief's office, he started shouting at them with threats to disarm and punish them on the grounds of rebellion.

Since the most competent people had been sent to negotiate, they were not afraid to look fear square in the eye. They set forth the situation to the "Red Czar" very clearly, letting the Russian authorities know that many people had been without food for the second day in a row.

The new government was now informed that many of the men brought to the area had already gone searching for food in the villages, but no one had been sold any food or been given anything free either. In addition, there were no opened shops in the town of Merkine. Therefore, they could not buy food there as well.

The fact that they were all armed had not helped the situation either. Who knew what incidents could have arisen. After all, hungry and angry people had been known to reach violently.

"As far as I understand, you've come here to threaten me. Am I right? I can quickly disarm everyone and turn you to the Tribunal for raising a riot."

"Here, I will turn my gun in to you myself," claimed one of the representatives stepping forward firmly. "But I must warn you, sir, that if we don't come back for a long time, it might be too late. Moreover, you might have to answer for that, since there are about a couple hundred starving people in this town. Hungry people become dangerous. We are not asking for anything else. Just give us some food. We are not asking it to be free, either. Most of us can pay for it. We have money. If you don't take this seriously, soon, maybe even tonight, this crowd will most likely start looting. Who then is going to be responsible when all this comes to light?"

While the representative was talking, the chief kept casting angry glances at him and the rest of the men. Now it was clear to him that even though he had the power to arrest the intruders, he could not control the outcome of the events. The situation was getting critical. It was not the same as locking up people and dumping them into a hole to be forgotten about. At the same time, he realized that it was impossible to feed everyone, too.

The chief wanted to shout again, but this time nothing came out of his mouth. He just stood up and walked to the window. Outside, he saw the courtyard full of armed men. He realized that despite the fact that his own crew of soldiers was very well armed, their numbers were too small in comparison to the crowd of people outside. True, he had two small caliber cannons parked outside. If a riot happened to arise, however, those men in the yard would turn and be on the opposite side. Of course, he could phone Russian authorities in Varena and require them to send a garrison to help suppress the revolt. On the other hand, the chief realized that he might be held personally responsible for the events. Therefore, he decided it would be better to come to an agreement in a friendly way.

The chief stood at the window for a while longer. Then, he turned around and walked up to the table where the gun of the representative was lying. He took the gun and handed it to the representative who had been selected by the crowd. He was the one who had done all the talking at this point.

Smiling, Chief returned the rifle to the man saying, "I agree that this situation is not normal, and we do need to take some action to fix it. I promise I will do whatever I can. Go back now and tell them that we will talk things over and give you an answer in about half an hour."

The representatives returned and laid all this out to the people outside, and this was exactly what they wanted to hear.

After good half an hour, a circle of NKVD people walked through the gates and quickly moved into the crowd. Soon, they began stirring up all the people there by telling them to go into the villages that were located nearby and, in small groups, search for food.

This agitation of the men lasted longer than an hour and frightened those who were already fearful even more. Feeling lost and helpless, they began wandering through the town in all directions. It stopped raining, and the sky had cleared. Low on the horizon, the sun had even showed its face.

Bronius walked out with the rest of the people. He felt so worn out, that he was lagging far behind the rest of the crew. A woman caught up with him. Adomaitis asked her about food. The woman did not answer the strange armed man at first. However, Bronius was very persistent. He talked and talked. He told her everything about how he had ended up here. Evidently, something he said evoked her trust, and the conversation between the two began. After a while, they talked to each other frankly.

The woman quite bravely and, without any dodging said, "People are afraid of you men because with your arrival you brought so many trouble and tears to everyone around. They hate you. You walk in groups all armed, and this is intimidating to them. I think if you went to the local farmers without your guns over your shoulders, they not only would sell you some food, but they most likely would feed you free of charge. However, if you go in pointing your guns at the locals and their family members like the Russian soldiers do, no one will give you anything. They would sooner throw their food into the river. They are scared. Many of them have had some relatives deported and detained or they know someone who has been deported. We have many people in the vicinity who have become the victims of the Red Army."

Adomaitis understood the woman regarding acquiring food. She was beginning to like this young man. She told him she would have given him some bread for nothing, but she lived about eight kilometers away from the town.

Upon separating from Bronius, she expressed her regrets of not being able to help more and advised him not to show up in locals' homesteads armed. According to her, this way they were more likely to be given some food.

Bronius caught up with the other men in his group. He told them about the woman's warnings. The others agreed that it made sense not having their guns out for everyone to see. Soon they turned off the highway and divided themselves into two smaller groups of three.

When Bronius's group reached the first homestead along their way, a half of the red orb of the sun had already been hidden behind the horizon. In a few minutes, it was going to be completely gone, leaving only a big red spot in the sky. Before long it would begin to show up on the other half of the globe shining to the people there and refreshing their environment and nature with its pleasant rays.

Standing by some bushes, the men discussed their plan of action. One of them would remain in the bushes to guard the guns while the other two went to the nearest homestead.

Upon entering the peasant house, they worshiped Jesus Christ first and then began politely talking to the owners. One man brought owners' attention to their difficult circumstances, and Bronius told them that they had not had anything to eat for almost two days now. The other man asked if they could buy some food from the farmer and his wife.

At first, the owner of the homestead looked at the uninvited guests unsympathetically as if he would at some intruders. The expression on his face did not show any promise either. Bronius and his companion thought the man might have something to sell, but he obviously had little trust in these two strangers.

The farmer had already quite a few wanderers have come into their home insisting that they get some food as well as the farmers' homemade brandy. Therefore, this time he listened to the young men more than he talked. However, the owner's wife, like a typical woman, soon became weak and started feeling sorry for them since they really looked tired and hungry. She did not dare to offer any food; she waited for her husband to say something.

"Mother, have you got some eggs to give to these young people?"

"I do have a few eggs that I could give to you," she said and she brought out a small basket. She took twenty brown eggs out of it and put them on the table.

"Well, I have got ten more left for my children."

"Thank you, thank you, Mistress. We don't want you or your family to go without food," Adomaitis said while pulling money out of his pocket.

"Don't worry about paying us," intervened the host.

"We have no intention of getting anything for free. We do have money to pay. If we took those eggs and did not give you anything in return, it would look very much like extortion."

"You are giving me too much money," the host protested.

"How much are your eggs? If there is too much money here, then could you also give us a piece of bread for the extra money?" Bronius asked.

"I can give you a loaf of bread free of charge. Thanks are to God, we have enough of it."

The hostess brought out a big loaf of bread. She cut it across the middle to divide it into two big chunks and left them on the table. Adomaitis took out another ten-ruble bill and placed it onto the top of the egg money.

"Young man, put the money back into your pocket. I can tell you are decent people," she said.

"No, we don't want to take anything for free, or it would be better to starve. However, we need food badly, and we'll be glad to take it with us. So, please take our money," Adomaitis said as he got the paper bills off the table and placed them into the woman's palm; then he bent her fingers closed. "There, I think it's the right thing to do."

"Would you boys like some boiled eggs? Or would fried eggs be better? You probably don't even have a place to prepare your food," offered the hostess.

"We sure would like to have a hot meal. Can you hear our stomachs growling? We don't want to cause any trouble for you, though. Frying eggs requires grease. I think that boiled eggs will do," uttered Bronius's companion.

"Mother, get some bacon out of the barn and fry the eggs for these men. Let them get their strength back."

"Okay, how many eggs would you like me to fry for you?"

"All of them, Hostess; we are really hungry. I have to tell you that there is one more with us. He is sitting in the bushes behind your house. "

"What is he doing there? Why didn't you bring him in with you?"

"He is guarding our guns. We didn't want to scare you by coming here with guns."

"Young men, those who have weapons usually are proud of being able to plant fear into peoples' hearts. It's easy to do, when most people are already scared of everything. During the day, Russian soldiers roam around the town with their guns slung over their shoulders. In the evening, those soldiers go to the villages where they knock on the locals' doors and, with various threats, demand food and vodka. My wife and I wish we lived much further from town. It looks like Russian underlings don't go far into the country as frequently as they come here, because they are afraid of partisans who are hidden in the forest. As for us, my wife and I have to put up with this misery, since they keep coming to our place in packs. We are so tired of the new hungry government that never can be pleased. The taxes are already unbearably high; they burden us with all sorts of obligations and tributes too. In addition to that, we must feed those drunkards and parasites."

"Well, go get your friend," encouraged the hostess. "What is he doing there alone in the bushes? Meanwhile, I will prepare you boys something to eat."

The woman brought out a big chunk of bacon, cut it into small pieces, and scattered them in the frying pan. Her husband laid a couple of bricks on the edge of the corner of a big stove over the old cast iron fireplace. Then, he lit up thinly chopped sapwood that illuminated darkening room with its cheerful crackling.

When all three soldiers walked into the kitchen, the bacon was already joyfully sizzling in the frying pan smelling pleasant and making the hungry young men feel even hungrier.

"You can put your weapons, young men, on the top of the chest of drawers. No one will touch them," offered the owner of the house.

"We would rather have them under the bench by the table out of everybody's sight," Bronius said as he placed the guns and kicked them out of sight with his boot. Now no one could see them, which mad the woman very glad.

The young men appeared to be quite humble and sincere. Soon, the hostess set the pan with the fried eggs onto the table while her husband lit a kerosene lamp. Then he walked out of the room. Soon he was back carrying two half-liter bottles of homemade vodka.

"Who wants to have a drink? I thought such simple, pleasant, and sincere men deserve to have some good stuff. It's homemade."

"You don't have to do that," spoke Adomaitis quickly. "Thank you so very much for saving us from our unfortunate situation. We can't find the words to express our gratitude."

"You don't have to say anything. You'd better sit down and have a meal and a drink," urged the man of the house.

As soon as the mistress brought the frying pan with the still frizzling eggs in it, the men instantly found themselves at the table. Without any argument, they grabbed forks and, with enormous appetites and scalding their tongues, began devouring the food. They took not time to cool down the tasty bites or stop saliva dripping from their mouths; in five minutes, the pan had been emptied.

The woman fried up another ten-egg batch and sat the pan on the wooden table, again urging everyone to eat. This time, however, no one attacked the food, since the first hunger had been subdued. Now, the owner poured himself half a glass of vodka. He first raised his glass to the health of all those sitting at the table and drank it to the last drop. Then, he sniffed a slice of bread and moaned aloud as if being choked by someone. After breaking off a piece of bread, he put it into his mouth and, almost without chewing, swallowed it. Then, he filled half of the same glass with vodka and passed it to the young man seated next to him. When it was Bronius's turn to drink, he just frowned and told them that he had never had vodka in his entire life.

"Are you serious? You are the first person I've met so far who does not drink. Even we women have a little once in a while," the hostess commented.

"You see, I haven't had time to learn drinking yet," Adomaitis tried to explain himself in order to avoid pressure.

"Everybody nowadays swills this stench," the hostess continued. "Even our priests drink some vodka. And as far as our officers go, they are just soaked in it. Those government officials who come from the district do not refuse a drink either. I can't believe there are people different than that in this world."

No matter how hard the woman tried to persuade Bronius to have a sip, she got nothing for her pains. He just kept joking and saying that it was better not to even try because, after all, he could get to like it, which could leave everybody with no vodka left. After emptying her second glass, she did not try to get Bronius to drink anymore.

Nevertheless, she did not stop wondering aloud either, "This man, this young man is a real angel! I just cannot believe that you don't drink at all. But maybe it is our fault; maybe I just don't know how to ask you properly. Maybe we, the simple people, are not good enough for you?"

Adomaitis expressed his gratitude to the hostess and apologized for not being a submissive guest, even though she had made him feel very uncomfortable with her comments. Soon, the third bottle of vodka was pulled out.

The frying pan was empty once again. Seeing this, the hospitable wife of the owner of the house filled up a big plate with pieces of bacon and slices of black rye bread. She encouraged the men to eat, but everybody was already full.

The master of the house struck up a popular Lithuanian folk song "Bait a Horse, Bait a Horse". Soon, everyone began singing along. His wife apparently liked singing, too, as she joined in humming along in her female voice. In the beginning, Adomaitis just listened to the others sing, but soon he also started trying to copy the refrain of the old folk song.

Finally, the vodka ended, but their singing did not. To the contrary, now it sounded even louder. Being drunk, they had not noticed when the hostess disappeared. The only one who saw what was going on around them was Bronius, since he happened to be the only sober person in the room. No one else besides Adomaitis noticed her return, either. In her hand, she held a half-liter antique bottle corked up with a white porcelain stopper. In such bottles they had had sold lemonade before Russians occupied Lithuania.

Now, the men at the table were so absorbed in singing national poet Maironis's song "Where River Sesupe Runs, Where River Nemunas Flows" that they probably would have not noticed anything.

The hostess interrupted their song, "Well, try my drink, and tell me which one is stronger. This is a magical drink. Look at how many different kinds of herbs are inside of this bottle. All of these grasses grow in this part of our country, the Dzukija."

"Okay, Mother, pour us some of your magical potion." After drinking half a glass, the husband could not recover his breath for a little while. "Oh, boy! Even tears gushed out of my eyes. Really strong," he confessed after collecting himself.

The other two men tried the drink and had similar reactions. That is how devilishly strong this magical potion was.

When the time came to say goodbye to this hospitable home with its residents, they hugged each other like the best of friends. The owner scooped up the rest of the sliced bacon from the plate and tucked it into the pocket of one of the three men. He also cut off a thick slice of bread and put it into Bronius's pocket, "Here, now you will have something to eat for breakfast tomorrow."

Singing loudly, the men staggered outside. Thanks to God, Adomaitis was sober. He pulled everybody's guns from under the bench and threw all three of them over his shoulder. He walked to the yard and thanked the owners for the warm reception.

Adomaitis's companions wrapped their arms over each other's shoulders and bellowed songs in their drunken voices all the way back to town, disturbing the calm spring night. It was already midnight when they reached the town.

They found themselves at farmers' marketplace in the town. Bronius noticed a truck leaving the courtyard of the nearby NKVD Building. Then, a second and third truck followed. Adomaitis immediately silenced the singing men. All three of them stood watching as the column of trucks quickly rolled down the street. Soon the first truck full of people came alongside them as they stood on the pavement of the street. Two soldiers, holding weapons in their hands, held onto the truck cab on both sides. The second truck drove by also accompanied by two armed soldiers. The lorries rolled by, one after the other, filled with people being guarded by their executioners.

"This is the fruit of our actions," Bronius thought. "How many tears and grief we have caused our brothers and sisters!"

Probably some twenty trucks rolled passed them. Soon, all the vehicles disappeared in the dreary darkness of the night. The roaring of the motors also quickly cleared away, and the three young men still stood and looked disgustedly the direction where the taillights of the row of trucks had faded into the night.

When they came to the Executive Committee building, everyone was asleep. Some men had lain down on the benches while others dozed sitting on chairs with their bodies leaning up against the wall. Snoring could be heard here and there. Bronius's two companions did not have to search for a place to sleep for very long; they fell on the ground where they were standing. Soon, they began to snore too. Adomaitis stretched out next to them and, with a gun under his head, he began dozing. After one and a half days without sleep and immensely tired, he did not even realize he had fallen asleep.

However, he could not enjoy his deep sleep for very long. A sharp pain in his cheek and stiffness on his right side woke him up. There was a red painful sore developing from where he had rested his face on the stock of his rifle. He turned on his other side and continued dozing, occasionally falling asleep and anxiously twisting his body. Thus, exhausted from lying on the hard floor, with much trouble he saw the sunrise.

Adomaitis was the very first to come out of the stuffy premises. He was happy to find himself in the fresh outdoors. Several times, he inhaled the clean air deep into his lungs and yawned. He walked to the well and drew a bucket of water from it. Bronius washed his face with the icy cold water, which immediately awakened him from unpleasant numbness. Feeling alive again, he wiped the face with a handkerchief. He did not want to return to the stuffy room that smelled like dirty sweaty clothes.

Instead, the young man walked to the Nemunas's River where the other river, Merkine, flowed as well. There, seated on a steep shore, he gazed at the water swirls that boiled at the confluence of the two rivers. Adomaitis attentively watched the powerful flow of the two rivers, which had been struggling day and night without any pause or sigh. For long time he enjoyed watching the Nemunas River carrying Merkine's waters, grabbing them into his powerful arms.

He thought, "This is real power!"

The current of the smaller river, against its own will, had to obey the force of the stronger and bigger river. Fascinated, he watched as a soft fog lifted above the water. Soon it rose above the banks and dispersed in the bushes. Nightingales twittered endlessly around him. Suddenly, emerging above the distant eastern horizon, the sun climbed to the infinite serene dome of Heaven, which predicted the approaching beautiful day. That was where the true paradise was hiding in Lithuania! Peoples' eyes, however, flooded with tears, could not see this beauty. Only the nightingales happily were singing their eternal song.

Although Bronius had seen Nature in its prime awake after a night's sleep, his soul was oppressed by some serious grief. He did not want to enjoy the wonderful morning at all, even though it was as refreshing as some curative balm. His torn heart sank into vast grief. Seeing all the injustice around him, he was flooded with endless sadness. His soul was filled with an enormous hatred for the invaders who drove people out, deported them, snatched them out of their homeland's arms, and cast them into various faraway strange places. What he could have done to alleviate this invasion of the Red Plaque? His little country was powerless to defend itself from the invasion of the cruel Soviet tyrant. It only suffered and shed its blood profusely.

Adomaitis sat delving deeply into his sad thoughts with his head down and face hidden in the hands. While he set a considerable amount of time elapsed. The mist over the Nemunas River had already disappeared, and the sun had risen high in the sky when he finally withdrew his hands from his eyes.

He got up with difficulty and, head down, and eyes fixed on the ground, returned to the Executive Committee building where almost everyone was up. Only his friends, after the previous evening's entertainment, were still sprawled out on the floor sleeping peacefully. Adomaitis woke them up and the three reluctantly walked to the local church and sat down on the grass in the shade of the trees.

The three men equally divided the bread and the bacon that the owner put into their pockets when they left the farm. After having fortified themselves with food, they lay under the trees a couple of hours more.

When they returned to the Building of the Executive Committee, they found almost all of the officials sitting in their chairs. Local people kept pushing themselves inside with all sorts of complaints. Some of the locals were barely literate. They begged for help in filling out applications. None of the officials was willing to come to their aid. Instead, they shouted at the poor, helpless individuals and drove them away like stray dogs.

The people really had a lot to complain about. Most of them had lost a sheep or a calf to the Russian officials, and some had lost their cows and horses. Several women while moaning and sobbing begged the return of their confiscated animals. Nevertheless, their efforts were futile. No one listened to them.

Bronius had difficult time watching this entire scene, and finally brought himself to help one elderly little woman write a statement. After what about ten more women went to him for help. He helped write new statements or fill out applications for each of them.

When he walked outside, the women he had helped surrounded him. Some of them slipped him a slice of bacon and others gave him a dozen eggs. Thus, Adomaitis supplied himself with food for several days ahead. He did pay the women for the foodstuffs, although they did not want to take money from him.

Day after day, armed men roamed in the town. Sometimes soldiers showed up in the surrounding villages also having been brought in numerous trucks. As soon as a truck full of armed men got close to a homestead, the owners ran away. They left their homes and hid in the woods. Only late in the evening, after all the soldiers were gone, would they return to their homes. Sometimes groups of ten or more locals gathered at another local resident's house. This way it was possible to get some rest from the invaders for at least a short while.

After Bronius and the other men had stayed in Merkine for a period of five days with nothing to do, they begged to be allowed to return to their homes. The Russian authorities did not want to hear anything they had to say.

On the fifth day in afternoon, the men began revolting and insisted on being delivered to the town of Varena. Tired of their threats, the officials finally agreed to let them go, but they refused to transport them to Varena. They were told to find their own transportation or walk on foot.

The crowd of men stood on the highway trying to stop a truck, but none of the passing vehicles stopped. Then about twenty of them stood in a row across the highway with their guns aimed at oncoming traffic and stopped four lorries. They planned to force the drivers to take them to Varena.

NKVD men jumped out of the cabs of the trucks and pulled their pistols from their holsters. They threatened the crowd by aiming their guns under the noses of the men blocking their path. At that moment, a few rifles were aimed, cocked, and ready to shoot the NKVD men. The stern looks of the men were aimed at the faces of the officers who were reluctant to take them to Varena. The atmosphere was so tense that it would have taken very little to have sparked this situation into a large and deadly incident.

The NKVD men got frightened and slipped their pistols back into their sheaths. Meanwhile, the men started jumping into the backs of the trucks. Bronius kept up with the rest of the crowd. He jumped into a truck, which was full of slaughtered pigs covered with blood. More people kept climbing and stumbling over the pile of dead animals.

Adomaitis found himself a pig smudged with least amount of blood and sat down on it. Thus, watching a red bloody sunset, four trucks, full of armed people, rolled out onto the highway.

The men had so severely trodden the dead animals under their dirty boots that it was disgusting to look at the scene. The blood on the pigs mixed with the dirt and turned it into a sticky paste. Riding in these conditions, they arrived in Varena well after dark.

The town was bustling vigorously as if some sort of revolution had taken place. Bronius heard drunken orgies coming from some of the houses. In another place, someone was slaughtering pigs who squealed with their piercing voices. In another yard, pigskins were being scorched and the fiery tongues of the hay fire licked the sides of the dead animals.

The men walked to the Building of the Executive Committee in Varena. The authorities who met them there were very angry. The officials threatened the crowd of men and ordered them to get back to Merkine. It was already night, however, and the men lay themselves down on the floor to spend the night.

In the morning, they again begged to be released to go home, and again they were told to return to Merkine. Almost all of the men tried to get rid of their weapons. No one would take them since it was against a new law to go to the capital of Vilnius when armed. Therefore, if they had a weapon, they had to stay put.

It was necessary to get rid of their weapons, but no one knew how to do that. A few lucky men were successful returning their guns. Adomaitis soon learned that in exchange for a few rubles, one could drop off his gun. He walked almost half a day around the arsenal and caught a moment when nobody was nearby. He went inside and handed his license, which he had folded in half along with a fifty-ruble banknote to a sergeant seated at a small low table.

As soon as the sergeant saw the corner of the bill, he immediately took the paper and placed it in the drawer. Adomaitis was able to return his gun right away and without any hassle. The sergeant even stamped a permit for a business trip. Adomaitis suddenly found himself a free man and he literally ran to the train station where he bought a ticket. An hour later, he was sitting in train car flying rapidly to Vilnius.

He listened to the metal wheels of the train cars monotonously rumbling on the railroad ties as if whispering into his ear, "To Vilnius, to Vilnius..."

At last, he saw the lights of the capital. He got off the train and found himself in his beloved city. It felt as if he had been gone for a whole year.

Bronius walked hurriedly toward his flat without looking around. The shame of the past several days tormented him. It seemed that even all the passers-by were staring at him with condemnation. Waling quickly, his thin body slipped through the people gathered on the streets. He was oppressed by black thoughts as if he had committed some horrible crime. Bronius wanted to escape from the crowds as quickly as possible and just have a good cry somewhere in total solitude.

Evidently, it was not meant to happen, since as soon as he found himself on German Street, very close to his flat, an old school friend stopped Bronius.

"Why are you running as if somebody is chasing you?"

"Oh, hello, Andrius. I have not seen you for ages! What are you doing here?" Bronius asked.

Unexpectedly caught, Adomaitis did not know what else to say. He liked Andrius. During gymnasium times, they had been close friends. Having a close friend who suddenly appeared right in front of him during such a difficult time made Bronius rather happy.

"Andrius, let's go somewhere to have a drink. Deuce take it, we are old friends, aren't we? I've so much to tell you. I'm anxious to spill it out to you. You are the only one I can share it with," Bronius said.

"You know that I have always been there for you. But what has happened to you? As far as I remember, you never drank. Even during the school graduation farewell banquet, you had never had any drink," his friend responded.

"Andrius, you don't know what has happened to me lately. You can't imagine. I will never forget May 21, 1948. I swear it was the worst day of my life. Until then, I had not known the taste of vodka. But now, I feel like having a drink with you. Maybe this way, some dirt can be washed away from my contaminated conscience. You, Andrius, have known me for years, and you know that I can do no harm to anyone. But this particular time, I was truly forced to do it."

"You've got me wondering now. For Christ's sake, tell me what you have done. I can't imagine it being so terrible. You could not even hurt a fly. Don't beat yourself up so badly. I'm sure it is just some trifle, which is not even worth mentioning."

"Let's go into a bar, Andrius, and I'll tell you everything in detail. Then you will probably condemn me because of my despicable behavior."

Soon, the two friends found themselves in a grim hole chock-full of people. Through the heavy, thick low hanging clouds of cigarette smoke it was almost impossible to see the portly bartender pouring drinks into glasses. The two old friends sat down at a small round table in a corner of the hall. Each one of them ordered one hundred and fifty grams of vodka and a portion of pork flank.

Soon they emptied their glasses. Adomaitis, having had strong drink for the first time in his life, could not recover his breath right away. Shortly after, both men repeated the same dose, and the frank and open talk began.

Adomaitis was relieved to have someone he could trust to confide in. He told Andrius everything he had done the past several days. While telling his story, Bronius kept shaking the head in disgust at his own behavior, despite the fact that he had been forced and that the Russian government brought it upon him. He understood now that those bastards and bloodsuckers were the only ones responsible for all the human torture.

"Andrius, the recently seen horrible images will never fade away from my memory. Even now, when I am at home, they make me disgusted. You have not seen how Bolsheviks treat Lithuanian people. What brutality! I saw one Russian soldier pulling an old gray-haired woman who had done nothing wrong by her hair. Then they snatched her away from her native homestead and sent her off in a truck to some foreign land. They did the same to many others. I can't handle seeing such repression. I can tell you right now, we are being shackled like slaves. 'Oh, woe unto thee, Jerusalem, and unto thy children…'" Bronius quoted from the Bible.

Bronius could not bear it any longer and started crying. A teardrop, severed from his eyelashes, fell down on his hand and shattered leaving only the wet trace.

"Bronius, calm down. This is not your fault. You were forced to carry out this job. You are not responsible for the violence and vicious mockery of human suffering. You said it well that God has forsaken us. I hope He just forgot about us. Maybe one day He will remember us and punish those sadists who only laugh at our bloody tears. Everything ends."

The high school friend paused to have a drink, and he continued, "Look at the history of the world. The Roman Empire that ruled Europe for so many centuries was also powerful. But it disappeared like a speck of dust. The empire of the Red executioners is built on human bones and is continuously being watered with innocent blood mixed with tears. It is not everlasting either. All nations hate colonial regimes, no matter what form they manifest. It doesn't matter what the regime is called, the Republic or some different name. Since the empire is subject to somebody's bayonet power, there is no talking about freedom."

"Probably at the time, our country is in the worst situation in the world. Oh, beautiful Lithuania, how much more suffering will you have to endure, how much longer will foreign conqueror trample you?" Adomaitis, with his head down, mumbled in a barely audible voice.

"Bronius, let's have another drink," offered his friend.

"Enough already, Andrius, I have gotten soused like a pig. I don't know how I will be able to show my face to my landlady. I'd better go home. I'm even getting nauseous just looking at the tipsy mugs here. Most of all, I am angry with myself. To tell the truth, at this moment I just want to die, so that neither my eyes could see nor my ears hear all the evils."

Tipsy, the two high school friends parted. Bronius, stumbling a little, walked up the stairs and unlocked the door of his flat. His property owner had been surprised to see him in the hallway. He tried to explain himself by telling her about the unexpected business trip and to apologize about not being able to notify her.

She simply nodded her head and told him it was exactly what she had thought about his disappearance. The nice woman did not reproach her tenant. Instead, she even offered him a cup of hot tea. Adomaitis refused it, though. He headed directly to his room, lay fully clothed on his bed, and fell soundly asleep.

.

FIRE

For a long time, Adomaitis could not forget the events he had to participate in lately, and he condemned himself for his actions. However, as most beautiful season of the year, the summer, was approaching he at last found himself being able to get away from the grim thoughts.

The quiet time kept flowing slowly weeks replacing days and the months replacing the weeks. Thus unnoticed, the autumn came. The sky became overcast, and the dark rollers of clouds were constantly handing low in the distant horizon. Sometimes it even seemed as if they fully merged with the ground below.

The rain began pelting repeatedly. Only occasionally, the sun glanced out of the low hanging clouds in the horizon, and even then, it seemed to be worried about something. Its rays did not feel warm at all. Only for a short while emerging from the thick clouds, they had no chance to warm up the air and the ground below.

Nevertheless, one or the other day sometimes happened to be sunny. Even then, neither the wind nor the solar rays could dry out stagnant water puddles flooding the country roads with mud. In some places, it was almost impossible to pass by.

True, everything in the city looked a lot different. Nobody had to trudge through the mud in the rain, since the water could escape through the pavement tiles and disappear down into the sewerage openings. In addition, as soon as the rain ceased coming down, the walkways would immediately dry out. Thus, it seemed as if it had never been raining.

Therefore, no person in his right mind would desire to leave the dry city and get into the dirty rural roads during such a nasty weather. In some places, it was even possible ladling mud over the top of one's boots.

Adomaitis could not get any vacation during the summer time. The recent events taking place, exhausted by his own thoughts, he felt extremely tired. Therefore, as soon as the first opportunity came by, he could not refuse taking some time off, even though there had already long been the cold and rainy autumn season.

Released from work for vacation, he immediately went to the crowded train station and bought himself a ticket. Soon he was sitting in the train which was rolling fast its metal ties making monotonous noise.

The train was taking him to his native land, where everything had been so dear and precious to him. There, he had had the most wonderful time in his entire life. So many all kinds of memories about the summer vacations, Christmas, and the other holidays entered his mind...

However, most of all, he longed to see his grandmother, whom he loved so dearly. When he'd been just a little boy, he used to sleep together with her. Almost every night, she'd told him fairy-tales. Often he did not feel when he had drifted asleep while listening to her calming voice. Although he had already known almost all her tales by heart, however, every time he listened to them again with pleasure, forgetting about the real world around him.

Sometimes he even had pictured himself taking part in those heroic battles of knights. Nevertheless, most of all, he had liked sitting on a warm inglenook and listening to the raindrops quietly tapping the glass of the window during the dark cold evenings in the fall.

He also had enjoyed the whitish purple evenings of the winter, when the frost pressed hard making even the wood of the fences to split. He'd loved those precious moments when the wind howling banged the window shutters up the outer wall of the house. Then, sitting on the warm inglenook, he'd used to cuddle next to his grandmother trembling with the fear.

It had appeared as if devil himself was dancing in the chimneystack. Often somebody also had whistled or hauled like a dog, or crackled so loudly as if the whole bunch of devils were tumbling down into the house through the chimney. Then, he had pressed himself even closer to his beloved granny seeking the quiet refuge.

Imagining that in some other world he was fighting the subhuman creatures, he finally would drift away into a sweet sleep. Upon waking up, he would always find the grandma toiling around the stove preparing a tasty breakfast. The flame tongues would be cheerfully licking the firewood, crosswise loaded inside of the ingle-stove, until they'd turned into the pink coal.

On that wood coal, grandmother used to bake delicious pancakes. Little Broniukas, her favorite grandson, had always been the first to eat a few pancakes while still in bed, covered with the blanket.

Rocking in the train wagon, Adomaitis was dozing away submerged into the most beautiful dreams he had cherished in his memory all these years. The atrocities of the recent events, however, started invading his peaceful thoughts again and breaking their stillness like some terrible nightmare. Moreover, even now while sitting in the train, he recalled several times those horrible deportations he had been anxious to run away from during his vacation.

He so eagerly had been waiting for the time off work that he even had started counting the hours before his last day at work ended.

Therefore, he was glad to break away from his onerous daily thoughts, and now he was happily wandering in his memory maze while being rocked monotonously by the train. Thus, dreaming he did not notice when the engine, blowing the steam, started slowing down and, then, stopped completely.

Bronius just now woke up from the torpidity, and soon he found himself outside. The train immediately trundled away. For a few seconds, he was standing alone in the small train station. The autumn darkness and the foul weather greeted Bronius spattering the tiny sharp specks of raindrops at his face. It was pitch-black around him. As the train disappeared in the distance, it seemed as if the sky has merged with the ground.

Bronius Adomaitis stumbling walked into the train station. After the war, a small shack was built, when the old train station building had burned down to the ground. Strangely, there were quite a few people inside. The wooden building was so small, that Bronius could hardly find a bench to sit down.

Therefore, he started looking for the place where he could lean onto the wall. There, in the corner of the waiting room, a kerosene lamp was glimmering barely lighting up the bleak room.

Bronius decided to stay here until the morning dawn. He had no desire wading through the mud in the dark. The distance from here to his parents' homestead was too long to walk-approximately seven kilometers.

Leaning against the wall, Bronius started dozing. Soon, however, the building door opened, and three armed men loudly walked inside-two civilians and one soldier.

They began examining everybody's documents. Shortly, they were standing next to Adomaitis. The soldier with the two men looked at his passport and the certificate of work history time from time also leering angrily at Adomaitis himself as if he had been some kind of criminal.

Finally, they completely suspended his documents. The three men already held in their hands passports of some other people in the room. "The chosen ones" got the order to follow the soldier.

All of the selected passengers were brought to the Militia Department for the interrogation. Their pockets were checked out as well, and they themselves were patted from their heads to their toes.

While searching Bronius's briefcase, officers unwrapped every little thing, where he had a few modest gifts packed for his loved ones.

All the other detainees were thoroughly examined. Adomaitis could not understand why he was threatened and asked to tell the truth. What truth?

Finally, he with the couple of men was released, but three more men were left there for the further quota.

Bronius, mentally exhausted, found himself in the street. He did not want to go back to the train station, even though it was the only place in this tiny town to take a shelter waiting until the morning.

Having felt the real taste of freedom, he did not want to go back there. Therefore, the only way left out of this situation was to walk the direction of his parents' house. Time from time stumbling onto the fences and some trees along the dirt road, he walked rushing to leave this unpleasant place far behind him.

When upon leaving the town he found himself in total darkness, his travel turned into a real misery. Not once being stuck in the mud hole, fumbling, he sometimes had to searched how to scramble himself out of the invisible pool of dirt stretching out almost along all his way.

Trudging and stumbling he kept walking while brushing away with his hand the sweat streaming down his face.

Finally, he reached the half way home. At that time, he suddenly felt so tired he could hardly drag his legs anymore. He saw an enormous shrub growing on the roadside. Then, Bronius gropingly got inside of it and found a thick branch to sit on. He decided to wait there until the sky lightens up a little bit.

However about an hour of time passed, and it was still pitch-dark around. The cold night's air began penetrating under his coat. His damp from sweat shirt was no longer sticking to the skin. Nevertheless, it felt very uncomfortable. With every little move, the debilitating cold pierced him. At some moments, it felt as if it penetrated down to his bones. He realized that little was needed to get a bad cold during such an inclement weather.

Therefore, he got out of the bushes and continued walking further. Bronius knew that by sitting there any longer, he could catch a cold or even get the pneumonia.

Again, he was wading through the mud in the somber darkness. The morning still was not breaking out. However, despite the difficulty traveling, he kept walking the familiar road.

Probably even blindfolded, he would be able to find his parents' house. Few times, he went astray in the dark, after what he found himself on some little path among the tall dry grasses. But then again, Bronius rambling got back to the main dirt road. Thus, fighting various obstacles in the dark of the night for a good five hours, he finally reached the boundary of his father's land.

Only now, standing still in a ravine and drawing deeply into his lungs cool morning air, he brushed the sweat away from his forehead. Now he could take his breath back. At that moment, he was happy, although, very tired and exhausted after the long and difficult walk.

He was looking at those precious and very familiar surroundings. His heart got instantly flooded with the loving warm feelings. Adomaitis realized he was at home. Looking at the east side, he noticed that the firmament had got significantly enlightened.

In a few minutes, all around began clearing up quickly. One could already distinguish the sky from the land. Observing closely under his feet, Bronius could see the tufts of the wizened grass.

He looked ahead of him and saw a few window lights in the distance. The dawn was coming, and some people have been already up.

He knew where his parents' homestead was. There were no lights in any of their windows', though. He remembered that the shutters always used to be closed for the night. The orchard next to the house slumbered isolated by the densely planted willow trees. During autumn and winter seasons, it was easy to discern the blurred contours of the homestead buildings through the bare tree branches.

To the contrary, during the summer time, when the trees got dressed in their thick green clothing, nobody would be able to suspect that there was a house behind the orchard. That was how well the big old trees masked it.

For some reason, Bronius's heart began palpitating hard in his chest. He could not bear any longer and began walking fast toward the first large birches ahead. While on the precious familiar road, bypassing the bigger water pools and jumping over the smaller puddles, Bronius his heart beating fast was approaching the fence that was surrounded by the branches of the willow trees on its both sides.

Bronius passed through the gates and found himself in the orchard, where the apple trees had still been slumbering in the turbid morning light. There were about ten beehives under their widespread branches. Near the dwelling house, there was a pigsty and a little farther away-the barn. In the northern end of the orchard, close to the river, the bathhouse rested.

Adomaitis looked at all the buildings. Nothing slipped away his watchful eyes. He could not notice any changes after the last time he had visited his family a year and a half ago.

The perfect order predominated everywhere. Household equipment was nowhere to be seen; every little thing was neatly placed where it had belonged.

However, in the other farmers' homesteads, all kinds of utensils used to be scattered everywhere, even in the front yard.

It had already been three years when the father got arrested, and nobody knew why. Since then, no news of him had been received, as if the man had had vanished.

Surprisingly mother did not break down; she did not become slack. Quite the opposite-she properly managed the household not letting it fall into decay. Now, she was the head of the family, and she alone had carried the double burden on her shoulders.

In spite of all this, she was in good health. She had always been a very tough woman. Because of her care, the perfectly maintained farmstead still gladdened the eye of every passerby.

Bronius found himself in the yard, where he saw that the pigsty gates were wide open. He walked a few steps to the well and stopped there not knowing what to do next. However, he did not have to remain there for long.

Shortly, he noticed an odd silhouette coming from the barn and moving slowly toward him. Even in broad daylight, it was difficult to discern from a distance who the person was.

Only when the creature approached the pig-house and threw down on the ground a big piece of fodder, Bronius recognized his mother. He wanted to yell out to her, but for some unknown reason, not a word escaped his dry throat. He just stood there stagnant his torpid gaze fixed onto her figure.

The woman grabbed a board from under the fence and took a solid step toward the well where the strange man was standing. Apparently, she held the stake in order to defend herself in case the intruder tried to attack her, or maybe she was planning to drive away the uninvited guest.

It appeared as if she was not afraid of him. It was obvious that if some stranger happened to show up in her yard, she would not hesitate to put her stick to work. She was a tall and strong woman. She could probably just with her bare hands strangle him. Nevertheless, if the stronger than her person came across, she would still have to strike him with the stake over his neck.

The mother was looming slowly toward her son, and Bronius understood that it was better to resort to some precautionary measures in advance. Therefore, he loudly shouted out to her, "Mom! Are you trying to meet me this way?! To consecrate me with the picket..."

"Jesus Christ! This is you, Bronius?" throwing the picket to the side, the mother broke into run. Kissing and hugging him firmly, the woman kept asking, "How did you show up here so unexpectedly, my dear? But look at you! You are all drenched through! Are you cold?" Feeling his coat, mother continued, "You should at least have written a few words to let me know that you are coming. Then, I would have arrived at the train station to pick you up. You shouldn't have walked all the way here. I don't think you take good care of yourself..."

"Mom, don't scold me, please. Aren't you glad to see me?"

"You kidding!? I think of you every day," she cut him short.

"Mom, I love you too much to trouble you at the nighttime. I have pangs already. Even though I have finished gymnasium and now I have a job, I'm not capable of helping you. Instead, you help me by sending packages with food. If not for the products that you kept generously sending to me, I might have not survived. Looks like even having a job can't save a person from hunger. That's not what I had expected when I studied at school. I thought, when I start working, my life will become a lot easier. But as you can see, I have remained the same burden to you... Forgive me please for being such a loser."

"Stop talking nonsense, sonny. You are my only child, and you will never be a burden to me. As long as I can afford it, I will always help you. I don't need your support, son. You yourself are a comfort and pride of mine. I'm happy just to see you healthy. Through this thought you're a loser out of your head. Now, it is so difficult to make ends meet; I'm sure quite a few of students living in the city suffer from hunger. However, I will never let you, sonny, suffer like that." The mother put her arm over the son's shoulder and continued, "Well, we have forgotten the time while chatting. Let's go inside. Do you know how much your arrival will cheer up granny? She has been talking about you almost every day lately. Poor thing asked me recently to write you in order to invite you for a visit. Granny has even fattened a rooster especially for this occasion, and she keeps weighing it every day. She is worried that it can lose any of its meat. She is so attached to you, that I heard your name being mentioned a few times when she prayed in the evenings."

On the way inside the house, mother was telling the son about her daily routine. Moreover, as soon as both of them entered the room, she accosted the old woman inside, "Mother, hurry up to meet the guest. Look who is here-your favorite grandson has come for a visit!"

"What are you, dear, talking about? How can he possibly come here at this time?" Grandma's voice came from the depth in the corner, where she was preparing breakfast.

"I also was surprised when I saw him. He appeared to have fallen down from the heaven straight into our yard. But soon, I realized this wasn't the ghost."

The granny came out from behind the stove with a kerosene lamp in her hand. She was so happy to see her beloved grandchild; she walked with her hands stretched forward ready to hug him. Bronius quickly took the lamp out of her hand and kissed the old woman on both of her cheeks that have been warmed up by the heat of the stove.

The grandmother was so overwhelmed with joy that even a few tears rolled down her shriveled cheeks. Hugging the grandson, she stroked his back reproaching him gently, "You, dear, have totally forgotten us. Why haven't you showed up for so long?"

"Grandma, the times are different now. When I studied at school, I used to get three vacations per year, but when I started working, I had to wait the whole year for a little time off. But wait… you might get so tired of me that you will start wondering when I'm going to leave," jokingly talked Bronius.

"Are you kidding? Shame on you for saying such things! Have we ever got tired of you yet? You know you are always welcome here. But it looks like your coat is all wet, dear. Why didn't you write us a note? Your mother could meet you at the train station. At least, you should have waited until the daylight and not walked at night in the dark."

"Yes indeed, it was pitch-black last night. However, I didn't want hanging out at the stuffy station all night long. I decided I would better go home. It's not that far away after all."

Bronius did not tell her anything about the interrogation and threats. He concealed information about the frightening incident at the train station that left him in a big discomfort.

"Well, grandson, throw off this heavy wet coat. It has been weighting your shoulders long enough."

After taken off his long heavy coat and washing the face with cold water, Bronius felt much better. Now, he was just feeling hungry and a little tired.

Mother went out feeding animals, while granny hurried to finish preparing breakfast. The p;'otatoes had already been fried before Bronius came. Nevertheless, after his unexpected arrival, the grandmother was trying to prepare something better than she usually did.

Toiling around the stove, she kept asking about life of her beloved grandson in the big city, and he barely could keep up with answering her questions. If not for her talking, he probably would already be sleeping right there at the table his head on his arms.

Bronius's eyelids were simply shutting down unwilling to submit to the fight with the fatigue. The circumstances, however, made him struggling further with the sleep; he did not want to appear a spoilt brat in the eyes of his mother and grandmother.

It had been getting lighter and lighter outside. Granny already turned off the lamp, and the shadows of the twilight began dissipating in the room.

Finally, mother returned after feeding the animals. She hurried to help grandma finish making breakfast. Soon, a frying pan with the frizzling cracklings was already standing on the table, and the pancakes were placed there too.

The mother opened a ten-liter capacity bottle of cherry juice and filled up the glasses up to the rim. Bronius his eyes following mother's manly movements was very proud of her, the strong and healthy woman.

At the same time, the feeling of shame started creeping into his heart. Being the child of the woman of such a great endurance, he started feeling himself frail and weak.

Even more now he was afraid to appear tired in her presence. He failed to realize, however, that there was another power in her called the maternity instinct that nature had deeply embodied in every single female.

"Well, son, let's have a drink. This juice is quite strong. After having a couple of glasses, you will sleep much better. You need some rest. I can tell that just by looking at your face."

"Okay, mom, to your and grandma's health."

After emptying the big glass, he drew air deep into his lungs and started praising the drink, "This is the incredibly delicious beverage. What a great flavor! Probably only ancient Roman consuls used to drink something like it in their subjugated countries. I am really fortunate having an honor to taste your wonderful wine."

Bronius cheerfully praised the wine trying to warm himself into her favor. Without waiting for a return compliment from his mother, he tore half of a thin wheat flour pancake and rolled it up. He immersed the piece of the pancake into the hot grease, pined a crackling, and put it into his mouth. While still chewing the food, he again began praising it, since he wanted to please his grandmother also.

"These are really delicious pancakes. It's been a long time I have eaten something like that. As far as I remember, it was a year and a half ago during my summer vacation. Everything for some reason tastes better when it's made at home."

"Son, I did not make this wine. Your father has produced it. It is over twenty years old now. Back then, you had not even been born. When your father and I had got married, we gathered our first cherry harvest. Then, we had made a lot of cherry juice and filled up with it a few ten-liter glass vessels. This bottle has been sitting intact to this very day. We made wine from various berries: strawberries, raspberries, blackberries, and others. Since then, we emptied many bottles of wine. However, we always left untouched this one ten-liter bottle. We decided to open it when some special opportunity comes along."

The mother gave a big sigh and continued, "We have more wine in the basement that is also very old. It could be ten or fifteen years old. After your father was arrested, I still used to make a few bottles of wine every year. Unfortunately, there is no one to drink it with anymore. The whole cellar has already been filled with the bottles. Since the time your father is no longer with us, our home is just not the same anymore. There is no more lively laughter and no songs here. I remember the times when we used to give such great feasts that amazed even our local priest with the doctor. Even they were not able to enjoy themselves as we did in our house."

Silence reigned for awhile at the table. Then mother resumed talking, "Back then, we had plenty of everything. Granaries and garners were full of grain and earthly blessings. The barn was filled with roughage up to its ceiling, and our cattle-shed was full of animals. Our fields, turning emerald green during summer time, used to vivify us with bountiful harvest, the earth's generous reward to the farmers for their endless labor. True, your father sometimes had to work hard even at the nighttime. However, the soil was fertile on its own, and it always blessed our family with the sizeable harvest. Our farm blossomed like some water lily after opening its magnificent fragrant white flower."

"I remember that," Bronius said his eyes sparkling and happy smile playing in his lips.

The mother continued, "Now, for some reason it is difficult to make yourself even to go to work. Whatever you do, it feels as if you work not for yourself anymore, but rather drag some serfdom. Parasites teem everywhere around campaigning on a daily basis, doing some dumb meetings only to distract people from their families and their business. They only want us feeding them and giving them more vodka. I don't believe in their collective farms. It's ridiculous farmers should give up all their possessions to the government!"

Now grandma joined the conversation, "There are many people who put their farms to perish, when they can live under a God's Bosom, in abundance. They are ready to unite themselves under umbrellas of those collective farms. I think they are just envious. They spread all sorts of rumors around about some miraculous kites that bring wealth to people. Nevertheless, they themselves have nothing, because they just keep idling their time away. They get up late, when the rest of the farmers are already eating lunches. No wonder such workers have nothing to show in their barns. The kites love those who work hard day and night rather than those who sleep until noon. Our farm is small-only ten hectares of land, but we have plenty of everything. However, some people are not able to grow enough grain even on hundred hectares of land. The same way they are going to work in the Russian farms. Soon they'll find out for themselves what the collective farms are about. In a meanwhile, the dumb people will keep believing, giving praises, and exalting this new way of farming."

Bronius was listening to his mother and thinking sad thoughts about the father. His gaze was fixed onto a big portrait hanging in front of him on the wall. Both the mother and the father were very young in it, probably about his age. A joyful smile was playing on their faces testifying about the happy life together. Bronius could not comprehend why cruel fate separated them. He was sad because their life now has been changed forever. He continued looking at the two precious faces surrounded by a halo of happiness.

Soon Bronius caught himself no longer listening to what his mother was saying. Nevertheless, he was feeling cozy and safe at home sitting like this submerged in his deep thoughts. However, his grandmother's anxious voice woke him up out of his stagnation, "Bronius, why are you so quiet? You have forgotten about the food. Eat, dear, your breakfast while it's still hot."

Granny moved the plate closer to the grandson.

The mother filled up their glasses with aromatic wine for the second round. She was the first to empty her glass and then she encouraged her son to have a drink too. Bronius followed her example; after emptying his wineglass, he asked timidly, "Mom, have you received any news about dad?"

"None at all… Several years already have passed after that terrible day, and I could not find out anything. As if the earth had opened up and swallowed him. I just can't comprehend that. After all, government officials were the ones who had arrested him. Why couldn't we find out anything from them? Where did they take him and why? I think they are the only ones who know the truth, but nobody is going to tell it to us."

"It must be very hard on you," Bronius said.

"Of course, it is. For so many years, your dad and I lived together and knew each other's secrets. Even if he wanted to hide something from me, he still could not have done it. At all times we used to be together. He never went anywhere alone. We used to go to the farmers' market together, we used to walk to church together. We worked together in the field. We always spent time together, and not even for an hour, we got separated. I am sure he never had belonged to any organization. Therefore, it had been an unjust thing to snatch him right out of his home and away from his family."

Tears filled her eyes when she continued, "How come you, me, our relatives, neighbors have not been driven into the graves yet? Why only he was chosen to be the victim? After all, everyone hates those foreign extortionists. They came here uninvited and brought the entire county to its knees. They force us to pray to their foreign ideas, worship their foreign gods. They tread our ancient traditions under their feet. They promised paradise on earth, but in reality, it is a veil of tears. I don't understand for what purpose we would need somebody from a foreign country, especially when they treat us like their slaves. In addition, they speak a language we don't understand. Don't we have our own language-the oldest living language in Europe?! We can be proud of our history as well."

The mother became so excited; she emptied all the wine in her glass and noisily sat it onto the table. Then she brushed her lips with the back of her hand and continued, "Son, I want you to know that five hundred years ago, Lithuania was the biggest and the most powerful county in Europe. Why should we listen to the strangers rattling their arms in front of us and threatening to destroy our country? Why would we need their foreign ideas; don't we have our own? Our ancestors had worked hard for ages. We, too, always worked from the sunrise until the sunset and even at night when necessary. We are not looking for an easy life the new government keeps promising. According to them, we are going to live in abundance without even having to work. According to them the machines are going to do all the work. Then tell me please who will produce those machines, who will repair them, and who will operate them? I don't know how people earn their living in big cities. However, I do know how farmers live. The only thing I can tell is that the machines can't do all the work without the help of a man. Without the help of a farmer, there will be no good harvest. Human and labor are connected in such strong ties that one cannot do without the other. Therefore, no matter who says what, the world cannot exist without the human labor. Imagine that for a moment everything stops. What a boring life that would be! True, it would be a good life for those who do not like to work, but there are not many of such people. The rest of us would suffer without having anything to do."

Bronius's interest kept growing as the mother continued talking, "In my opinion, a human being is happy only when he is fully occupied. If a person lacks something to do, he gets restless and unsatisfied. For example, look at people being entertained during a wedding. In our village, wedding celebrations last the whole week. Usually people invited to the wedding look forward to having fun. However, halfway through the wedding celebration, it becomes old and they are glad when the celebration is over. Ironically, we feel at peace again only when we get back to working. That is how closely we are connected to labor. But looks like from now on we are going to be forced to loaf. We don't need any collective farms or tales about the kites. The labor itself is life! The more work we can accomplish working for our families, the better will be our lives. Remember, son, those words of mine, the old crow…"

After hearing his mother talking, Bronius felt very proud of her. For the first time in his life, he had seen her like this. True, he always had had regarded her as a tough and strong woman. This time, however, he saw her in a very different light. She managed to fill his heart with deep respect. Now he saw her as a person of a strong character, who had conquered the biggest storms in her life. She was standing in front of him like a tall rock firmly rooted into the earth. She never became sluggish and she'd not given into a slight breeze. She bravely looked life into the eye as if saying with the sneer, "Well, savage fortune, we'll see which one of us is stronger…"

Immersed in thought, Bronius poured another glass of wine for himself. His hand froze halfway when he glanced at the mother sitting in front of him. She appeared so majestic and unconquerable. He saluted her in his mind and gulped the wine down.

"Well, I think, it's time for you, sonny, to take a nap. There are still a lot of things that I would like to tell you. But we can do that after you get rested."

Bronius drank another cup of wonderful cherry wine and, feeling a bit tipsy, walked to the bedroom.

There he slowly undressed. Feeling tired, he lay down and quickly fell sound asleep. It was lunchtime when he woke up. Suddenly, he felt some gravity on his heart. Bronius tried clearing his throat, but the pain under his chest started really bothering him. At first he ignored it. However, as soon as he lifted his head off the pillow, he started feeling dizzy.

Most likely he would have fallen down if he was standing on his feet. He did not pass out only because he was lying. Bronius felt giddy, and his entire body felt like on fire. He gave it another attempt to get up. This time he was able to sit down. At that moment, the mother walked into the room.

Seeing her son sitting on the edge of the bed, she said, "I'm glad you are awake. It's lunch time. I have come here to wake you up. I thought you won't be able to get asleep at night if you continue sleeping. Granny did not want me to wake you up. She said-let him sleep. Well, it's great you have slept for so long. But now it's time to get up. It's such an unusually fine sunny day outside."

Bronius tried to stand up on his feet, but his efforts were fruitless. He only gave a moan and slumped back on the bed.

"What's a matter with you, sonny?" asked the mother in a frightened voice and ran up to him.

"I don't know. My head swims. Everything has just gone dark in my eyes."

The mother sat down onto the edge of his bed, laid her palm on his forehead, and exclaimed in a frightened voice, "My God! You Bronius are burning. What has happened to you? I will prepare a cold compress for your head."

This was when motherly instinct awakened in this strong like steel woman. Soon, already two broken hearted women were standing beside him.

After returning home, he spent almost a week confined to bed. Finally he got up. In was afternoon. Despite feeling weak, he put his clothes on and stood up onto his shaking legs. Carefully like a child, who has just learned how to walk, he came up staggering to the window, through which cheerful sunbeams have been penetrating into the room and spilling out onto the wooden boards of the floor painted brown.

He set down onto a small stool standing below the windowsill. There were a few hens pecking around in the yard. In the middle of the flock, a handsome rooster was twiddling. Upon finding a tiny grain or perhaps a bug, he called the chickens to come closer to him. As if being trained, they immediately ran to him.

Bronius counted the chickens, since he had nothing else to do. It was not easy counting them, though. The birds never stayed in one place; they kept running all over the yard. There were twelve hens, and the rooster was the thirteenth among them.

Feeling better, Bronius was enjoying the scene out of the window. He noticed how much more dense the apple trees had become in the orchard. He was happy the strength returned to his body.

As soon as the grandmother saw him sitting there, she quickly turned him away from the window asking to go back to bed. He obeyed her wishes without any resistance.

Towards the evening, however, he got up again. Only this time, Bronius did not listen to her. After kindling the fire in the stove, he opened its little metal door and turned his knees against the blaze to keep them warm. The skin under his pants got so hot that he had to draw himself away, since he had started feeling as if the material over the skin could melt down.

The next day since the early morning, he felt totally fine. Only his eyes were still a little bit sore. He lounged fretting the whole day in the house from one corner to another.

When the evening came, he went to bed earlier than ever, right after dinner. Soon he was sound asleep. Only healthy people could sleep like that. Next morning, as soon as it grew light, he got up and, after breakfast, went outside.

The day happened to be extremely beautiful. Sun was shining. There was not even the slightest breeze outside. After quickly crossing the yard, he found himself in the orchard, where dry apple leaves kept rustling under his feet with every his step. Bronius inhaled fresh air into his lungs. It had a slight smell of the decaying leaves. He enjoyed this smell, and it was very joyful on his heart.

He walked slowly the whole orchard. The apple trees stood without leaves, and there were beehives lined up under the bare branches, about ten of them total. Bronius did not linger there for very long.

He quickly found himself by the wooden fence. Now he joyfully marched along it, where on the other side a narrow brook murmured. Its banks covered with thick bushes had shielded the orchard from harsh north winds during cold winter times.

After passing through the gates, he found himself at the riverside. There he walked down the small wooden steps and onto the low precipice that had led to the water. He approached the osier its branches drooping into the river and sat down onto its thick ramification. The branch did not even move.

For a while, he was sitting and gazing at the opposite bank of the river through the large opening in the brush. It appeared grubbed by the force of the rushing spring waters.

Nevertheless, the water itself looked so incredibly clear. Sunbeams were filtering into the river's steam, and bottom fine sand with the little rocks scattered here and there could be seen despite the depth there being well above one's head.

While sitting on the trunk, Bronius remembered when as a child he used to jump into the water from this same willow-tree. Thus he spent almost two hours in his favorite spot recalling the beautiful carefree years of his past.

How many times he'd bathed in this bay! During the summer heat, probably six or more times a day. He had got so used to doing it that even on the foggy days he'd still liked to swim there even just a couple times per day.

In addition, in the evenings, the sun beginning to descend and the mist starting to rise from the river, the water used to become so nice and warm. He had hated to come out of the river then. He could just sit there for hours feeling like in some bath. That is how warm the water in the bay behind the willow bushes sometimes used to be, just like the tea.

Only when coming out of the river and dressing up, he had his teeth chattering. The home was near, though, and the caring hands of his grandmother had had always made a soft bed for him. He used to come home and fall into the bed, where his teeth had stopped chattering. Then he would sleep sound like a baby until the sunbeams filtering through the curtain woke him up the next morning.

Every day had offered the same lovely time at the river fishing, swimming, and sunbathing. He had loved laying on the grass, looking at the cloud formations in the sky, and listening to the birds singing. He himself had even felt as free as a bird.

Those times had been the best in his entire life, with no worries and no pain.

While living in the city, he had a few responsibilities. Doing his homework after school had been one of them. Bronius had always been a good student. Some of his classmates had got left to repeat an old course the second time in a row for the following year. However, Bronius had always managed to learn his lessons at school the very first time.

In addition, he had never got left to re-pass his exams along with some other lazy students during summer holidays that had always lasted for a period of three months.

Now things changed so drastically. Bronius often felt lost in thoughts, and he continually anticipated for something bad to happen. He had been dealing with the depressing mood for a while, but there was nobody he wished to share this with.

Although he had had some friends from his school times, their paths had diverged. Bronius had left alone, isolated not only from them but also from his own family.

Moreover, his life circumstances became intolerable. Who could take him out of this impasse? Bronius reconciled himself with his loneliness. He decided he was going to remain rotting in that abyss, alone and misunderstood.

However, he was wrong, very wrong! He was not alone, even though he had been fallen into the deep depression. He did not realize yet that the time had come for this crisis to end and for him to step into the new right path of life. The time began for him to fly somewhat very fast, skipping.

While he was sitting on the willow tree branch drooping over the water, the gloomy thoughts began bothering him again. Bronius tried to get rid of them, but it did not work.

Moreover, he relived in his head some of the past events repeatedly until he started feeling completely exhausted. Accompanied by his sad thoughts, he got off the branch he had been sitting on and climbed up the steep river slope.

Now, he was walking home his head hanging low. When he reached the house, he did not feel like going inside. Instead, he sat down on a bench under the window.

He sat there his head leaning up the outside wall of the house and fixed his gaze into the distance. He looked with the dull eyes in front of him but did not see anything.

It felt as if the time had stopped. For a moment, it seemed there was nothing around. However, in reality, the life continued. The surroundings were so beautiful, and the sun was shining brightly.

Bronius started feeling too warm. He had to throw his coat off and hang it beside him over the bench. He sank back into his thoughts time from time letting out a deep sigh or a quiet moan.

It was not know how long he would continue sitting on the bench lamenting painfully if not for his mother who approached quietly awakening him from the senseless torpidity.

"Sonny, you have only recently risen from the sick bed and you are already sitting outside without a coat. Do you like to be sick? Put your coat back on, please."

"Mom, it's such a nice day. It's too hot with the coat."

"Then, at least, keep the coat on your shoulders."

"Well, if you want, I will do that. But I want you to do something for me too. Sit down over here on the bench. I want you to forget about all your chores at home and just relax for a few minutes. Enjoy the sunshine with me," saying this, he removed the coat and covered with it his back while making room for her to sit down.

Bronius uttered, "I know that you seldom find time to just sit and do nothing, and enjoy the moment."

"I have come, son, to discuss some business with you. Therefore, I am more interested in talking to you, than I'm interested in enjoying the weather. It is my duty as a mother to find some time to talk with you from the heart."

"Mom, you always worry too much."

" Maybe I am. I always have plenty of work to do at home. Nobody, son, will do my chores for me. If your father still lived with us, everything would be different. Now, I have to do all the work by myself. I hope you also don't wish for our household to fall apart. But I haven't come here to complain. I already came to terms that I would have to live my life alone, without your father long time ago. My own parents had a difficult life. My biggest concern now is you, son. I want you to know that I'm worried because you don't take good care of yourself."

"Mom, it just seems to you this way. And I understand why. To every mother her child is always little. But you know that I'm an adult now, and I can take care of myself. This is not your fault I am barely making ends meet. Although I have used your help many times, I want you to know that I don't intend to be a burden to you any longer. I could even quit my job that is of little use anyway and come back home. An extra worker can do no harm to our household. Then you, mom, won't have to do all your chores alone. I can help you."

"Let's be honest with each other. I don't want to diminish my concern regarding the way you act. Both you and I know very well that life shatters the weak while it helps the strong. For example, those who fight with calamities do not sob. They don't give into failures, they are led by their improvements. It's pathetic you are such a weakling. We both have been struck by the same disaster. You lost your father, and I lost my husband. This fate, however, did not bring me down to my knees. I fought with the difficulties. Often my heart wept bleeding profusely. Despite that, I managed to get up and go to work. Only then, I discovered I would find the solace and forget all the wrongs. And look at you… You, son, became inert and tripped down the halfway. But the worst thing is that it looks like you don't even try to draw yourself up. You've blindly submitted to your fate entrusting your entire future to it."

Bronius did not say a word.

The mother continued, "True, life has not been spoiling you for quite a while now. Tell me please are you going to give up and come back home? Have I put you through school only to have you help me in the field later? Of course, our household can use extra work hands. But if I had wanted to turn you into an ordinary worker, I would have not thought of sending you to school. The education you have been acquiring in the capital is not needed in our homestead. Maybe it is difficult for you to understand, but what has happened now is you are neither a highly qualified specialist nor a good agricultural laborer. Nevertheless, if you continue studying, you can become everything you want to be. You just need to strive for that. I exhausted my every effort to put you through the best school in the entire country. Naturally,

I don't want our dreams to go in vain. You yourself could not handle hard agricultural work disrupting the entire household within a year or so. In addition, I would hate to see you with a dung-fork on a pile of manure!"

"Mom, I don't understand you," Bronius sounded surprised. "According to you, I'm worth nothing at all?"

"That's right... until you finish the school," answered the mother with determination, after what an uncomfortable silence fell between them.

Bronius was instantly covered in cold sweat. He found no strength, however, to break this oppressive silence.

As always, the mother demonstrated her superiority to son by resuming the conversation first, "Don't despair, son. I will be frank with you because I mean well. I would like you to change your outlook on life. By continuing to think this way you will hardly make your bread. And even then it will be bitter. You should think about an easier life. Therefore, you should continue studying, after what you can choose your path in life. You understand that you will have to choose your profession, don't you? You've studied before and you are used to that. Now you could pick some other specialty, such as the civil law or something else. Whatever you decide to learn, all your efforts will pay off at the end. You'll have a better job in return and, therefore, a better life. Look at your current life. All day long you sit at the office for a minimum wage. You cannot even support yourself. Son, your main goal at the time being is to pursue education further. As long as our farm has not been ravaged, I can help you. I only pray for you to wake up from this hibernation. You're not the only one broken morally. Look at me. Look how I keep fighting with my destiny. I don't give in to the calamities, even though I have had more problems in my life. Go on further with your education, sonny. I will continue helping you even if I have to give away my last shirt."

Mother's eyes filled with tears, and she wiped them out with her hand callous from hard work. Bronius seeing such her devotion instantly forgot all the reproaches. He took her hand into his unmanly soft hands and kissed it.

Then he said, "Forgive me, please. You serve as a live human example. From you I can gain energy and stamina. You have opened my eyes and convinced me. You are right because I have been such a patsy. But now it's over. Tomorrow without fail I am going to Vilnius, and I will make every effort to enter university again. It's not my fault that father was arrested. Because of him I got expelled from the University, even though I'd already been in my second year. His arrest put a stigma on me. Moreover, it practically has crippled my life. I know that my father was innocent. And even if he had done something wrong, why should it impact my life in any way? I should not have been kicked out of school because of my father. Have I hurt anybody? What did I personally do wrong? This dark shadow of bad luck has been following me since. No, I will not be silent! I will lay myself out to prove that I had nothing to do with it! The truth must come out to the surface. There must be somebody out there who will be on my side."

"I approve your reasoning, son. God bless your endurance, and I wish you to remain spiritually strong."

"I will try my best, mother, to make it happen."

"I'm glad you've finally made your decision. I will be at peace, if you succeed in re-entering the University. Maybe I should go with you to Vilnius? Perhaps I can grease somebody's palm. It must be an inconvenience for you to do that, and perhaps you can have some problems because of that."

"No, you really shouldn't do that. I don't feel guilty. Therefore, I'm not going to give anyone even a rusty copeck. Let everybody croak. The truth must prevail. I did nothing wrong."

"Bronius, don't be naive. Your father did not commit any crimes either. In spite of that, we don't know where he is now. There is no justice in this world. Isn't it also pathetic when people have to seek justice with the palm oil?"

Bronius shook his head in disapproval.

Then the mother began talking again, "You don't believe bribes help? Soon, you will see for yourself how powerful they are. Since many people live half-starving, without being able to make ends meet, it becomes almost impossible refusing any graft. This is why bribery is so widespread."

"Mom, I will go by myself. Nobody has to take my hand and lead me everywhere like some little boy. Those days are long gone, and they will never come back. You have a lot of work to do at home and all kinds of worries to deal with. I can manage my affairs all by myself. I've firmly decided to go alone. But I want you to know that I am extremely grateful to you for everything you have done for me."

"Ok, go alone. Just don't forget to write us about what's going on in your life. And remember, if you aren't be able to establish yourself at the University, then I will come and help you. I must go now. The animals are thirsty," having a sigh of relief, said the mother.

She got up from the bench and walked towards the cottage leaving her son lost in thought.

Bronius did not remain sitting by himself for long though. He walked across the orchard toward the river occasionally stopping to draw the fresh air deep into his lungs. However, he was in no time to reach the river, since the mother all out of breath caught up running with him.

"What is wrong with you, mom? Why are you running?" Bronius turned his face to her.

"Bronius, let's go home! Look at the other side of the river. See all these troops there? There is something happening. I am afraid it could lead to a firefight with our local people. We need to run."

Having said that, the mother seized her son's hand and pulled him running after her.

Bronius ran into the house and quickly threw off the coat of his shoulders. Then he walked up to the window. The mother joined him and both fixed their frightened gazes onto the bodies of the soldiers quivering through the tree trunks.

Probably more than ten of them were on the other side of the river. Bronius occasionally exchanged glances with the mother, but neither one of them uttered a word.

Nevertheless, he could not perceive anything wrong with this view. He was hoping they would disappear just as quickly as they had mysteriously appeared seemingly out of nowhere.

The mother, however, had a different opinion about what was going on there. She had envisioned something bad happening; she just did not dare to reveal her fears to the son.

Bronius still appeared indifferent while taking a detached look at the scene in front of them.

The mother seemed to calm down a little bit. So far there was no sign of the soldiers doing any harm. Finally, she managed to tear herself away from the window.

Now the granny replaced her. She was standing there and observing the soldiers with the frightened look on her face while silently mumbling prayers under her nose. Occasionally a heavy sigh slipped out her chest and she started a new prayer in oblivion.

After finishing her prayers, she crossed herself with her right hand and said, "We all are at God's Will."

The mother began preparing something for them to eat while Bronius remained by the window sitting on the chair. However, he was not longer preoccupied with the soldiers. Now he was absorbed in thought, when suddenly he saw a column of smoke rising into the sky.

There was neighbors' homestead burning across, on the other side of the river, and the wind slowly blew dissipating smoke toward Bronius parents' house. Being surprised and confused, he initially could not comprehend what was happening. It was scary to think the neighbors' house has been on fire. Only when he noticed the flame tongues consuming the thatch he realized that everything enfolding before his eyes was real. He instantly jumped off the chair screaming, "The house is burning! The house if burning!"

"What is burning? Where is burning?" the mother sounded confused.

"The neighbors' homestead is burning!"

"What are you prattling?" the mother was so terrified she could barely talk.

"Mother, look! Lopinis's homestead is burning."

The grandmother grabbed her head with her hands and quietly as if afraid that someone might hear her whispered, "Oh, Dear Lord… Jurgeliavicius's house is also on fire."

The mother was standing as if rooted to the ground, afraid to come closer to the window. Only after a few minutes, she approached them fixing her eyes onto the flames that have been submerging the two houses of the neighbors.

About a dozen of the soldiers were walking around and shouting something. Two woman and Bronius have been standing at the window not able to utter a word.

Suddenly a few of the soldiers showed up on their side of the river. They were marching directly towards their homestead. For some time, the creek delayed the soldiers who had difficulty getting across its cold water.

"Why are they coming here?" fearfully babbled Bronius in a trembling voice. "Maybe they are going to set our house on fire too?"

Finally the men found a little footbridge and crossed the creek. When they approached a bathhouse, one of them pulled out a filament of straws from under its roof and ignited it. Then he threw the burning tuft onto the roof. Soon the whole sauna was engulfed with thick gray smoke, and all the walls of the building started blazing like a torch.

After seeing that, the mother jumped out of the house and broke into run through the orchard toward the bathhouse. She stopped in the alley of the apples trees. With her hands spread wide open she attempted to block the soldiers' way. It was obvious they were headed toward the homestead now.

Bronius like in some dream saw how the mother fell on her knees. He could not hear her voice because of the distance separating them. Only from her behavior he understood that she was begging for mercy. He observed strong gestures of the soldiers, who bawled something loudly while swinging their arms.

Then the mother, crawling after one of them on her knees, grabbed the edge of his overcoat. The soldier harshly kicked her away with his black leather boot.

Seeing all this, Bronius's heart gushed with blood, and he hid his face in the palms. When he lifted his head and looked through the window again, he saw the grandmother running across the orchard now her long disheveled gray hair fluttering in the wind.

The granny ran up to one of the soldiers', fell on her knees, and reached for his hand in an attempt to kiss it. The soldier angrily forced his hand out of her callous palms. At that moment, the old woman lost her balance. She fell on the ground and was not able to get up.

In the meanwhile, the mother ran up to another soldier. She was still begging for mercy. Therefore, she was not in time to help the grandmother get up. However, the enraged soldier did not want to listen to her.

In front of Bronius's eyes was looming his mother's bloody face. The soldier with his boot had kicked the kneeling before him woman on her cheek knocking her on the ground. Bronius heard both the mother and the grandmother lamenting something. The horrible scene broke the silence and peace of the day.

Bronius's heart kept bleeding profusely when he stood numb by the window watched this tragic view. He had no desire to leave the house. At the moment, he just wanted to burn in the flames and be buried under the pile of the ashes.

He could not hear anything anymore. He did not look at what was happening out the window. It seemed to Bronius as if he could not even comprehend anything. The vociferation of the angry soldiers', who had been sent by the NKVD authorities, and the prayers of the two helpless women dissipated into the air.

He just stood rooted into the ground all stiff, his blunt gaze fixed onto a single point ahead of him. He had been waiting when the soldiers light up their home too and he start suffocating from the smoke and the heat of the fire.

It felt as if an eternity had passed by. However, in fact, it was only a few minutes which had put their lives the head over the heels.

The door of their cottage soon opened up, and the whole regiment of the soldiers bust inside. Bronius could only hear them. He could not see the soldiers, since he was at the other end of the house.

He was hearing the male voices, but he could not understand all the words spoken. Nevertheless, it seemed as if the mother with grandmother had managed to appease them and soften their harshness a bit.

Soon, grandmother found herself standing by the stove. She laid two bricks sideways on the top of it. After chopping some splinters, she struck the match, and the dry wood started crackling merrily. Then, she placed a big heavy black skillet onto the top of the stove, cut up some bacon into thick pieces, and laid them on the bottom of the pan. In a few moments, the frizzling bacon began spreading tasty smell which made everybody's mouth watering.

Meanwhile, the mother brought a full ten-liter bottle of homemade wine and placed it on the table. She also dragged in a big bowl full of honey. She did not have to encourage those "benefactors", who had turned the homesteads of the neighbors to ashes, to eat the food. They sat down at the table without any invitation themselves and like some hungry wolves began scooping the honey out.

For some time, just the loud puffing and smacking could be heard. Only when the officer, who evidently had been in charge of the soldiers, gave a command to stop they ceased gobbling the honey and put their spoons down.

The officer got up from under the table and walked to another room to check how soon the promised fried egg meal was going to be ready.

Suddenly he saw Bronius sitting there by the window. Their angry penetrating looks intertwined like the swords of opponents' fighting a duel.

The officer with lightening speed grabbed the handle of his gun, pulled it out of the sheath, and began waving with it in front of Bronius's pale face.

Grandmother frightened retreated backwards, when the soldier commanded in Russian, "Hands up!"

Bronius could not immediately perceive what was required of him because he was extremely puzzled by all that had been happening in their house.

When the officer, however, shouted at him for the second time, he rose up off the bench and slowly raised his arms up.

The officer called a couple of the soldiers to come and search Bronius's pockets. First, he had to turn them inside out himself and submit his documents for the officer's review. After looking at the papers, the officer dropped them onto the small table standing close to the stove.

Suddenly, the soldiers went on the rampage again threatening to burn the whole homestead. The mother blocked one of the soldier's way by falling on her knees in the doorway when he was trying to walk out with a box of matches in his hand. She cried for mercy and begged not to burn anything. The woman tumbled over the officer with her whole body trying to prevent him from getting outside.

After kicking her into a stomach, he left the house, after what all the rest of the soldiers flocked outside after him into the yard. The order to get outside was given to all of the dwellers of the house as well, since the soldiers were just about to ignite it.

Weeping and nearly fainting, the two women their heads hanging low slowly walked out of the cottage However, Bronius left inside. Then, the officer ran into the house his face distorted with anger, and he shouted at Bronius to get outside too.

However, Bronius refused to walk outside insisting it had been his native home. He bravely declared that he was not some criminal trying to get through the intruder's head that he had never had any ties to any offenders. Bronius kept repeating he had no intention to leave the house, even if he was to be burnt alive together with the whole building.

The officer was shocked to experience the unexpected resistance. Bronius took advantage of the momentum and started persuading the stunned officer trying to convince him of not having anything to do with any government wreckers or any other groups of saboteurs.

Moreover, he began thoroughly laying out all about his job and telling about his vacation, which he had come to spend here, in his homeland. Finally, it appeared as if his sincere and relatively calm explanation had slightly softened the hard-hearted officer.

Then Bronius fell silent, and the officer didn't say a word too.

Grandma was already back at the stove. The sound of the frizzling bacon could be heard again, and the bluish clouds of smoke began forming in the air.

A chimneystack was not in time to suck all of the smoke. Therefore, it was slowly dissipating in the room. The sapwood turned into live coals, which became almost white covered with the layer of ash.

The officer abruptly turned around and left Bronius standing. Apparently not the Bronius's talk made the biggest impact on the callous man. Most likely he just did not want to leave a big bottle of wine standing untouched on the table.

Grandma beat twenty eggs into cracklings, and instantly the sound of sizzling resumed in the air. Soon the whole frying pan was sitting on the table.

The hungry soldiers simply gorged the eggs with bacon rinsing everything down with the homemade wine. After they emptied the frying pan, the second round of eggs with bacon was prepared for them.

In addition to that, the grandmother brought two plates of smoked sausage with black rye bread and placed them on the table.

The soldiers consumed the food so fast that they had not left anything even for the officer, who had been doing his propaganda talk while everybody was avidly eating. In a meanwhile, the soldiers guzzled the food as if they had had nothing to eat for the entire week.

After they emptied more than half of the bottle, the officer gave an order to invite Bronius to join them at the table. The officer poured a full glass of wine and urged him to drink. Ironically, it turned out that the invaders started treating him to his parents wine in his own home.

Being afraid to complicate the situation that had seemingly been growing softer, Bronius drank to the dregs without arguing. Setting the empty glass on the table, he did not know what to do next-to leave or to stay. However, he didn't have to debate for long, since the officer ordered him to remain at the table.

When the bottle was emptied, the mother brought another one exactly the same size. The soldiers drank it down to the bottom too.

Bronius grew so drunk, that he started seeing the entire masquerade as if through the fog. He did not remember much of anything happening after that. He just felt one of the soldiers embracing him while talking to him all the time in Russian.

Upon separating, a couple of the soldiers even kissed him. All of them stumbled out of the homestead. The soldiers with the officer left the same time a red sunset disappeared below the horizon.

Miraculously, they had not set the house on fire, even though they had had threatened to do that in the beginning of their vicious visit.

Everybody was drunk, even the grandmother. The poor thing got filled up so badly that she couldn't even get up off a chair.

Bronius did not remember how he went to sleep. Only after feeling sick, he woke up at midnight. He found himself laying in bed with all his clothes still on. He felt so nauseated that it seemed as if he would start vomiting any minute .

He got up with difficulty and could hardly walk. Holding onto the walls, he staggered to the bucket with the water. He downed two cups of water and felt a little bit better. Then he returned to bed where he undressed, got back under the sheets, and quickly fell asleep.

This time when he woke up, there was already broad daylight. He saw his mother toiling by the stove and greeted her.

"How do you feel, son?" she asked.

"Not so good, mother," replied he in a quivering hoarse voice. "Where is the grandma?"

"Grandma, Bronius, is ill. Those pigs yesterday literally forced the old thing to drink. No wonder, she is barely alive today. How much an old person can handle? At least, they did not set the house on fire. Thanks to God Almihgty! What terrible times have come!" painfully moaned the mother.

Bronius got into his house slippers and walked to the bed where his grandmother was laying. For awhile, he gazed at her droopy, deathly pale face. The grandmother appeared barely alive and could only intermittently breathe.

He wanted to wake her up in order to give her a cup of water. Nevertheless, at the same time he felt so sorry for her that he did not dare to touch the old woman. Feeling sick at heart and still being hangover, he wobbled back to bed himself.

"Bronius, maybe you should get up. Have breakfast, drink some hot tea. Soon you should feel better."

"I don't want to. I feel like throwing up."

"Have a cup of tea, and you'll feel better."

"I'm not sure if the tea can help."

"Just try."

"Okay, I will."

Bronius rose up with difficulty holding his head in his palms. For a few minutes, he listened to his blood pulsating in his temples. Finally, he gathered his strength and suppressed the desire to vomit.

He got up and poured himself some water into a big metal bowl. Then he threw the shirt off his shoulders. The water was cold and he hated to wash his face and neck with it.

Bronius gave a sigh and washed his face first. Then he started quickly rubbing his chest until the cold water made his flesh creep. Even then, he did not cease washing himself. Finally, he began vigorously rubbing his body with a towel until his skin turned red. He quickly put on a clean shirt and a warm wool sweater over the top of it.

As he walked into the kitchen, the mother poured him a glass of strong black tea. Bronius placed a hard square piece of sugar into his mouth and began sipping the hot tea. Time from time he kept blowing the air through his lips in order to cool it down. He had to drink two big cups of tea before he started feeling almost as he usually did.

The hot tea even made him sweat. Wiping his reddened face with a handkerchief, he walked up to the window where a small stool was standing under its sill.

Everything outside looked like always. The day was hazy, even though the sun had cheerfully shone yesterday. The thick fog was hanging over the river, and it was almost impossible to discern its bank on the other side . Even the beehives under the somber dark tree branches looked somewhat mysterious.

Despite everything looking the same, a strange feeling something had been missing overwhelmed him. Only he could not understand what that something was.

He remembered yesterday's events as if through the mist. Now it seemed to him as if it had happened long ago, perhaps even a few years ago.

Suddenly the picture emerged into his mind of his mother with blood on her face and begging for mercy while kneeling in front of the soldier. Another picture flashed of his grandmother with her white dispersed hair. In his mind's eye, he also saw the tongues of flames ruthlessly licking their neighbors' farmhouses and the black smoke hovering above their own burning bathhouse.

How strange it had been seeing their over the decades acquired assets burning! The shock his family had experienced was so immense that everything appeared almost surreal. At some moments it even seemed as if the mother with the grandma hadn't paid serious attention to what had been happening as if not theirs but somebody else's property had been burning.

Moreover, they had entertained their worst enemies to the meal and the homemade wine! Neither the mother nor the grandmother had looked at the finishing to burn bathhouse, even though it had been ready to collapse at any given moment right in front of their eyes, like some house of cards.

Bronius got overwhelmed with the strange feeling that prompted his cynical laugh. Then he uttered in an undertone, "I feel like some perpetual pilgrim, who is in search of the Holy Sepulcher that probably has never even existed."

"Are you talking to me, son?" turning her face to him, asked the mother.

"I'm just talking to myself."

"What are you there talking about to yourself?"

"I am tired of the humdrum of the daily living, which the foreign invaders keep hauling us about. I cannot handle this any longer. I don't know where to resort to, but I have to immediately change my attitude and start handling life differently. We are humiliated by them, treated not like normal human beings, but like some animals or things that belong to them. Enough! We don't have to live this way. We must defend ourselves. We need to express our concern in regards to that, so that other people wake up, too. The crimes of the foreign government should not be crowned. It is vital to let the folks know all about what is going on. New generations living after us should be horrified by the atrocities that had been done in the middle of the twentieth century. Paradoxically, everything is happening at the same time together with the fast evolving technology, flourishing science and culture. This barbarism in the highest degree has reached the culmination in the countries subjugated by Russia. Millions of innocent people are doomed to perish or to drag this inhumane yoke while placed into the most awful conditions."

"But what can we do, son, about that? We just need to clench our teeth and be silent waiting until this cruel barbarism ends. The horrible torture of Lithuanian people cannot go on forever. Over the time, humanness should prevail. Then, there will be real paradise on earth. There will be no oppressors and, therefore, no need feeding all these parasites who are just swarming all around us."

"Has it ever occurred to you, mom, that after driving local farmers into the Soviet collective farms, their so called Kolkhozes, the new government could completely destroy the entire agriculture in Lithuania? Then things could get even worst. So far, people have been able to raise piglets, and almost every household had a cow or a few. Therefore, everyone had their own meat and milk products to feed their families. When the Kolkhozes get established everywhere, then nobody will have even that much left. Nothing good is being foretold for the future either. It feels as if the humdrum existence wrapped up the entire universe... It is such a boring period in our lives! However, the life must go on-the nature itself requires us to do that. It's too bad when a most powerful beast, the man, can't control his own destiny."

A good hour of time elapsed while he was talking with the mother. Bronius started feeling better, and he was no longer upset.

He put his coat on and walked out of the house. As he was walking in the orchard, he immediately noticed that things there were no longer the same as they had been before. The bathhouse that had been standing for fifteen years was no longer there.

At that moment in his memory an image emerged of his father building the bathhouse. Back then, he had been just a little boy who was running over the building materials interfering with the dad's work. Nevertheless, the father had not got angry with him. His dad had always been nice to Bronius when he was little. Moreover, he was always supportive of him when he was growing up.

Now, at the same place where just yesterday their bathhouse had been standing, only the dismal emptiness was lingering about. The same way on the other side of the river, about a half kilometer away, the two homesteads had been standing next to each other. However, only the gray sky mournfully was shining through there now.

Bronius with the heavy feeling on his heart slowly walked to the place, where just yesterday family's precious building had stood. Here, the scene depressed him even more, since not only the whole structure was burnt down to its foundation, but the bare branches of the dead black willow trees where hanging stiff all around as well.

The fence separating the orchard from the river had been burnt too. An old apple tree that had been growing next to the bathhouse was also severely burnt. Only its black trunk was menacingly shooting up into the sky its bark peeled off and hanging like some huge protruding lips just about ready to cry.

"Only the stone foundation has left to tell the story of the building that stood here before," Bronius was talking loudly to himself.

He circled on foot the fire scene a couple times more and slowly walked away from it and went along the riverside.

After walking about half of a kilometer, he reached the water inlet where people from all the vicinity used to go swimming at their lunchtime during the summer time.

Sometimes the entire herds of horses used to be brought here for bathing. How much fun everybody had in this place during the warm summer days! Children splashing in the water had yelled in frenzied voices of joy. The adult laughter had mingled with the neigh of horses, and all the sounds had been heard far away.

What great times were then! Nobody had experienced any government violence. All the people had managed living according to their ability and free of any agitation, any persuasion, and intimidation. It had been nothing like lately, when everybody trembled for no apparent reason and lived without knowing what lies ahead of them.

Bronius sat down on the top of the hill and planted his eyes on the bay. It appeared as if the water was not moving. After observing the currant more attentively, however, he noticed the long water grasses flowing downstream like some green flags where the river got narrower.

Sinking deeply into his sad thoughts, Bronius did not feel relaxed in this quiet corner of the nature.

He did not remember how long he sat there, but there was no necessity to count minutes anyway, since he had nowhere to rush. Suddenly, a man's voice spoke to him. The person had approached him completely unnoticed.

Bronius came back to his senses only when he just of a suddenly heard a hollow greeting from behind, "Hello, Bronius."

It was an old man Lienys, whom he had known since the childhood. He had been old already then. It appeared to Bronius as if he had looked like that from the times immemorial. The only difference was that back then Lienys had been much more mobile. He also had not carried a cane.

Now, the very old stooped man leaning on his wooden cane was standing next to him. No one knew exactly how old he was. Moreover, he himself probably had long forgotten his age. Bronius heard that Lienys had been the oldest man in the vicinity, maybe a hundred years old or so.

When Bronius had been just a little boy, this man used to make him a basket out of the thin branches of a willow tree or a little pipe, or to model him some laughable figure out of clay.

Maybe that was why they had become such close friends. Therefore, even as a grown up, he always visited this dear fellow when coming home for vacation.

"Hello, hello sir," Bronius jumped to his feet and welcomed the neighbor.

"So you've come to visit your mother again? How long are your going to stay this time? It must have been three years I haven't seen you," spoke Lienys in a quivering husky voice occasionally having a fit of coughing.

"Let's sit down, son, and have the talk if you are not in big hurry," suggested the old man.

"I have nowhere to rush, we can talk," Bronius helped him to sit down on the ground by holding the old man's arm.

"I came home for a visit probably a year and a half ago."

"Somehow it appeared to me I have not seen you for a very long time. I'm glad I have recognized you at all. Let me, son, take a closer look at you. My eyesight has got weak. I feel so very old that it has become real misery for me to live anymore… My strength is no longer the same. My vision is so bad that I see you as if through some kind of fog. Well, tell me how life has been treating you. Are you still studying?"

"No grandpa. After my father had got arrested, I was expelled from university. Maybe you have already heard about that?"

"Oh, yes. I remember. I think you told me about that yourself. But maybe I heard about that from others. I don't remember it now. Lately, my memory has got impaired so badly that I forget everything. You know that old age, son."

"I think you look good. Still going strong…" Bronius made an attempt to sound polite.

"I don't have much strength left, but as long as I can move, I will continue strolling about. It bothers me, though, that nobody needs me anymore. To tell the truth, I have become tired of this kind of life myself. But I still continue walking and boring everyone I meet on my way. Probably God has forgotten about me, too, since He hasn't called me Home yet… And the times are so difficult also. Look what a horrible day we had yesterday. The disaster struck our vicinity sweeping off two farmhouses on the river. I heard that Russian soldiers have burned your family's bathhouse too."

"Yes, we have also been affected by this disaster. Our loss is small, though, in comparison to the loss of the neighbors'. Nevertheless, it is unfortunate that my mom's bathhouse is gone. At least, they did not burn the entire homestead, like they had done to Lopinis and Jurgeliavicius' families. It almost happened to us, too, but the mother and grandmother managed to appease those villains. You are right- the times are terrible! Our homes are being burned right in front of our eyes. A decent government would not leave people without the shelter. In addition, there is nobody to complain to about that. We just have to bite our tongues and suffer through this violence!"

"Don't you, sonny, know why Lopinis's homestead was burnt to the ground?"

"No, I have not heard anything about it."

"People in the village were talking that some men had been hiding in his house. Did those soldiers, who had had gathered oat from the local people to feed their horses, stopped at your place yesterday too?"

"Yes, and they had visited us the day before yesterday in the morning. Mother had given to them some oat also."

Old man Lienys replied, "I bet, they were the same soldiers, who had gone to Lopinis and Jurgeliavicius'. They had not found any of the local men hiding in my house. However, when the soldiers had opened the pantry door in Jurgeliavicius's house, they saw two men hiding there. The soldiers shot the men immediately, and they took their bodies to the forest. They buried them there and covered the top soil with the branches of the fir-tree. That is why Jurgeliavicius himself has been arrested and his house was burned down."

"But what does it have to do with our family?" Bronius asked.

"That I don't know, sonny. No one knows why your family's bathhouse was burned as well. Most likely, because they wanted to intimidate the locals even more."

Bronius replied in aggravated voice, "And they succeeded at that... What can be worst than leaving people without the shelter and without food?"

Having a chat, they sat at the riverside until noon. The day was nice and warm, so both of them were not in any rush. When the lunchtime came, however, the old fellow rose from the precipice. Bronius followed him.

Lienys waddled heavily along the river, and Adomaitis walked beside him. For some time they were walking in silence. When they reached a footbridge on the left side of the river's bank, where the trail through the trampled down grass led through the bushes, the old man was the first to utter, "Well, our roads part here. Goodbye, sonny. Probably when you come next year, you won't find me anymore. I will have gone to a better world..."

"What are you talking about, grandpa. Don't ever wait for the death. It will come to its own accord to all of us."

"Dear, I am already tired of living anyway," the old man replied.

"Don't say that grandpa. You need to enjoy life, whatever is left of it because we are only guests in this world. Any person visiting this planet should feel lucky. One could get bored living in the other world, too.

"You are right, sonny, but I already have got tired visiting this planet especially because I know I've pestered everyone to death. I feel that some people just cannot wait for me to die. You don't know how many times I've heard my daughter-in-law saying, 'Here this old man has come dragging again...' In addition to that, I get only reproves from my grandchildren. I don't understand why they hate me so much. I have not done anything bad to them. I'd never expected the last years of my life to be so difficult. Many years ago, everyone in my family had accepted me because I had been strong and kept feeding them. But now, they've become strong, and I've grown old turning into a burden to everybody around," the old man shared his pain while wiping tears. "Well, sonny, goodbye. I wish you a happy life and better senility than mine..."

"Grandpa, maybe you should swing by our house? We can have a drink. I want you to taste delicious wine that my mom makes. I swear, one could swallow his tongue while tasting it!"

"Maybe some other time. Your family is probably also sick of me. But I have to admit that every time I have dropped in when passing by, your mother always treated me to a good meal. She is such a good woman. It's too bad that her beautiful life has also collapsed. She had a great husband, whom those bastards had taken away from her. Your family had been exemplary in our vicinity. The entire household had been taken care off to perfection. No wonder, they sent you to university in Vilnius accordingly to the family's wishes. You are the only educated person in our village."

"My mother, grandpa, is not one of those phony women. She is the righteous person, and she never pretends to be who she is not. Feel free to dine with us. I really love listening to you about good old days in our countryside. After all, we have been good friends since my childhood. Come with me, I know my mother will be pleased to see you, too."

"Well, maybe I should drop in. You are so good at persuading."

"Please do that!"

The old man Lienys accompanied Bronius home. As soon as the old man entered the house, he first asked after the grandmother's health. The old woman was still in bed, but she already was feeling much better.

"Mother, will you give us something to eat? We are hungry," asked Bronius.

"Adomaitiene, don't worry. I only have come by to see how you are doing," a little confused Lienys tried justifying himself .

"It's great that you decided to swing by. You are welcome to all I have. It would be rude of me not to spend some time with such an honorable guest. I have to admit I'm very happy you've been associating with my son."

"Mom, I love this man the most out of all the people living in our village. No wonder, I've always missed him. Pour us some of your wine you'd treated me to earlier."

"Well, sit down. Don't be modest," Bronius's mother said in good spirits while taking a white tablecloth out of the dresser.

She covered the table with it and added, "I'm happy to see you, Adomas. I have just made some tasty hot meal."

Adomaitiene picked up a copper with the cabbage soup off the stove and ladled a full bowl to each of them. Then she encouraged, "Please, try my soup. I have saved for you something even better than that for later."

After finishing to eat the cabbage soup, the kind Adomas Lienys has not tasted for years now, the mother brought the plate with a big steaming piece of pork and a ring of boiled homemade sausage placed around it. She sliced the meat and sausage and then brought three glasses along with a liter-jar of cherry juice. When she filled glasses with the juice, the pleasant aroma of cherries started lingering in the air.

"Let's have a drink," the hostess spurred the guest. "I would like to have a drink to Bronius's health first. He is my only son. I always look forward to his visit. Now that I have grown old, nobody wants to talk with me anymore. Simply put, nobody even appreciates me as a person. But Bronius is so educated, and he is always so pleasant to me. He is really the great son. To your health, dear. I wish you a good life."

The old man Lienys also raised his hand in order to clink glasses and emptied his wine. The mother took after him, and Bronius was the last to follow their example.

After having a few more drinks, Lienys became even more talkative. Now without a moment's respite he was rattling about the old and the present times.

Only well after dark, he thanked meekly for the hospitality and left. Bronius walked Lienys to the gate of their fence in the yard. All this time, Lienys kept repeating, "I was treated like some kind of priest…like a priest… a priest…"

For some reason melancholy embraced Bronius after he saw off the old friend. The sad thoughts were flashing through his mind. Therefore, he decided to go to sleep, but then, he couldn't get asleep for a long time.

Only in about two hours, he felt asleep. Nevertheless, his sleep was somewhat shallow. All sweaty and worn out by the anxious dreams he woke up several times.

Then he woke up again at dawn and laid in bed with his eyes closed. He heard his mother rising, dressing up, and lighting a kerosene lamp. Her steps were slow and heavy like a man's. She walked out of the house and came back only a good half an hour later.

Bronius has been familiar with the each sound in this house. He lifted his head off the pillow and, resting his elbows on the mattress, kept listening further.

Now he heard his mother quietly toiling at the stove. Shortly after, the firewood started crackling loudly. Mother walked up to Bronius sitting in bed and asked, "Son, you're not sleeping any longer?"

"Yesterday, I went to sleep earlier than usually, so now I've prematurely made up for the lost sleep. But It's still difficult getting out of the warm bed. I feel like a little kid. You spoil me too much. If I lived at home for about a month, I would probably become very sluggish. Maybe I should start thinking about going back to the city. Instead, I just keep lounging around without any purpose. It's high time for me to pursue something more serious. I'm learning from you, mom. You have something to do from the early morning until the late evening every single day. I, to the contrary, only waste my time. I feel ashamed living this way. I ought to go back and start taking care of my school business today. That ruddy fire has destroyed my composure and messed up all my plans."

"Maybe you could stay for a few more days and rest?"

"Mom, I've already been late, since the school year has started quite a while ago. It's too bad my determination to fight for my destiny did not strike me earlier. But now I feel like on fire, as if my entire future is in trouble."

As soon as breakfast was served, grandmother also got out of bed. She walked with unsteady steps to the kitchen table and sat down. Then, she slowly drank a glass of tea and ate a couple of pancakes. Despite feeling unwell, she did not go back to bed no matter how much Bronius and the mother tried persuading her.

Moreover, now that she found out Bronius intended leaving so suddenly the grandma began crying with vexation. She had not had enough time to enjoy her grandson. After all, right upon arrival, he had fallen ill and spent nearly all week in bed. Then, as soon as he recovered, the soldiers invaded their homestead after which she got sick herself.

Now, so unexpectedly, he decided to leave. The old woman was very distressed. Pacing the floor with her trembling legs, she kept uttering unhappily something under her breath.

Indeed, the next day Bronius was already sitting in a one-horse cart on a pile of hay covered with a blanket. The mother was making the last preparations before taking him to the train station. Finally, she came outside and fixed the edges of the blanket tucking them under the hay in all four corners of the cart.

The grandmother with a sad look on her face was observing them through the window.

Then, the mother jumped onto the carriage after grasping with her hands the edge of the cart. She sat down next to her son. After slapping a couple of times with the whip, she urged the horse to trot forward.

The wooden wheels rolled out into the dirt road. Bronius kept looking back at the homestead and waving. With his gestures he kept showing the granny to stop crying.

Only when the trees covered the view of his native homestead, he let a heavy sigh out and made himself comfortable in his seat. Then he glanced at his mother and fixed his gaze down on his knees.

For some time, they were riding without saying a word to each other. Both of them were absorbed in their own thoughts. However, soon the one and the other started searching for words to break the silence.

Bronius was the first to utter, "It's not easy departing from home. My whole life has been evolving out of this place."

"It's too bad, Bronius, the times are so difficult now. I only hope that you can study again, this time, without the hassle and humiliation. But don't despair, sonny. If you fail entering university, write me immediately and let me know. I will do everything I possibly can in order to help you. Please write me soon. Remember that I will be thinking of you day and night. The uncertainty can be very oppressive..."

While having a chat, both of them did not notice when they got to the train station. There were about two hours left before the arrival of the train. Bronius tried to talk the mother into going back home, but she did not listen. They were waiting for the train in silence.

Bronius started feeling more comfortable only when he finally was sitting in the train that was rolling fast to Vilnius.

STUDENTSHIP

While sitting in the train, Adomaitis remembered various events and relived all kinds of moods that would never fade away from his memory. He summed up and analyzed those events in his mind, since he had sufficient time remembering his past without any outside interference.

Therefore, he let himself to relive some of those moments two or even a few times in his imagination. The images of the same scenes danced in his memory like in some slow motion movie.

Metal wheels of the train wagon kept monotonously tapping up the metal tracks disturbing the silence of the fields, that he was observing his head leaning up the window glass. Bronius was looking at the wide planes of the meadows and forests appearing and disappearing in front of his eyes.

He was so absorbed in the troubled thoughts that he almost did not pay attention to the continually changing views. He felt comfortable sitting on the wooden bench in the train compartment his gaze fixed on the melancholic late autumn sceneries flashing in front of his eyes.

The goal he had set for himself, however, was giving him the most anxiety at the moment. He did not know if his plans would come to fruition. The thoughts were bouncing in his head. What should he start doing first? Whom should he turn to for help? What must he do if he gets rejected?

It was painful to even think that the answer could be negative. His soul, prompted by some hope, was longing to overcome all the obstacles that had been rising like a wall in front of him and blocking his road to success.

He had a presentiment that it would be difficult to achieve his dream. At the same time, he found it difficult to believe he would have to pay such a high price for his education.

Nevertheless, he was happy to have discovered the higher purpose in his life. He knew he would be pursuing his goal in spite of the consequences awaiting for him.

Bronius did not notice when he arrived at Vilnius train station. Standing in a big square in front of the main city's train station, he felt at home. He had his two big suitcases full of food sitting on the ancient cobblestone ground. Bronius drew moist air deep into his lungs, and suddenly a strong desire to get into the giddy vortex of the capital life overwhelmed him.

He hired himself a coachman. Soon Bronius was sitting next to him with his collar fixed up as if hiding from somebody. The two men were passing the old part of Vilnius when they found themselves in a little narrow street. After the coachman reined the horse, Bronius paid him and climbed out of the carriage. Hauling his heavy bulging out suitcases, he turned into the familiar tight, long courtyard.

Panting heavily, he climbed the narrow stairway onto the second floor. The apartment building was very old, and it was obvious that the same stairs had been used probably for more than a hundred of years.

Today, though, the stairway appeared to him narrower than usually. Maybe it seemed this way only because he carried the heavy suitcases in his both hands, which kept brushing against the metal railing fixed onto one side of the short narrow staircase.

It was well after dark. Obviously his landlady was already in bed, even though it had not been that late after all. However, there were no lights in the two windows of their flat facing the courtyard.

Bronius had to knock loudly on the door several times until the old woman finally heard him. Therefore, he had to stand outside the door in the dark for several minutes until she got back to her senses. Apparently, the woman could not perceive right away what was going on. When the door finally opened slightly, she still was very sleepy and looked much older than she really was.

He heard her frightened voice coming out of the dark, "Bronius, is that you? What has happened? Maybe you had some problems at home? My understanding was, you intended spending the whole month at home."

"Things are going pretty good at home. But you are right- there is a reason for my early return here," spoke Bronius while crossing the doorstep.

"Are you hungry? Maybe I should make you some tea?"

"I don't know. It might be good for me to have a bite. Otherwise, my growling stomach won't let me sleep at night."

"Hang on. I will quickly make you a sandwich. Are you cold? The weather is very nasty. It had rained earlier. It seems as if this cold dampness penetrates right into the bones," spoke the landlady while turning the electric stove on.

"Maybe you, auntie, should go to sleep. I woke thee up. I can heat the tea myself."

"Oh no, sonny. You must be tired after the trip."

Although she was not a relative of his, Bronius never called her the 'landlady'. Instead, he called her 'aunty', most likely, because she was exceedingly nice to him. Another reason for that was because he had been renting a room in her flat for six years already. During all this time, he had not heard even one rude word from her. Moreover, she had been taking care of Bronius as if he was her own son.

She would make him a modest breakfast every morning before he left for work. Upon coming from work, the steaming hot supper was always awaiting for him too.

True, he used to eat his lunch at their dining room at work, since it was too far away to walk home. During his first year at university, though, the auntie used to prepare a delicious sandwich and slip it into Bronius's pocket.

Because of her motherly caring, Bronius had become attached to the aunty very much. It was impossible not to love her!

Even his shirts were always washed and his bed carefully made each morning. However, she began feeling unwell more often during the past two years. The old age kept increasingly bending her to the ground. Thus, approaching her seventy-fifth year, she had grown almost completely week.

Bronius remembered well those few years spent living with her. The times came to life in his memory when she had to stand in long lines at the bakery during cold winter days, so that she could buy a loaf of bread for both of them. Upon coming home from the store, she had never complained. She always had a smile on her face as she had showed a loaf of bread she had had purchased.

However, Bronius also always treated her with respect. Several times a year, he used to go home, and he never had returned back empty-handed. He always had brought with him a full suitcase of bacon, lard, sausages, flour, onions, and some other goodies. All that food he used to give to her.

Time from time, his father with mother also would come to visit him in the city. They, too, never had showed up empty. Auntie's flat had been the place where Bronius felt just as comfortable as he had felt at his parents' house.

He remembered his school friends complaining about the owners of the rooms they had been renting from. Often those owners used to eat all their roommates' food keeping them almost starving, not to mention the laundry that his classmates had to do themselves.

On the contrary, Bronius's clothes had been kept clean and ironed. It was impossible to even compare his life to that of his school friends'.

In spite of all this, it was strange that Bronius knew very little about the auntie's past. She was Orthodox by religion, since she had been Russian by her nationality. Before the World War I, she had had lived in St. Petersburg, but she had been driven out of there by the ranging Civil War.

A couple of times, Bronius had heard from her about the terrible life of the Russian people during that period of time. However, she'd never gone into the details, and he had never asked any questions either.

Furthermore, she was very reserved, and she had no relatives. And even if there had been any, they'd never come to visit her.

Once in a while, Bronius used to see her bringing books from somewhere written in Russian or English.

Few times after walking into her room, he had noticed tears in the old woman's eyes. Nevertheless, she had always tried hiding her pique away. At first, it had been difficult for him to understand why she was distressed.

As the years went by, though, he began realizing there must had been a reason for that. Nevertheless, he could never bring himself to inquire about it. Bronius was reluctant to appear as if he had only been trying to satisfy his human curiosity. In addition, he had not wanted to re-open her long-standing wounds.

Thus, his own shyness had prevented him from learning more about auntie's secret that she had always tried to cover up. He loved and respected her as if she had been his own mother. Moreover, Bronius considered the old woman to be a person of the noble heart.

Auntie brought a kettle with hot tea and sat it on the table that Bronius had already loaded with the food all over, that had been taken out of his two suitcases. She poured the steaming dark brown liquid into two beautiful porcelain cups that she had got out of the sideboard in the living room. Auntie moved a sugar basin closer to him and encouraged him to treat himself to some sugar cubes.

"Drink, dear, while it's still hot. I have not heated the room today, so it might be cold for you to sleep tonight."

"I'm sure it will be fine. Don't worry, auntie, I will wrap myself into a blanket. After all, it's warmer in the room than it is outside, and this is not even wintertime."

"This year could be worse than the last year as far as the firewood goes. We'll probably have enough of it just for half of the season. Hard times are coming, and we'll have to suffer through that cold."

"Well, auntie, we might have to freeze a little bit, just like everybody else. There are people who could not afford to buy any firing. One of my co-worker's family is so poor they had not heated their flat for several years in a row now, and they are still alive. Therefore, we also should somehow adapt to the cold weather. It can always get much worse," Bronius comforted the troubled mistress while sipping his tea.

"There is not much we can do about that. Many people struggle. In spite of a war being long over, life has not become any better. Such is phony government for the people that does not make any efforts to meet those peoples' needs. The same was in Petrapilis (St.Petersburg), in 1918. Then, authorities also had lied to the masses promising to create the paradise on earth. Instead, the people kept suffering hunger and cold."

"How was it back then?" Bronius encouraged her to continue.

"Everything had been so tragic. You could see a person walking in the street and then suddenly falling down onto the sidewalk... People literally had died from starvation, just like flies. Nobody had bothered trying to ease the life of those suffering. The government officials had endeavored to seize power, so that only they could have a better life. The rest of the Russian nation kept only sinking deeper and deeper into poverty while suffering hunger and being constantly persecuted. The times had been so terrible that just remembering about them the sadness mixed together with horror takes over me."

"Is that why you had come to Vilnius?"

"Yes. The people kept falling sick had been struck by that "red plague". The bloody epidemic had raged all over the St Petersburg which had been the capital of Russia at that time and up until the year 1918. Many people had simply been afraid to come out of their dwellings into the streets. Nevertheless, the hunger had been merciless. It had huge eyes and drove the unfortunate outside looking for food. Thus, folks had not lived. They'd just existed being hounded by the fear and all kinds of repressions."

"I'm glad those times are long gone, auntie'" Bronius said.

"Bronius, history always repeats itself. There is nothing new under the sun. I sometimes wonder where has the humaneness of the century disappeared that so many men of wisdom had exalted. Moreover, life is still getting worst with no visible clearing… The same violence and oppression has come here from the east, the basis for which had been laid in the 1918, in Petersburg. What rather progress the Soviet government had achieved during its reign years? According to its officials, they had founded the International body of the society. However, it had only turned out to be that those people who had been nobody became somebody. The Russian Duma had been rooted out, but the other exploiters, just called by the other name- the communists, had replaced their seats. Satiated and paunchy, they had remained for years in the governing positions getting paid huge salaries. They had lived in luxury apartments in a kingly way."

"Looks like not much has changed since then, auntie."

"No wonder, officials love the Soviet government that had given them this kind of life! That is how, dear, the International has been created… People have again to suffer pulling their heavy yoke on their shoulders. The communists have led to the collapse of the agriculture and the industry, which are now unable to equip ordinary people with the most elementary everyday needs. What should we expect from the government that does not serve us?"

"I completely agree with you," Bronius said.

The auntie got so worked up that she could not stop talking, "Let's take for example you, Bronius. I have known you for a few years now. You have never belonged to any political group. You have always lived the life of a neutral person, and you had a beautiful dream to climb the heights of the education and live a virtuous life. The arrest of your father had started haunting you and has stirred up all your life the wrong way... Why had you been expelled from the university? As if it was not enough, you are still being constantly chased like some animal wounded by the hunter. And there are many more people like you."

"The new government does not like people who have many assets. According to them, my parents had too much land ," Bronius said.

"It's was not your parents' fault they had assets. They hadn't stolen any of them. I would dare to say that the new government steals farmers' assets by nationalizing their estates. Together with destroying the working intelligentsia it destroys the country's future by hurting their children as well. Why the entire generations have to be persecuted because of their ancestral past?"

"Auntie, some people are doomed to be persecuted. I think the new government has special files created, where it keeps the information about certain people. I have no doubt there is information compiled about their relatives arrested or living abroad as well. In my case, my father had been arrested, even though we don't know why. If I ever learned that it had been a mistake, I still could not support this system. I would never be able to reconcile with my destiny because of my father being gone from my life. Also, I would never be able to come to terms with being persecuted because of that. There are many more innocent people like my father and me who have been tossed in the vortex of such horrible nightmares. This system could never take a root in peoples' minds."

"I'm afraid that a revolution might happen," the old woman added.

Bronius continued, "This system will never justify expectations of the people, no matter how hard the officials keep exalting it. Their new "friends' order" is not any better than the old one- the "rotten Tsarist regime". A popular Russian slogan "Struggle for the existence!" very accurately describes the real face of the Bolshevik life. We do not live. Instead, we only exist. We live just according to this slogan. We exist by being kept in permanent poverty, by being harassed and driven away like some sorts of homeless dogs. I have come back to Vilnius before my vacation was over in order to find out the truth. I want to know why I had been expelled from the university, what crime had I personally committed. I would like to put a period in this story and, thus, put an end to it no matter if it was a good or a bad one…"

"You will not gain anything, sonny. You will not find the truth. It's impossible breaking through the stonewall with one's head … The only thing you could achieve is ruin your life. Many people have already perished in Lithuania trying to fight the system. Almost all intelligent, cultured men of Lithuania have been decimated. Over the past few years, not only their bodies have decayed but even their bones have also turned yellow."

Bronius had never been engaged in such an open and sincere conversation with his landlady. Their talk was different because he learned about her view on government politics.

Now she appeared to him even more mysterious. Bronius began wondering more about her past and her personality. He had tried before solving her mysteries, but his efforts had gone in vain.

After talking with the landlady, Bronius was laying in bed his gaze fixed onto the ceiling. It was dark in the room. He was thinking about the events of the past days and the open talk with the auntie. He also was pondering over his plans for the future trying to figure out what it takes to put his goals to fruition.

As he relaxed, the words of auntie started ringing in his ears, 'You won't gain anything, sonny. You won't find the truth. It's impossible breaking through the stone wall…'

Bronius kept turning from side to side unable to get asleep, but he failed to isolate himself from his thoughts that gave no rest to him almost all night long. Just after being totally worn out, he finally fell asleep at the dawn. However, his sleep was shallow and restless.

Bronius woke up several times afflicted by the nightmares. He just kept kicking off his covers. After wiping away the sweat of his face, he rolled over onto the other side. Finally, without having had any rest, he got up late in the morning.

After washing up with the cold water, he finally came to himself and ate a modest breakfast that auntie had been already prepared for him as usually. The meal totally dissipated his tormenting night dreams.

When Bronius left the flat, rainy cool weather shrouded him that totally drove all the nightmares out of his head. Nevertheless, as soon as he remembered where and with what purpose he was going, his head got flooded with anxiety.

Shortly after, he found himself in a long corridor of the University, where he spent almost all day walking from one office to the other. Bronius met few teachers. Some of them chatted with him sincerely expressing their compassion because of his father's arrest, while others only briefly stopped most likely just out of politeness.

There were also those who did not wish talking to him. They passed by quickly as if being afraid catching some terrible incurable disease. Bronius noticed that many of his previous instructors were not only reluctant talking to him, but they were even avoiding him all together.

However, the most painful moment was when one old acquaintance of his, the senior lecturer, accelerated his step upon seeing Bronius. The man quickly turned into another corridor in order to avoid their encounter.

However, there were some sympathetic people, who most likely were also afraid to be noticed talking to Bronius by professors at the University. In spite of that, they found some time to say a few words of comfort. They were the ones who revived his soul, gave him strength and determination to proceed on pursuing his goal.

He saw many students he had only known by sight. Some of them beckoned him from far away. A few of them stopped to talk without any fear asking how he was doing, what he had been up to and the like.

Nevertheless, there were students who passed him like some stranger. At those moments, Adomaitis's heart would give a twinge, and he just felt like screaming with vexation.

The biggest blow to him, though, was when he came across one of his best friends, with whom he had also studied together at school. Bronius noticed him unexpectedly and got very excited. He extended his hand in attempt to greet him. To his big surprise, the friend did not hold out a hand back to Bronius. Instead, he eluded and walked away leaving him totally stupefied, standing alone in the middle of the narrow corridor.

For a few moments, Adomaitis stood there deprived of speech. He was hearing a ringing in his ears and saw dazzling in his eyes. Being overwhelmed with grief, he wanted to moan, but no sound escaped him. Bronius had to lean his arm on the windowsill in order not to lose his balance.

After standing there for a while, his eyes finally began to brighten up. He felt the feeling of resistance creeping up his throat. He was asking himself what he had done to deserve such behavior, especially because it was coming from an old friend. He wanted to know where this hatred was coming from. Maybe someone's filthy tongue had slandered his reputation?

Bronius could not stand there any longer. Some spontaneous force suddenly drove him to come to his senses. The unknown power propelled him taking to his heels the direction, where the receding figure of his friend could still be seen at the very end of the long narrow corridor.

"Alfa!" shouted Bronius upon caching up with him.

No response followed although he walked next to him for a while.

"Alfa, why are you acting so strangely? What have I done to you so terribly wrong so that you don't even want to talk to me? Only enemies behave this way."

"And we are enemies," Alfa grumbled not slowing down his step.

"Who managed to defame me to you so severely?"

"You yourself have, who else?"

"You, Alfa, are delirious. Better explain to me what has happened."

"I don't want to talk to you."

"But what is the matter? Whatever it is, I'm sure someone has only misled you. Why do you have such a bad opinion about me now?"

"If you are just a meek lamb, why then you were expelled from the University? Are you trying to say that government does that to innocent people?" Afla finally stopped and cast an angry look at him. Then he continued, "People like you are really impudent. Maybe you think I should defend you or stand up for you?! Are you trying to make it appear like some kind of a mistake? No one will believe you. You've made your bed, and you must lie in it!"

"What have I done wrong? Why are you so harsh to me?"

"You have done wrong not only to me, but you've also fouled the entire class."

"Alfa, you don't really mean it…"

"Yes, I do. You are no good, and I can repeat that to you a hundred more times."

Then he turned around and walked away again leaving Adomaitis rooted in the spot, his fists clenched.

"No good… Why no good?! What have I done so vile to deserve such an unjust blame? You yourself are no good, not me! You are worst than me; you are a venal creature…" Adomaitis grumbled under his nose angrily.

Who knows how long he would had stood there, if another high school times classmate did not start the conversation. Bronius had never really liked him. Therefore now, suddenly spoken to at this difficult moment, he almost snapped at him being all agitated. In his mind he still was reviling Alfa.

"Don't get mad at me, but I was standing just around the corner when I accidentally overheard your conversation with Alfa," the former Adomaitis's peer said, fearfully looking around .

"Deuce takes it! Why are you all loaf around giving deep sighs like some ghosts? You, too, are looking around as if you are afraid of something… What does this all mean?! As far as I remember, you had been not the bravest one during our school years either… Are you even afraid of your own shadow? Yes, I had been kicked out of the University! It's easy for you to judge. Nobody will have any compassion towards me."

"Bronius, this is not the place for those kinds of debates. Let's go somewhere and talk. Then I'll be able to tell you in detail about the prevailing sentiments at the University."

"I'm sick of those talks! Just during one day today I have already heard plenty of nonsense!" Bronius turned around getting ready to leave.

However, the thought suddenly struck him that it might be beneficial talking to his former classmate. After all, he could find out something very important in relation to his personal mission.

Therefore, he suddenly turned around and quickly agreed, "Okay, let's go outside."

"You, Bronius, walk towards Castle Street, and I'll catch up with you there."

Without delay Bronius went outside where he crossed a couple of old courtyards and found himself in the Castle Street. There, he joined the stream of people.

His friend caught up with him before he had a chance to reach Saint John's Church. Even in the street, he was the same timid person and kept looking around as if here, also, somebody had been following him.

"Well, where are we going?" asked Bronius his fellow traveler.

"Let's go somewhere where there are less people."

"Maybe let's go to the bar. We can have a beer there and talk freely," Bronius offered feeling more relaxed.

"I have to admit, Bronius, that I'm lacking the funds. I receive only a small stipend that enables me barely to survive in this harsh world, and I do not get much help from home, either. Our family is big; I have two sisters. Therefore, it is not easy for my parents to support all three of us. Maybe lets go somewhere to the city square where we can sit on a bench, and we can talk there."

"I've got a couple of rubles. I'll not ask you to return me the treat. I make enough money at work. In addition, I've got my vacation allowance with me."

Both of them walked into the first snack bar they happened to spot on their way that was located on Great Street. Inside, it was crammed with so many people, and the air was so full of cigarette smoke that they could barely see a chubby barmaid through the thick cloud of the smoke. She was standing behind a counter pouring vodka into big thick glasses and preparing fast snacks.

There were no seats available at the tables. However, the two young men had not even wanted to sit at the table. Instead, they settled at the empty barrel. Bronius grabbed a couple of wooden wine boxes sitting next to it and turned them into their seats. Meanwhile, his friend got to the end of a line of half-drunk people at the counter.

Bronius left to guard the place at the barrel so that nobody could occupy their seats. It was a problem finding any free corner to have a drink in this somber hole. All the dregs of the city used to gather here and, after having a few strong drinks, they would become exceedingly loud. The men used to get so drunk that they couldn't even comprehend what was happening around them.

After standing good fifteen minutes in line, Bronius's friend ordered two glasses of vodka, a couple of bottles of beer, two portions of liver with onions, and one portion of herring. He alone brought everything on a tray and put it onto the top of the barrel. Then he sat down on the empty wine box using it as the chair and handed the glass with vodka to Bronius.

"Let's raise our glasses, Vitas. You are a good man. Not many students could bring themselves to go somewhere with me... Everybody avoids me as if I'm some kind of a leprous man. The only difference is that not my body is contaminated, but my reputation is."

Both clinked their glasses. Bronius quickly drank half of his vodka. Then he put the glass onto the top of the barrel, shook his head vigorously, and washed the taste down with a few big gulps of beer. After that Bronius began eating with appetite his portion of liver. He had had nothing to eat since the early morning. Thus, he cleaned out almost all his plate at once. His friend did the same. When only a few pieces of herring were left, Bronius and Vitas put their forks down.

"Bronius, I see you are surprised that distrust dominates among the students at the University. I can assure you there is a reason for that - namely, we are afraid of each other. One can never know who is his friend, and who is an enemy. Many students have been dismissed from the University over the past few years. You are not the only one. Moreover, a few of the students had mysteriously disappeared... I heard one of them along with a teacher had been taken away straight from the rector's office and the other two vanished afterwards. No wonder then, that the rest of the students don't trust each other. For example, there is a student at the University by the name Alfa. He is a real devil! Quite a few of students have already endured extreme hardship because of him. He behaves as if he is next to God and, therefore, he has a right determining the other students' destiny. He is a Secretary of the Young Communist League. That is why he had turned his nose so high up. Every student appears suspicious to him, but he talks very highly of himself. To tell the truth, I'm not too afraid of disappearing myself.

I'm more afraid of being expelled from the University. My family would die out of shame…"

"I understand. That's how my mother feels about my situation now," Bronius interrupted him.

Vitas continued, "After all, I have already climbed into my fourth year, and the finish line could be seen in the near horizon. It would be extremely unfortunate after having studied for so many years in vain… I maybe am poor now, but, at least, I have hope finding a good job after I finish my education. In addition, authorities at the University provided me with the room at the students' dormitory where I can stay. What would I do, if I didn't have this opportunity? The school is my only salvation. Bronius, you can't imagine how much I suffer from those red fleas myself. It seems as if they can never get satisfied by drinking my blood. However, a pay time will come one day… When I get my degree, I'll spit at Alfa's ugly face. For now, however, I must clench my teeth and keep silent. I also don't have a father, and my mother had to raise three children by herself. She gives all she has to me and my two sisters while suffering hunger and walking ragged herself."

Falling silent, he gulped remaining vodka and wiped away tears from his eyes with the sleeve. Then he put the last piece of herring into his mouth and swallowed it together with all its bones.

"I feel for you, Vitas. I wish I could help you. You, too, have become a victim like the rest of us. We all had set high hopes on our studies. However, life has crippled me, and there is no one to complain to. Moreover, it feels as if only evil hyenas and poisonous snakes are swarming around. Those creatures are just lurking in the anticipation of a painful bite. Thus, you can find yourself feeling alone and lonely like in some Sahara desert. I've kept silence long enough, but now I decided there is only one way out of this situation, and that is by reaching my goal."

"It wish you came back to study with us, and I hope you'll succeed in fulfilling your dreams."

They chatted for a good an hour and only after dark both friends parted away.

Bronius came home. It had already been pitch black in the room when he lay down on a sofa. He was staring at the darkness plunged in thoughts. In his mind he could see himself happy and having a nice family in his distant future.

A thought came to his mind asking his mother to come and visit him in Vilnius. Suddenly, some unknown force pushed him out of bed. He got up and immediately wrote her a letter. Then, he slipped it into a metal mailbox that had been hanging on the front of the outside door of the flat. The mailman always picked up their outgoing mail straight from their mailbox. After that Bronius returned back to his room and fell sound asleep.

Next day Bronius went to the Ministry of Higher Education, where he managed obtaining a permission to meet with the Minister himself. Bronius talked with that handsome tall man for a long time. After spending more than half a day in the ministry, he returned home tired and disappointed.

Couple more days went by with him crossing doorsteps of some more agencies, but all his efforts were in vain.

On the third day Bronius's mother arrived. He told her all about his problems and plans in detail. At the end they decided that the best thing would be going to Moscow, since there was little hope achieving anything at home. Lithuania fully belonged to Russia. Therefore, local government could not settle the slightest thing without a consent of its government above.

Soon they started making arrangements for the travel. The mother with difficulty obtained a ticket that she had paid double for, and Bronius saw her off to the train station.

He himself remained in Vilnius eagerly waiting for her to come back from Moscow. Days went by turning into weeks, but she had not shown up. Finally, his vacation ended, and there had already been a few days when he went back to work.

There still had been no news from his mother. Bronius even started reproaching himself for sending her there. The thought that she could be in some danger drove him insane. He even forgot about his dreams and goals.

Only terrible thoughts in relation to his mother's disappearance kept flashing through his mind. He could not comprehend where to search for her or what to do next.

Being overtaken by this new misfortune, Bronius was walking sad in the street, when he again met Vitas. He could not remember time when he had been so happy seeing his friend.

Bronius almost by force dragged Vitas to a bar, where he ordered vodka for both of them in expectation to suppress his pain. After having a couple of drinks, he started complaining to Vitas about his mother's disappearance, and tears appeared in his eyes. Only well after dark, he returned home feeling dizzy.

This particular evening, he did not chat with his landlady as he had usually done. He did not want to listen to her talking either. Bronius had come home feeling giddy and did not want to be bothered by anyone.

Therefore, after eating supper, he immediately lay down and quickly got asleep. Bronius slept so tightly that he was unable to hear when his mother arrived. Apparently, vodka that he had been drinking with his friend the night before contributed to his good sleep.

Only upon waking up in the morning, he learned that his mother had arrived from her long trip. She herself was sound asleep. Being prompted by unappeasable curiosity, he did not dare, however, waking her up. Bronius only stood near gazing at this so dear to him woman who was breathing loud and deeply on the couch.

In spite of not being able to find out anything, he walked to work not feeling ground under his feet. The reason for his happiness was the mere fact that she had returned home alive and in good health.

Thus, in high spirits he came to his office. The day lasted long as never before. He managed, though, to suffer through lunch, but the second half of his workday lasted even longer.

It felt as if the time had stopped. A wall-mounted clock was loudly ticking its hands seemingly never moving forward even an inch. Bronius kept impatiently looking at the big white clock dial. Then he realized that namely because of that the time had been dragging so slowly.

He tried to concentrating on his tasks, but that had not been working either. No matter how agonizingly slow the time was crawling, he waited until his workday was over.

Bronius was the first to get outside, where he broke into a run home. He didn't have much hope his mother had succeeded in achieving anything positive during her trip to the capital of Russia. However, the mere fact she had been back home provided him with relief and joy.

However, he was pleasantly surprised to learn that she had spent three weeks in Moscow not in vain. She had brought the documents to her son allowing him to re-enter the University!

Adomaitis was so happy; he felt like in seventh heaven. At first, he even forgot to ask about the trip. Only when both of them calmed down a bit, the mother began telling him about her Golgotha road she had had to go through.

She began laying out how she had stood for hours in the corridor outside the doors of some Russian government officials. In spite of receiving an audience beforehand, she had spent days waiting in line in order to obtain the necessary documents for her son .

She had begged and sometimes she'd almost forced the Russian administration to make an appointment for her to meet some important government official. Few times she had even squeezed some golden coins into the officials' palms in order to make them more submissive…

Thus, sometimes with truth, sometimes with lies, and sometimes with the bribes she'd received all the necessary papers that her son needed to continue his education.

She had to spend so many days lingering in the corridors of the various institutions until she'd managed to reach the right officials hiding behind their fancy big doors.

No wonder, the same had happened when she'd had requested seeing Kalinin. A couple of weeks had had to pass by before she had been allowed to see him.

True, the mother had not been able to see Kalinin himself. Some of his representative sitting at the huge luxurious writing-table issued her the most important document. Namely this document with a big golden seal on the bottom of it appeared most promising to Bronius. The mother also managed receiving a few additional documents from other authoritative persons of the NKVD in Moscow.

For long time that evening, Bronius spoke with his mother. She told him about the trip in detail. He learned that she had also inquired about the father while in Moscow. However, she had not been able to find out anything about him. He had had vanished as if into thin air.

While listening to his mother's story, Bronius's heart was gushing with blood. It was obvious that she had gone through a lot of trouble during the last few weeks, and she had done all this just for him.

He was thinking that he would had never gone to this extent for himself. Despite being more educated than her, he felt much weaker than she had been. Bronius would had never thought of taking the same measures that his mother had had resorted to. The only lesson he was able to learn after her trip was that a person could not accomplish anything in this new system by doing the right thing.

The mother wanted to stay in Vilnius until Bronius will have established himself at the University, but he persuaded her going back home. He insisted on handling all his school affairs by himself.

Immediately, he started taking care of the matters of his education. Everything was going smoothly enough, even though it had not been easy. The whole process took considerable amount of time and cost him a lot of stress.

Bronius had to walk from one institution to another. A big improvement he experienced was that the officials gave no refusal anymore after they had read his documents. It was clear they regarded the commandments of the authoritative officials from Moscow.

Despite that, they kept referring Adomaitis from one place to another as if being afraid to solve the question themselves. After a couple of weeks, though, the things at last turned out to go a better direction.

All the obstacles had been overcome, and Bronius finally succeeded at securing an appointment with Chairman of the Supreme Soviet of the Lithuanian Soviet Republic himself. He was the one who made the final decision in Bronius's favor.

Bronius was amazed at how much suffering he had to endure in order to arrange his going back to school! He still kept pondering over his past life. After all, he had never belonged to any political group and never violated any laws. Bronius was not able to understand why this blown out of proportion affair had not been resolved at the University by its staff.

However, he became overwhelmed with happiness when he learned that he had been allowed attending his classes again! He immediately hurried to notify his mother in writing of the joyful news.

He wanted to thank her and to make her proud. After all, it was her merit... He imagined what joy this letter would bring to her after she reads it. Adomaitis wanted to share his happiness with the closest and dearest people in his life. In Vilnius, he did not have any close people besides the landlady of the flat he had been renting a room form. Other than that, he could not think of any schoolmates who sincerely and without hypocrisy would rejoice over his accomplishments and winnings.

Upon coming to work, Adomaitis with joy wrote his resignation notice. Only when it had to be turned into Director, he for some reason began hesitating while standing at his office door. He started reasoning there was nothing to fear, since soon he would no longer be the subject to this institution.

After gathering his strength, he knocked on Director's office door. Without waiting for a response coming from behind it, he opened the large door upholstered with the black leather himself.

Adomaitis slowly walked to the large desk. The director lifted his eyes from a stack of documents. He took his glasses off and greeted Bronius himself, "Oh, hello hello, please sit down."

He appeared to be in a cheerful mood while pointing at an armchair across his desk.

"I've good news for you. My understanding is that you might have learned about it first, since you have come here to see me," Director said.

Adomaitis timidly sat down onto the edge of the armchair.

"But maybe you yourself have some business to share with me, or maybe you have some request... Do not hesitate telling me about it. Well, go ahead and lay out your business first."

"Sir, I have come to you with a personal matter. It's linked to my past. Therefore, it is very important to me..."

"I'm listening. I will be glad to help you if it's in my power to do so. I can tell just by looking at you that it is very important to you. Besides, you never come to me without a necessity. What kind of assistance do you need from me? I am ready to help you in any way I can."

"I have to quit my job, sir. This is the reason I've come here," Bronius laid down his employment resignation statement written in beautiful handwriting onto the table.

"Are you serious or you are just teasing me?"

"I wouldn't dare teasing such an authoritative person like you."

"Then, my dear, maybe you will have kindness explaining the reason why you wish leaving your job," asked Director in a different tone of voice.

"I don't know how to explain it, but I'll try giving you the facts about what has been going on in my life lately. I think of you very highly as about a person who has a very positive outlook on life. Therefore, I don't intend hiding anything from you."

"Go ahead. Maybe after learning about your situation, I will be of any use to you."

"Thank you for being so nice to me. I hope I won't bore you too much by making you listen to my story. You are welcome to interrupt me at any time. My story goes like this… When the Soviet Army liberated us from Germans that had invaded Lithuania, I had just finished a gymnasium. I'd been overjoyed learning that the University of Vilnius had inaugurated its new era. I had been dreaming to study there. Later my dream came true, since I rally found myself in that wise temple. Totally dedicating myself to science, I spent countless nights at an old university library deriving knowledge from the books. I lived life of the highest spiritual degree. In addition to that, I had everything I needed materially, although, there had been quite a difficult economic situation in the country. None of this, however, did seem to touch me. True, out of a scholarship alone which I had been receiving then along with the food cards, I would had hard time making ends meet. Nevertheless, I was better off than most of the other students. My parents had been supporting me from my native village, where they had a rather small but arranged in an exemplary manner farm. That always came to my rescue. Later on, I even refused to take the student grant, so that the other students who needed it more could have it. Months had been slipping by while I was studying medicine. My biggest dream had been to become a doctor, but I did not plan limiting myself with just an ordinary doctor's degree. I desired to continue improving and thought of going on studying further. Thus, I completed my first year course at the Medical Faculty and climbed into the second year. However, just of a suddenly, all my plans for the future fell apart like a little house of cards. My efforts unexpectedly turned out to be of no purpose. I'm not sure if I should continue… maybe you, sir, have got bored or don't have time hearing out my story…"

"Oh no, continue, please. To the contrary - I'm very curious learning more about your life."

At that moment, there was a knock on the door of Director's office. Some man opened it widely without even waiting until he would be invited to come inside. Most likely, he was a customer, but Director immediately asked him to wait outside so he could finish his business with Adomaitis.

As soon as the door closed, he turned his face to Bronius and encouraged him to talk, "Well, go on. What made you quit the school though?"

"I myself would had never quit the university. I was expelled from it because my father had been arrested. I still have no idea what had happened to him. The only thing I can tell you is that I have become a double victim - I not only had lost my father, but I lost the right to get education too. I had never committed any offenses. Prior to my dad's arrest, my classmates had always respected me. Suddenly the incident with the father, however, had turned my life upside down. I'd tried hard to find out the reason for his arrest, but all my efforts had been in vain. Then, I came to work for you. I thought my career as a doctor was over. Therefore, I reconciled myself to the fate, and I stuck to work not wishing to see or hear of anything else. I have to admit, though, that heartburn of the loss visited me quite often until eventually some words uttered by my mother made a big impact on me. They made me feel so small and worthless that I was ashamed of myself. That prompted me to make some efforts fighting for my future."

Director became restless in his chair. Nevertheless, Bronius continued, " Thus, without even finishing my vacation, I came back from my native land to Vilnius in hopes of finding out the truth, but my efforts were like the sound of a voice in wilderness. Like some pilgrim, I cried for help to the Lord. Nobody wanted to talk with me. I felt like in a desert, where without a sound of the sand being blown by the wind, I could only hear hissing of the snakes. Finally, I lost all my hope. I spilled out my entire sorrow in a letter to my mother. Few days later, my mother came to Vilnius. I told her in detail about all my problems at school, and she decided to travel to Moscow. After spending almost an entire month there, she brought documents that allowed me to return to the university. I can't describe what she had to go through in order to get those papers. I think she had not told me everything about her trip. The only thing I know is that namely those papers from Moscow helped me re-enter Vilnius University. Now, you know my entire story. Mainly because of the classes at the University, I decided to quit my job. Pardon me please for taking away so much of your time trying to explain all this. I couldn't have explained everything in such detail even to my closest friend."

For some time director was silent apparently reflecting on just heard story. Finally, he got up off the chair and started walking back and forth in the room without saying a word.

Then, he stopped at the window and started gazing through the glass somewhere into the distance. He said, "Even under those circumstances, Adomaitis, I don't recommend you quitting your job. I admit that your situation is serious, and I would be happy to help. I think there is no reason for you to make such a drastic decision. Keep the job, and you will not depend on anybody. Studying at the University will only make everything better. What I can do in your case is to create the favorable conditions for you, so that your job would not interfere with the attendance of the lectures at the university. A supervisor of your department has long ago asked me to replace a foreman. Recently we talked about you, and he did not have anything against your candidacy... Salary there is considerably higher there too than the one you are getting now. I will personally ask your supervisor to make sure you can attend the school while being able to work at the same time. One more thing... I would like to ask you personally also not to tell anyone at work about your personal matters. Moreover, no one has to know about this our conversation..."

"I understand. I would have never dared to quit in the first place if I had known there was an opportunity working and studying at the same time."

"We already have a few people in our office who work and study at the same time. Of course, it's not easy, but it is possible. I advise you to take advantage of this opportunity!"

"Thank you very much. I can't find words to express my gratitude."

"You can withdraw your application and go home. Come to work tomorrow. Starting tomorrow, you can work in the department."

Soon Adomaitis was walking energetically down the street. Although the day was foggy, his heart had been filled with joy like on some careless and sunny spring day. It was the first such a cheerful moment in his past few years.

He did not remember when he unlocked the flat door. However, even when at home, he could not find where to put himself. His heart was overflowing with joy. He without a moment's respite kept pacing from one corner to another. Then he sat down onto the chair. Once again, he jumped and began walking around the room caught with the ecstasy.

Finally, Bronius found himself outside breathing moist air while aimlessly walking along the pavement. He did not see anything that was going on around him. He had a feeling as if he at least doubled in size, and that others around were looking at him like at some celebrity...

After good night's sleep he got up well rested and in an unusually high spirits. When sitting in an auditorium at the University, he listened attentively to the lecturer while writing down almost every his word. At the end of the lecture, he was the last to come out of the auditorium.

He carelessly walked waving a notebook in his hand. When he was walking along the narrow corridor, some human figure as quickly as a lightening shot out of the sharp corridor curve of the ancient building of the University. She hit him with her head right on his nose with the biggest bang! Bronius immediately saw stars in his eyes. In a few seconds, warm blood poured out of his nose. The notebook fell to the ground as Adomaitis grabbed his face.

The girl apparently hit herself hard enough too. Perhaps she got also frightened seeing blood streaming from his nose. She jumped backwards away from him. With horror in her eyes and her fingertips pressing tight the pale cheeks, she was gazing at Bronius not able to utter a word.

Finally she came to herself, bent down slowly, and came back up holding his notebook in her hand. Timidly, she extended it to Adomaitis while uttering in a barely audible voice, "I'm sorry, it was an accident. Don't know how it has happened…"

"Well, what happened that happened. Would you happen to know where I could find some water to wash myself up?"

"We can go to my auditorium. There is a drinking water reservoir where you can wash your face. And I will help you clean these few drops of blood off your shirt."

They hurried off in the long narrow corridor. Soon, they both got down to an empty classroom. Adomaitis tore a clean sheet out of a notebook and dampened it with water. He began wiping his face. His nose had not been bleeding anymore.

The girl waited until he finished cleaning the dried up blood off his face. Then she moistened her handkerchief and began gently rubbing spots of blood on his white shirt. No matter how hard she tried, the spots were still visible.

Adomaitis was watching her dexterous, slender fingers moving fast. He only now noticed how beautiful the girl was. With curiosity, he again glanced at her perfect face which had been so close to his. The only thing he could not see was her eyes, since she was looking down at his chest. Despite that, she was so attractive that he did not even dare to keep staring at her any longer.

The girl did not succeed removing the stains completely. She regretfully looked at him, and their eyes met… but Adomaitis was unable to withstand her gaze. He was the first to look away; he blushed like a teenager. Bronius got so embarrassed that he did not know what to do or what to say, or maybe even not to say anything at all.

The girl, who turned out to be bolder, rescued Bronius, "I'm unable to fully remove the stains. The shirt needs to be washed. You could bring it to me tomorrow, and I'll wash it for you. It was my entire fault… Therefore, I will do anything to remove those stains. I'm terribly sorry because of this."

"It's nothing. All this is already in the past. My landlady will wash the shirt; she always does my laundry for me. The spots can barely be seen anyway.

You already have done the clean part very skillfully," gaining his courage back, joked Adomaitis.

Thus chatting, they found themselves in a students' dressing-room. Adomaitis took the girl's coat and helped her to put it on. He himself was buttoning up his raincoat while walking beside her.

When they got outside, fine autumn rain began to drizzle at their faces. The weather was nasty, but Bronius was feeling lightness and content inside of his heart.

"Which direction do you go now? But maybe we get to walk the same way?" asked he looking at his beautiful companion.

"I'm going to Pylimas Street."

"Then we do go the same way. I hope you don't mind if I walk with you."

"I don't mind it at all. The sidewalk is wide; there is plenty of room for both of us," jokingly said the girl.

They both walked leisurely. Even though the two of them had not known each other from before, they were not lacking a conversation. The further they walked, the more one and the other wanted their walk to last longer. The happy times, however, run out fast. Therefore, they did not notice when they got down to the Pylimas Street.

"Well, we've arrived. Even though we didn't hurry, we've got here quickly," Bronius said.

"I have to turn to the right now, and what about you?'

"And I to the left."

"Our roads part here. There is no knowing when we will meet again. Such opportunity might not arise anymore," he said regretfully.

"I am getting an impression you don't regret what happened today..."

"I don't. Otherwise, we have never met. I'm very glad that happened..."

"It's only a pity that you were injured. There are better ways to meet... If not a secret, you are also studying medicine?"

"Yes. Currently I am in my second year."

"And I am in a first year. This is just a start for me. I wonder why I haven't seen you before. In spite of being new at the University, I know all our faculty students at least by sight. However, I've never seen you. I don't understand how I could not have noticed you."

"It's not surprising. Today is my first day at the University. I had been expelled from it before. Otherwise, I would have already been in my fourth year now. However, one unfortunate twist of fate had had mixed up all my plans. Nevertheless, I've been lucky to be able to continue studying again. We have been talking for quite a while… and I still don't know your name," Adomaitis first introduced himself stretching out his hand to her.

The girl answered the same way, extending to him her trembling little, soft hand.

"Tilzyte, Ema. I'm sorry, but I have to go home now. Farewell, my new school friend… Oh, and pleases forgive me for that hapless incident at the University today…"

They parted. Adomaitis walked, his head down, carrying a beautiful image of Ema in his heart. She had been stamped in his memory now.

However, Ema felt quite differently. When she heard that he had been expelled from the University, she got frightened. Therefore, she hurried to say goodbye to him.

Now, with the troubled thoughts flashing in her mind, she was quickly walking the opposite direction. The girl had no desire to be mixed up with some kind of a scapegrace, who would pursue her endlessly not leaving her alone. Nevertheless, she had to admit this meeting had made an impact on her, too.

Next day, Adomaitis left his last lecture as usually. Only this time, he came to the coatroom and was not in any rush to leave… Instead, he tarried.

When he saw Ema, his heart began beating faster, and his face flushed. As the girl was walking by, she greeted Bronius by giving him a nod. He came up to her and helped to put her coat on.

"It looks like our classes ended at the same time. We can walk together again."

"I'm not going home yet; I still have to run to the teachers' office. "

"Maybe I can wait for you outside? I'm not in any kind of hurry."

"You don't have to. I don't even know how long it's going to take," Ema said and, without waiting for his reply, she left.

Next morning, he again was the first to show up in the University's coatroom. As soon as he saw Ema, his face turned red and his heart started beating fast again. He came up to her and helped her dress up, just like yesterday.

This time, too, she went to talk to some teacher. Bronius finally got the message… He understood she was avoiding to talk with him. In spite of that, he still wanted to see her.

Since the first time he saw her, he could not throw her out of his mind. Bronius decided to wait for her outside. Ema noticed him in the street and asked, "What are you doing here?"

"Ema, you are avoiding me. It feels as if you don't want to see me. Why do you keep running away from me?"

"Do I have to do everything you ask me to? I am just as independent as you are. I can go or do anything I want. I don't want to have any commitments. Besides, we have known each other only for a few days. You shouldn't demand from me any more than from any other students. I hope I did not violate any courtesy rules…"

"I'm not asking for anything from you. It just seems that there is some other reason you are avoiding me. It almost feels as if you hate me. Whatever it is, forgive me please. I won't bother you anymore. Maybe you are just imagining something. I am not experienced in relationship with girls. However, I want you to know that I have good intentions… I don't want you to be afraid of me. Don't worry – I'm not going to stalk you. In fact, I need to turn to the right now, since I've some business to take care of. Goodbye."

"But this is the wrong street for you to take home…"

"Under these circumstances, I should probably take this street…"

Bronius hurried away and crossed the street. Then he turned into a first alley on his way not even knowing where he was going.

Ema walked home reproaching herself with speaking rudely to the young man whom she liked so much. She had been very cautious, however, and she got frightened sensing that he was making every effort to meet with her. In addition, she did not want to get into a relationship right away, without analyzing the situation more thoroughly.

However, the fact he had been expelled from the University concerned her the most. The girl was worried because of a possibility of him had been mixed up with the wrong people. She realized that could damage her own reputation as well.

At the same time, some tender longing feeling was beginning to nag her, and Ema started reasoning that maybe tomorrow she will see him again. Then, she would have an opportunity to rectify her mistake… and she certainly wouldn't be so tough.

She thought he would be waiting for her in the street again after their lectures. Maybe this time, he would be standing and waiting for her in a different place in the street.

Even though Ema decided to be more polite, she still was afraid getting into a close relationship with him.

For the rest of the day, the same longing was tormenting her. She knew that Bronius was the cause of it.

Even Ema's mother noticed the change in her behavior, and she anxiously asked, "What's wrong, honey, are you not feeling good?"

"Nothing, mother. Everything is all right," she answered a little irritated.

Ema was approaching her nineteenth birthday. Since she was still very inexperienced in life, she found it difficult to conceal her uneasiness. Therefore, she understood that her mother is sensing her anxiety, and she tried her best to hide it.

Next morning, Ema was in better spirits, because she had hope meeting with Bronius soon. She spent the morning thinking and dreamed of him.

At first, she imagined how she was going to scold him even more than the last time. She even created a scene in her mind of him kneeling down on his knees and kissing her hands while asking her for forgiveness. She saw him begging her not to be mad at him and allow him to see her home.

Later, the scene in her mind changed into another one. Now, she saw herself asking for his forgiveness for her rude behavior.

Those thoughts accompanied Ema until she reached the University. She was somewhat absent-minded during her classes. The day wasn't very successful for her. In her head, everything had been mixed up.

She felt better only after the classes were over. Without any delay, Ema the first came to the dressing-room.

To her biggest dismay, he wasn't there. She quickly dressed up and ran outside.

Ema walked down the street looking around all the time, but when she got down to the place where she had expected Adomaitis to be waiting for her, she did not see him. She could barely keep herself from crying out of vexation.

Suddenly she got overwhelmed with the desire to set herself right with him. However, he was not there. Then she thought that maybe he would catch up with her.

Therefore, she began walking very slowly hoping that she might soon hear the steps behind her... However, she could hear only the sound of her own steps. There was silence around. She wanted to glance back and see if anyone was following her.

Ema thought that it would be good meeting some acquaintance in the street even if the person happened to be her worst enemy. At least, that would give her an opportunity to stop and look around as well as glance back at the street behind her. Then, she could wait until Bronius caught up with her...

She was thinking that he wouldn't probably start a conversation first. However, she expected that he, at least, would say hello to her. As luck would have it, though, no familiar face was seen in front of her. She thought that it would be great if even an entire stranger stopped her to ask some question, for example, 'what time is it now'. However, nobody cared about the time either.

Then, she with curiosity turned back and looked. Now, too, she did not notice anybody following her.

She continued walking slowly again hoping that, sooner or later, he would catch up with her. After all, he had to walk the same street home.

People one after another kept passing her by, but the one her heart was so eager to see still had not emerged.

Suddenly, upon noticing an advertisement board in the street, the idea to stop and read the ads sprang up in her mind. Maybe then, she would see him coming from behind.

Without hesitation, she came up to the stand and began to explore it while looking back from time to time. After standing there for about five minutes, she finally realized that her efforts were in vain. In addition, it appeared awkward to her to stand here any longer, since some other student could had walked up to her and started talking.

After being convinced that Bronius was not there, Ema went home feeling sad. All evening she was upset, but she did not entirely lose her hope meeting him again.

Next day, she got up not fully rested. However, she felt relief, since the tiresome sleepless night had already been in the past.

As she found herself in a classroom, she eagerly waited for the classes to end. After her last lecture, she did not rush to leave like the day before but delayed in the classroom. Then she slowly walked to the dressing room.

She slowly put her coat on and turned her head slightly to look back. Suddenly, she saw Adomaitis standing few steps away from her. Although she was very eager to see him, it was still unexpected to her.

Seeing Bronius, unsettled her a little bit; she did not even notice when her gloves fell down on the floor. Bronius quickly picked them up. Extending his hand with the gloves to her, he uttered, "I'm sorry, Ema, but I haven't intentionally looked for an opportunity to meet you…"

Without waiting for her reply, he took his coat and walked out of the lobby while still dressing up. Confused Ema remained standing. For the second day, she had been cherishing hope to see him. And now, their meeting turned out to be so fruitless.

After Adomaitis vanished from her sight, she could barely keep herself from crying. She could allow herself the luxury of crying if there were no other students around. Ema knew that if one teardrop fell out of her eyes, the whole flock of her classmates would had presented itself to comfort her.

With the heavy heart, she found herself in the street. She did not notice when she came home. However, even being all by herself, she could not relax.

Her parents, too, sensed their daughter was being distressed. Ema tried to hide her feelings. She realized that by showing her sadness she would not only be hurting herself but she'd also be drawing her parents' attention.

Therefore, she sought to soften the situation at home. She was smiling, although her heart was breaking into pieces.

Ema continued cherishing her hope to meet with Adomaitis again. Now, she dreamed becoming friends with him. She even changed her opinion about him.

She was sure it was love from the first sight. He managed to maintain a very good impression on her after the last time they'd talked.

She only feared a rapid and strong feeling of attachment that she had never experienced before. In addition, the fact that he had been expelled from the University somewhat bothered her.

Moreover, she was troubled because he so quickly and easily left her after hearing just a few tough words. That alone was extremely painful to her.

After all, she used to talk this way to other students, too. Only, they had paid little attention to her words. Few times, some of them had said something silly or funny back. And if some classmates had got mad at her for some reason, then she herself did not pay attention to them.

This time, though, things were different. Now, every time she saw Bronius, Ema became anxious. Her heart would stop beating and her cheeks turn bright red.

Two weeks full of tension went by, a she had not ceased hoping to meet Bronius. The situation was becoming even more complicated because he was seemingly avoiding her. Soon, it got to the point where she did not know if the conversation would ever resume between the two of them.

Ema noticed he was reluctant meeting with her. Nevertheless, his behavior incited her further to want seeing him again.

Upon learning about dances coming up at the university, she decided to go there in anticipation to see Bronius.

She sometimes used to go there dancing before. Those kinds of recreational events at Vilnius University had been held every second Saturday of the month.

Ema particularly waited for this coming Saturday, though, because she was almost sure that she would see him there and maybe even manage to revive their relationship.

The long awaited Saturday came. All dressed up, she impatiently waited for the evening to come.

Ema a few times changed her hairdo, sprayed herself with most expensive perfume, and went to her girlfriend's home. The girlfriend had already been waiting for her so that they could go dancing together.

As soon as both of them showed up in the lobby at Vilnius University, they heard the sounds of music coming from a sports hall located on the second floor.

The girls quickly took their coats off and left them in the coatroom. They walked to the dance hall which was already crammed with students. Half of them were spinning in the middle of the room on the parquet floor. The rest of the students kept swaying at the beautiful waltz music while standing along the walls and in the corners of the big hall. Few of them were sitting on the chairs placed along the walls.

As soon as Ema walked into the dance hall, some student immediately ran up to her and called her out for a dance. Next moment, she was already happily spinning on the floor. At the same time, she was looking around while searching for Bronius.

To her surprise, he was nowhere to be seen. She did not rule out an option that maybe he was sitting somewhere in the corner and watching the couples dance, or maybe he went out into a corridor to cool off.

A couple of hours passed. She finally got convinced that the one her heart had been so eager to find was not there.

Despite this, she still waited for him to show up in the densely crowded dance hall. Ema lost her desire to stay there, however, she was reluctant to leave in fear Bronius might show up the last minute.

Therefore, she was the last one to leave the university dances. When she returned home late, the concerned mother reproached her. However, that caused her less pain than the failure of the evening.

Weeks dragged by. At last, winter holidays came, which all students had been looking forward to, except Ema and Bronius.

Both knew well they would have no opportunities meeting each other for a while. While attending classes at the university, there had not spent much time together either. Nevertheless, they had been happy to see each other just from a distance.

Ema and Bronius would cast a glance at each other so quickly, that neither one of them managed to notice their undivided attention. Sometimes, however, they had those happy days, when they would just run into each other in the hallway during their break between the lectures.

Their relationship had been rather formal. Just out of courtesy, they greeted each other with the nod of a head, barely audibly mumbled "hello" under the nose, and then quietly passed each other by.

Ema did not miss even one dance event at the university always hoping to meet him there. She knew that not only he could call her out for a dance, but she, too, would have an opportunity to do the same during the "girls' dance". Naturally, a conversation should begin between them. She would have an opportunity to rectify her mistake and, this time, she would certainly be more gentle with her words... Now, she realized the price she had to pay for her careless words.

Neither Bronius, nor Ema rested well during their three-week holiday. Bronius had to work. Therefore, his vacation passed by practically unnoticed. During the work hours, he only occasionally remembered Ema, because his working conditions did not let him constantly dream about her. Keeping himself busy, protected Bronius from sad thoughts. Often, he did not even notice when the time came for lunch.

In addition, Bronius frequently stayed working overtime in order to compensate days he had been late for work because of his classes at the university.

He gladly worked for two people after sending his apprentice home. Upon coming to his flat afterwards, Bronius would still spend a few hours at the table loaded with schoolbooks. Only late at night, he would fall exhausted to sleep.

Even then, he managed to dream about the beautiful Ema right before falling asleep. He often saw her in his night dreams, too. During those dreams, he always saw both of them reconciled, chatting sincerely and happily.

After waking up in the morning, the feeling of sadness would overwhelm him, since he realized that it was only the dream.

Ema had difficulty coping with her loneliness, because she did not have a job. While at home, she could not find any pleasant activity for herself. Not having anything to do, made her feeling bored and lonely. Even her head often started hurting toward the evenings.

She brightened up only when her father returned home from work. Then, the family would sit down at the table. While they were eating the supper, he would tell all about his day at work. That pulled Ema out of the world of her monotonous thoughts.

Sometimes, she would read a book, which also helped distracting her attention from the empty dreams about Bronius. During those rare occasions when Ema was alone at home, she talked aloud with herself.

She imagined speaking to Bronius, "Easy for you when you don't love me. No need to suffer… And look at stupid me. What are you doing to me… It would have been better if I had never met you. If not for that ill-fated, bloody encounter in the corridor at the university, I would still be living at peace…"

Sometimes, though, Ema went with her girlfriends to see a movie or watch a show at the city theatre. Most of the time, however, she stayed at home which caused her going through the agony of love.

Finally, the tantalizingly long vacation ended. Both Ema and Bronius eagerly waited for it to end.

After her lectures, Ema delayed picking up her coat in the dressing-room. She was looking for the one who had taken her peace completely away from her.

However, this time, she did not see the face that had been so precious to her. Most likely, schedule of his classes had been changed.

Ema, heartbroken, left the university. She wanted to meet him badly, but the pride prevented her from actually making this happen. Thus, she continued suffering with longing.

Nevertheless, the next day already, an opportunity knocked on the door… Coming down the stairs to the lobby, she met Bronius at the main entrance, and their eyes unexpectedly intertwined. Both of them were so perplexed that they even lost their balance for a moment.

After a few seconds, Bronius realized the need to say hello. Then, without waiting for an answer, he added, "How was your vacation?"

He regained confidence but, after a few seconds of silence, a thought crossed his mind that she probably did not wish seeing him.

Since she had still not said a word, he decided taking a further step, "I'm sorry that I have crossed your path again, just like some black cat... Really, I don't want to come across like some nuisance to you. "

"No, you're not any kind of nuisance to me. As about the vacation, I had a great time!" Ema began turning as red as a poppy. "And how was your vacation?"

"I can't brag I had a very pleasant vacation. Rather, I did not have it at all."

"So, why didn't you use your time to get some rest?"

"Of course, most people during their vacation have plenty of time to rest and go places. I didn't have such opportunity, because I had to work."

Making the small chat, they walked to the dressing-room. Bronius helped Ema dressing up by holding her coat.

She walked beaming out the front door of the university building. Meanwhile, Adomaitis found his raincoat among dozens if not hundreds of other coats. Somebody had apparently hung it in another place.

Bronius did not attempt following Ema. She walked ahead very slowly. If Adomaitis paid close attention, he would had realized that she was helping him catching up with her...

Nevertheless, driven by pride, Ema slowly but firmly continued walking while secretly hoping that he would be walking alongside very soon.

However, Bronius did not even dare to look her direction afraid to make the nuisance of himself.

Even though Bronius did not catch up with Ema, she remained very happy with their sweet encounter.

The news he had the job was extremely pleasing to her. That made her think he had been expelled from the university by some mistake and not because of debauchery or some kinds of intrigues.

Ema continued reasoning to herself that even if he had been mixed up in some dirty business, then he was probably quite a reformed character now. At least, such was her wish. For some reason, Ema tried justifying him in her mind. She wondered if she would had done the same if she was to learn that he had committed the biggest folly…

One day, the Secretary of the Young Communist League at the University approached her. He had been agitating her to become a member of the Komsomol for quite a while.

Ema used this opportunity to ask him, "Alfa, do you know why Bronius Adomaitis was expelled from the university?"

"Why are you asking about that villain?" responded Alfa angrily. "Don't ask anything about him and do not attempt to enter into a relationship with him, either. He is a dangerous character. I can assure you his days at the university are numbered… In time, we will clean out our school from those kinds of suspicious characters. Why are you asking about him anyway?"

"I'm just wondering. I thought you are the one who knows everything about everybody at the university. As far as my relationship with the other students goes, it's my personal business who to associate with! I don't care about Bronius's affairs. I just think you should show more interest in him. Maybe he had put himself together with a bad crowd… I know it's always easier to expel students from school, since it is more difficult to help them…"

"Ema, this guy is dangerous with respect to politics. Thus, he should be avoided at all cost. More than that, such characters should be isolated from the educative society all together. It is partially our duty, here, at the Komsomol, to work on it. I have to warn you beforehand to not have anything to do with him! Otherwise, you will regret it…"

"You, Alfa, don't have to worry about that. I will never engage in any political affairs. There is a reason why I have chosen a profession which is close to my heart. I don't have anything to do with the politics; I don't even understand it."

"Quit making fool of me! The mere fact you have not joined the Young Communist League serves as the evidence that you do care about the politics… If a student is equipped not with us, then it means he or she is against us."

"And my understanding is quite different. Somebody who does not support either party is the person who does not want to have anything to do with politics…"

"It just seems to you this way. We, at the University, need to think the way our Communist ideals teach us."

"Alfa, I have already said - the sphere of the politics does not interest me at all. I don't know what your duties at the university are, but my duty is to study as diligently as I can. I put everything else aside. The politics is not the girls' business anyway, and I don't even want to think about it. Please, don't bring this subject to me anymore, because I'm not going to join any groups."

"What do you mean? How can you compare the Komsomol with some sort of groups?! In general, how those kinds of thoughts even come to your mind? The time could come when you'll feel sorry for these words... Then, you will remember our conversation. Although, it could be late... With such thinking, you might not finish the university after all... Fine, don't join the Young Communist League! Get together with Adomaitis... he will take you down the same path he is going himself..."

After casting a furious glance at Ema, he suddenly turned around and walked away leaving unnerved Ema behind.

She had to suffer double pain, since, now, she feared not only for herself but for Bronius as well.

He could be expelled from the university at any given time! She realized there was nothing she could do in order to help him. How could she rescue him? Ema knew it was up to her to notify Bronius of the trap that had been set before him. She thought he would inevitably find himself in it again.

In addition, a thought that no one should see her talking to Bronius started haunting her.

If not for the conversation with Alfa, she could be looking for another opportunity to draw closer to Bronius. Ema realized the relationship with him could lead her to perdition. At the same time, however, she understood that without having this conversation, she would had never learned about the danger lurking ahead of Bronius.

Ema kept reminding herself about being obligated to warn Bronius about the possibility of being expelled from the university at any time again.

Being haunted by those turbulent thoughts, Ema waited until a most beautiful season of the year, the spring, arrived. The sunshine dissipated all her fears and depressed mood. She, like the nature itself, revived after the long severe winter.

Birds had already returned to their land from far countries. The starlings had been joyously singing on the branches of the trees their buds swollen to the point where it seemed as if they were just about to explode. Even the air had been filled with some magical promise.

Any day now, all the plants around were ready to cover in transparent verdure while basking in the bright, warm sunrays. Everything was so beautiful around… Coming to life, the Mother Nature was breathing out vitality.

Only Ema had been feeling a little anxious; she had to carry a dreadful secret in her heart.

She had been desperately seeking an occasion to reveal that secret to Bronius. She felt obligated to do that. Ema's only concern was that maybe she should had told him all about the ill-fated conversation with Alfa long ago, at the time she had had learned it.

Ema feared that delaying to inform Bronius about her conversation with Alfa could do further damage to him. No, it was impossible to continue waiting and putting it off any longer! She needed to notify him about it immediately. That would enable him to defend himself before it was too late.

One day, after her classes, Ema consciously decided to wait until Bronius came out of the university. Upon seeing him walking down the street, she followed him. For a while, there was a distance of about fifty meters between them.

Most of the students had already been scattered in all the directions of the old town. When both of them were far enough from the university building, Ema dared to look around making sure she didn't see any acquaintances.

She was afraid to be seen together with Bronius after her conversation with Alfa.

Being driven by her tender feeling, though, she wanted to warn Bronius of the danger awaiting him. This moment was her only opportunity to accomplish this task.

After she adjusted her pace in order to catch up with him, the distance between them kept decreasing fast. Finally, Ema caught up with Bronius.

Now, she was walking next to him her heart beating fast in her chest. She badly needed to talk to him. Therefore, without waiting until he would turn his attention to her, the girl looked at him first. Their eyes interlocked.

Now, there was no time for delay; it was necessary to act quickly. At the same time, she lost all her courage. Ema simply did not know how to get started, even though she realized that she needed to begin the conversation.

Upon such unexpected meeting with Ema, Bronius also became utterly lost. However, he reacted quickly to the situation and tried mumbling something first.

Ema got ahead of him feeling the need to carry out her duty. Out of breath, she uttered, "You are running so fast like during some kind of marathon..."

Freed himself from the difficult situation, Bronius was feeling relieved. This time, he did not want to apologize to her for anything, although he himself had secretly sought an opportunity to meet with her.

"Indeed, I walk fast. But you've managed to catch up with me."

"I've tried to do my best," out of breath, Ema uttered.

"Where are you headed?"

"I was walking fast because I wanted to catch up with you. It's such a beautiful day. I don't even want to go home."

"Yeah... Was there some other misunderstanding that has prompted you to do this?'

"No, Bronius, there is no misunderstanding this time. I've just accidently seen you in the street. To pass you by without saying hello, seemed to me a little awkward."

Thus, they came to an exact place, where they had separated sometime in autumn after Ema had had said some harsh words to Bronius. They stopped.

He said, "Our roads part here. You'll go to the right, and I'll turn left..."

Bronius was ready to leave, when he saw tears in Ema's eyes. That stunned him a little. He even took a step back."

"Bronius," with trembling voice uttered Ema while getting red in her face. "Why do you avoid me?"

"I don't know how to explain everything to you. First of all, you warned me yourself to stay away from you. Second… Well, that I should probably keep to myself… I've learned that sometimes it's better not to say anything at all. Or, I could fall into your disfavor again…"

"Keep talking, Bronius. I will not get mad, even if it hurts…" asked Ema in a trembling voice.

"I don't know what to say. However, if you really wish to know, I will tell you. I don't want to hide anything from you. I avoid you because I fell in love… don't know if you believe in love at the first sight… Of course, I shouldn't say things like that about the sacred feelings that I foster together with my most beautiful hopes for the future. I just don't know how to put it into words…"

After hearing these few sentences, Ema began feeling dizzy with happiness. She was so stunned that she had to step back and lean against the wall of the standing nearby building. She never expected hearing such strong words coming from his mouth so soon. Therefore, she remained standing in silence still not being able to recover from the unexpected "blow".

Observing her behavior, Bronius became confused and started mumbling, "I thought that I should not tell you this… Forgive me… I will never bring it up again."

"Wait, Bronius, don't leave. Could you please accompany me home?"

"Accompany you… I would be happy to," said Bronius.

Ema regained her balance and said in a serious tone of voice, "I have to tell you one very important thing. Namely because of this, I followed you today. Let's go."

"I hope you are not making fun of me…" Bronius said.

"I am serious. This conversation can't be delayed any longer. Admittedly, I have long wanted to talk to you, but I kept postponing it. For some reason, I didn't dare…"

Both of them were walking along the street, where ancient buildings were standing on both of its sides. At first, the conversation was not happening between them. Besides, Ema did not want coming to the point right away herself. She turned it over in her mind that as soon as she told him about her conversation with Alfa, both of them would separate again.

Therefore, Ema was enjoying her time with Bronius. She didn't know if such an opportunity would happen again. And it was so great knowing that he loved her!

Bronius did not know she had been up to her ears in love with him herself! However, now, a scale suddenly and unexpectedly tilted in her favor.

She remembered her suffering while dreaming about him. The memories of lonely countless evenings emerged in her mind. Ema remembered how depressed she was thinking he did not care about her. Those times had been eating her heart out with sorrow.

For a split second, Ema got overwhelmed with a desire paying him back for all the pain he had caused her. She thought that she could lead him by the nose for a while.

Ema knew she would not take advantage of Bronius.

Her home was very close. Therefore, time had come to tell him about her conversation with the Secretary of the Young Communist League at the university.

She started, "Bronius, as I said earlier, I have to tell you one important thing. However, you have not shown even a slightest interest in hearing about it."

"I've been waiting for you to tell me about it yourself."

"Your reaction surprises me. After all, it has something to do with you."

"What is it all about? You make me anxious. Maybe it's better not to even know... When I don't know anything, I feel as if it doesn't concern me. If you don't want, you don't have to tell me anything."

"Bronius, that does not affect me personally, but I am concerned about you. It looks like you are in a big trouble. I heard that a conspiracy is being plotted before you. Recently, I found out that you could be expelled from the university."

"It doesn't surprise me at all. Once, I already had been kicked out of it. Of course, all the cards are in their hands. Therefore, they play their game the way they want to. I can only watch that from aside."

"You are acting so indifferently, as if you are not worried about it at all. Bronius, you shouldn't remain so unmoved. You need to fight against your enemies. Do something so that those rascals couldn't engage in any deception against you!"

"Ema, I understand what you are saying. Not many things can surprise me anymore. I am firmly determined, though, completing my studies at the university despite all the nooses the others have been setting for me."

"I, Bronius, admire your decision, but I still have to tell you what I recently learned. I had a conversation with one of the students whose name is Alfa. He is a Secretary of the Young Communist League in our faculty. With threats, he warned me not to associate with you. According to him, you are a very dangerous political criminal. Alfa said the arrangements had being made to kick you out of the University. He told me that he would not be able to settle down until he accomplished this. Therefore, I felt an urge to notifying you about this mean plan."

"Thank you, Ema, for being sincere with me. However, this is nothing new to me. I know he is not a friend. I would not want having anything to do with him. However, has it ever occurred to you that if I was some kind of the political criminal, then, regardless of Alfa's wishes, I would have probably been sentenced to death by now? But as you can see, I am alive and healthy… and I'm still a free man!"

"I know your aren't the political criminal. They had just blown everything out of proportion themselves!"

"Ema, I can tell you why I was expelled from the university."

"Yes, I would like to hear that."

"I had studied before at the medical faculty. At that time, I already had had finished my first year there. That was when the whole hell broke loose. The university management learned that my father had been arrested. For that reason alone, I was excluded from school. They reproached me with not disclosing information about my father in the questionnaire upon my entering the university. However, at that time, my father had not been arrested yet, and, therefore, I had not been able to mention about it in the questionnaire. Then, they began accusing me why I did not report about that after my father was actually arrested. Nevertheless, then, no one asked me about it, and I myself was unaware of the need reporting something as personal as that. That is all I can report about my "criminal activity"."

"Why should your father's arrest affect your studies? This is so unjust!" exclaimed Ema.

The two of them reached Ema's apartment on St. Anne Street. They stopped by a brick fence, and Ema pointed at the wooden gate, "This is the place where I reside."

She placed her graceful little hand on the small opened door of the gate and said, "I have to go now. Before I leave, though, could you tell me why you never come to the university dances?"

"Well, there is probably not one but a few reasons why I don't go there."

"What are those reasons?"

"First of all, I do not know how to dance. Second, I don't want to trouble you by making you teach me dancing. Third, I feel lonely, because everyone avoids me. Some people hate me without any apparent reason, just because I live... Others are afraid meeting with me, since they know that I had been expelled from the university. This fact alone gave a stigma to my reputation. Many of my classmates would gladly be on friendly terms with me, but they are afraid of being persecuted because of that. And forth, I would feel uncomfortable standing alone somewhere in the corner of the ballroom while others are dancing... In addition, there is still another important reason that I have not mentioned yet. And that is my work which takes away from me the rest of my time."

"If it were not for those reasons, would you come to the dances then?"

"I'm not an old man to not want having any fun. Soon I will be twenty-three years old. Of course, I would like living a carefree life just like the rest of the students. When else to have fun if not now?"

"Well, if those barriers were removed, would you come to dance with me?"

"Yes, but I still can't see how they can be removed... My circumstances do not allow me to go dancing."

"Bronius, I will teach you dancing. Being busy, you won't feel lonely. Can you see how the two of your reasons have already fallen through? I have to point out to you that your third reason is unfounded as well. You are not troubling me at all. This is only in your head. Therefore, now you have only one reason left, and that is your job . That obstacle is real, and you must take it in consideration. I still think, though, that if you truly wanted, you could spare some evening now and then to have a good time. You cannot entirely forget about yourself. Time flies so fast. You won't even notice when it's gone... We'll want neither to study, nor to have fun when we grow old."

"You, Ema, won't have enough patience teaching me. Being so clumsy, I will only keep stepping on your feet. You won't have good time dancing with me."

"That's not true, Bronius. You have no idea how great it is teaching the others something new! I really want you to learn dancing. Then, I would know that I also have accomplished something positive in this world."

"If I knew that I can give you even the slightest satisfaction, I would definitely come. I also am the same way like you - I always want to do something good for others."

"Does this mean that you've agreed to come dancing this Saturday?" Ema asked smiling.

"Let it be, I agree. I can't say no to you, even though I doubt I could dance without constantly stepping on your feet."

"It's my duty to teach you dancing, and your duty is to cooperate and participate."

"So what time does the dancing start?"

"Somewhere around nine o'clock or maybe earlier. But I usually come in at nine."

"I can't come so early because I finish my work at ten in the evening."

"Okay, then come in after that."

Ema was happy being able to persuade him. After trampling a little in one spot, she said, "Well, I have to go now. Probably I already wasted enough of your time. Just don't forget to come on Saturday. See you soon." She stretched out her hand to him.

Ema did not remember when she unlocked the door or when she entered the room. She only remembered herself running with joy like a lamp lighter up the stairs.

She so noisily broke into the room that even her mother came out of the kitchen to see what was going on. Girded herself with an apron and still holding a steaming ladle in her hand, she said while standing in the middle of the hallway, "Calm down! I thought you have brought the whole crew with you."

Then, seeing the glowing face of her daughter, she just reproached her gently, "Sweetheart, you shouldn't make so much noise; you can accidentally break something."

"Mommy, I'm so happy! Just don't know how to explain everything to you..."

"Where is all this energy coming from? Tell me what has happened to you?"

"Mom!" The girl ran up to the mother, hugged her, and whispered happily, "One guy declared his love to me today..."

"Baby, you're too young..."

"Mom, there are a lot of girls who are already married at my age..."

"Ema, don't forget that you are still going to school. In your case, what good does it do dreaming about the marriage? Think - what would happen to your studies? Do you want to quit the school?!"

"Mom, don't exaggerate!" turning serious, spoke Ema. "The idea of marriage has never even crossed my mind. Is it so bad being friends with somebody? According to you, I should remain a spinster for the rest of my life?!"

"I'm not trying to say that you should never get married. I just think that at this time in your life it is little premature to be thinking about creating the family..."

"Let it be as you wish. Children must obey their parents. On the other hand, the time always comes to leave a native nest... In addition, I would be afraid to remain alone forever. And as far as the marriage goes, I don't have any plans regarding it yet. I just think that there is nothing bad in dating a nice guy. I could even be acquainted with a few of them at the same time. When I graduate from the university, I will be twenty-three years old. Thad is the perfect age for getting married. If I can't find a friend for life now, then when can I find him? Later on, it could even become impossible at all to do that."

"What you are saying is true, dear," looking straight in her eyes with compassion, spoke concerned mother. "Marriage itself is not a bad thing. I'm not as much afraid for you to associate with this guy or any other guy, as much as I'm worried that you are still so inexperienced in life... Many boys seduce girls and then leave them. That is the thing I am afraid of the most. You cannot even imagine what a big pain that can cause you. I'm simply trying to protect you from a disaster. You would see everything in different light while being over head and ears in love, and you would always be forgiving toward him even if he hurt you. You need to be careful, my dear. Remember that in one brief moment you can ruin your entire life forever. I would suffer greatly, too, because of your downfall."

"Mom, don't worry too much about me. I'm not some light-headed person, and he is not some kind of impudent boy, either. Otherwise, I would tear him by the roots out of my heart. Believe me, I would never allow feelings to overcome my mind."

"Your thinking is probably right. Nevertheless, life can throw at you surprises you have to take in consideration. Sometimes you need to be ready to repel... You really have to use your head and evaluate the situation carefully. Please, don't forget about your father. He loves you more than anything in this entire world. Think, how much he would worry about you! Having in mind his age, any problems at home could drive him straight to his grave..."

"Mother!" exclaimed Ema horrified. "You are acting as if I'm planning to do something bad to both of you. If you wish, I can immediately end this relationship, even though we have already made arrangements meeting at the university dances this Saturday. Despite the fact that he declared his love to me, I myself did not give him any promises. To tell the truth, he hasn't asked anything of me. He even said he had thought I didn't like him. I think he expressed his feelings for me just because he was certain I had not been interested in him."

"So, the two of you have already known each other for some time?" calming down, asked the mother.

"Since the autumn of last year."

"Who is he? Do you know anything about his family?"

"I don't know much about him, and the little that I already know, I, too, have learned only by chance."

The mother and the daughter, like some close girlfriends, were chatting from the heart while sitting on the couch.

"I only know this much about him that, three years ago, he was expelled from the University."

After hearing this, the mother painfully moaned. It was hard to tell what thoughts were going through her mind. It was only clear by an expression on her face that it was painful to her hearing about that.

"Mom, I understand how you feel after learning about this... I reacted the same way myself when he had told me that. At the time after I'd learned it, I did not even try to find out the reason why he had been removed. Afterwards, for some reason, my heart cried from longing during dark winter evenings. In spite of this, I still managed holding onto my principles. Then I accidentally found out he had been expelled in connection with the politics. In addition, I learned that a trap has been set for him now as well. For the second time, they want to remove him from the university."

"So, he is back at the university? Is he studying again?" the mother sounded relieved.

"Yes, mom, he is the student of the same faculty I am. Only, he is in his second year now. If they hadn't expelled him, he would have already been studying in the fourth year. They had removed him from the school because his father had got arrested. I asked him why he never comes to our dances at the university. That was when he told me that he loves me... I think he just doesn't want to cause me any troubles. That is all I know about him so far. Also, he told me that he works in the evenings. Most likely, he is from a poor family, even though you couldn't tell that by the way he dresses."

Both of them chatted amicably until the father came home from work. He loudly walked into the room. Both Ema and the mother jumped off the couch directing their eyes at him which made him alarmed.

"Why are you both looking so puzzled? What happened?" asked he.

"We spent long time chatting with Ema, and I've totally forgotten about the supper. You already home from work, and I haven't even started cooking."

"No need to rush. Today, I came home an hour and a half earlier. There is plenty of time to make supper. Better share with me what you both are up to, unless you have some secrets from me..."

"We don't have any secrets from you," said the mother confused.

"So, what has happened? I've got an impression it is something important," sitting down at the table, said the father with concern.

"To tell the truth, I don't even know how to start," muttered the mother under her nose.

"You've already started. Now, you just need to finish it. Come on, get it out! I'm not some kind of a stranger from whom you ought to be masking the family matters."

"That's right. Maybe, that's why I don't know how to say it…"

"What are you, mother, talking about? Perhaps it is something very serious…" Stunned father glanced first at the mother, and then he scanned with his eyes his daughter from her head to her toes.

After jumping off the couch, Ema was still standing and looking down as if she had committed some crime.

"Mother, it's not necessary talking about that," said Ema not looking up.

After hearing daughter's indecisive words, the father became even more worried. He quickly stood up and walked up to his daughter. He took her hand and squeezed it firmly.

"Ema, tell me what happened. Your mother and you are hiding something from me…"

"Paul, calm down. Nothing bad has happened to Ema. She is quite able sticking up for herself!" the mother took him by the hand and seated him back at the table.

"If you are so persistent, then I will tell you. Looks like Ema has found herself a boyfriend…"

Then she fell quiet, and dead silence set in the room. The father did not say anything awaiting for the mother to add something more.

However, the mother was silent also. It seemed to her that with those few words she already had said a lot.

It was clear that the news of their daughter's relationship with a student from her school suddenly broke the peaceful life of the family.

Ema remained still while standing silent between her father and mother, growing red like a poppy in her face.

"Why are you standing as stiff as a poker!? What else happened?" The father rather angrily broke the silence.

"That's all I know," babbled frightened mother.

"Ema, has your mother told everything?"

"Yes, father. One guy really declared his love to me, There has been nothing more between us... This coming Saturday, we are meeting at the university dances. But if you, daddy, forbid me to go dancing, then I won't go."

"Sweetheart, maybe he had just said that. Many young men do this trying to seduce girls. Today, he maybe confessed in love to you, and tomorrow he will say the same to another girl. You should use sound judgment in your situation. Love is sacred, but only when it is sincere. The holiness of love, however, can be used gaining the insidious purposes as well. This way, a lot of girls of weak disposition have perished."

"Daddy, I understand your concern, but, I swear, I will not incur shame upon you even if I had to tear out this love of mine by its roots out of my heart. If it turns out to be impure, I surely will disavow it myself. However, his words appeared sincere to me. I have no doubts regarding his conduct, either. He has not suspected yet that I am also in love with him. Otherwise, he had never declared his love to me. In fact, I did not respond to his words the same way and did not even show they had made any impact on me. Dad, this is all I can tell you about Bronius."

"So far, I am not seeing anything that would make it worth worrying. I just don't understand why your mother and you are behaving as if you have lost everything you own. What I have learned so far, seems to me quite within the normal range. This is what one could expect. Those kinds of things happen according to the laws of the Mother Nature. Especially if it is the real love, love without cheating. Mother, have you already forgotten our own youthful years? We ourselves had been still in a gymnasium when we had fallen in love."

"In those days, everything was different. We had dated for a long time. You could say that we had known each other since the childhood. We also had known each other's parents. Therefore, it had been relatively easy for us making the right decision. Here, we have a total stranger. We do not know anything about him; we haven't even seen him."

"There is no need worrying about that. Ema should introduce him to us before she decides to tie her destiny with him. Parents always have more extensive knowledge of life. Therefore, our advice can come in handy. Isn't this true, Ema?"

"Of course, daddy. I will definitely introduce him to you if the close relationship develops between us. I find it hard making important decisions in my life without your and mother's approval. And if you won't endorse my choice, I will keep your will."

"Mother and I don't have the right to decide your destiny for you, dear. It is totally up to you. We can only give our opinion or advise you. You are the one who would have to live with the chosen one. This is one of the biggest tasks in any person's life, which he or she can only accomplish alone. If you seriously are thinking of having the relationship with this young fellow, then you should introduce him to us. You could invite him here on your birthday. That would be the best opportunity for us to get acquainted. After having some wine, people tend to become more open... and it would be easier for as drawing conclusions about him afterwards. I think, we have agreed on this. It's always best to discuss the things like that in a close family circle first. Well, now let's leave aside all the debates and get back to our business."

Soon everybody dispersed into different corners. Father sat down at his writing desk and took a book written in English out of the drawer. He had been translating it into Lithuanian for quite a while now. In a few minutes, he got fully integrated into another world.

Ema went to her room, where she situated herself at the window trying to read notes of her last lesson. However, the studying was unsuccessful today. She had still been overwhelmed with her heart matters.

Ema was trying to read the same paragraph over and over again only to discover that she could not understand the meaning of the writing.

She was steeped in the most beautiful dreams. She could not help looking out the window, where a few young, slender apple trees with Japanese cherry bushes have been growing.

She felt some unexplainable lightness and goodness in her heart. Not being able to stand reading any longer, Ema went to the balcony. She rested her stretched arms onto a metal railing and leaned her upper body forward over the hurdle. Then she took a deep breath of the fresh air into her lungs. She understood that her chance of doing any homework this evening was equal to none. Therefore, she decided it was not even worth trying.

Meanwhile, mother in the kitchen was hurriedly preparing food. In her heart, two opposite feelings were interlocking - the joy and the frustration. On one hand, she was happy that love unexpectedly had visited their daughter. On the other hand, she feared that this stranger could deceive their sweet girl, their only child who had still been so inexperienced in life.

Although the mother was late to prepare the supper, nobody complained. The father and Ema realized the important matter for the entire family had been discussed today.

At last, the mother opened the kitchen door and let both of them know the supper was ready. Since Ema was not showing up, the father went to her room looking for her. She was not there either, only her school notebook was laying opened on the windowsill. He was going to leave the room, when he noticed something moving in a balcony. It appeared that Ema was sitting there in a rocking chair. He crossed the room and opened the balcony door with a big window installed in the upper half of it.

"Ema, the mother is already calling us to eat supper," he told Ema who was indulged in reverie.

An uplifted mood was hovering in the room. While eating their meals, all three talked very little. In spite of that, each of them felt unusual lightness in their hearts.

Ema, in particular, appeared happy and serene as never before, even though she tried not to make a big deal out of her recent discovery. Now, she for some reason became a little reserved.

Several times, the mother gave an attempt renewing the latest discussion, but she did not succeed.

The father did not elaborate her. After the supper, he again found himself at his desk and was quickly absorbed in his work.

Ema went back to her room, but she did not want to stay in the balcony any more, although the evening outside was still alluring with warmth and fresh air.

Instead, she sat down at a small table, where she had been doing her homework since her early years at school.

Meanwhile, the mother was in a hurry cleaning in the kitchen, where she washed dishes, the table, and the floor. She was anxious to finish her dirty chores that, over the years, had been making housewives so bored and exhausted.

All three family members were busy at home, each in his or her own corner. Thus, nobody interfered with each other.

The mother was thinking of going to her daughter's room after she had finished cleaning in order to continue their previous conversation that seemed not over yet, only cut off by the supper.

The mother walked into the room, where the father had been submerged into his translation so deeply that he did not even lift his head from his papers.

However, she herself did not wish to linger there any longer. Instead, she went to her daughter's room. As soon as Ema heard the mother walking in, she looked at her and said smiling, "Are you done with your chores in the kitchen already?"

Then she again got back to reading her homework material. The mother realized that if she stayed in her daughter's room any longer, she would only interfere with her studies.

Therefore, she also found a quiet corner for herself. She picked up some book along with her glasses and went out to the balcony, where she sat down on a rocking chair and started reading.

However, the book did not spark her interest, and she caught herself reading the same paragraph repeatedly. At the same time, it started growing dark outside. Mother put the book aside and plunged into a thought. In a few minutes, she began dozing.

Ema walked up to her and said, "Mom, I brought you a scarf. Evenings are still cold. You could catch a bad cold."

She covered her mother's shoulders and disappeared. Soon, she was back studying again.

The next day at the University, Ema did not see Bronius, even though she loafed about in the corridors for some time in no hurry to go home after her lectures had been over.

Upon coming home, she found her mother cutting hems of her dress.

"Mom, what are you doing?"

"I want to make a dress for you for this coming Saturday. You said that you are going dancing. You need to look beautiful. This material is very nice. It should turn out to be the beautiful dress. You could not find the expensive fabric like this in any store."

"What have you done, mom! This was your most expensive dress! I have plenty of dresses already, and you cut up your most beautiful one..."

"I've had no need for beautiful clothes for a long time now. Your father and I have not gone out anywhere lately. This is your time to dress up... I find it to be fascinating when young people dress fashionably and stylishly."

"Mom, when dad discovers you ruined the dress that he had bought you for your birthday, he will be very angry."

"Don't worry about that. I'll be able to calm him down. You will see for yourself what a wonderful dress you will have for this coming Saturday. It will probably make you look the most beautiful girl out of all the girls there! That boy of yours will like you even more then. Hopefully, he is a good person."

"Mother, don't worry about him. I can see with my own eyes, and I can sense with my own heart what kind of person he is... Don't think that I'm still a child."

"Yes, dear, you are already almost an adult. Nevertheless, you will always remain a child to me. Until I meet this young man myself, I won't settle down."

"Mom, your words frighten me. That could break up this beautiful friendship, even though it has not even begun."

"You said he loves you..."

"So what?! That does not mean that we have already been engaged."

No matter how hard Ema resisted for her mother's old dress being disassembled, the woman remained implacable.

She maintained the same by insisting she no longer needed it, since she had already had found her good fortune in life.

As soon as the father returned home from work, Ema immediately rushed to him and complained about the mother's decision. However, after some negotiations with the mother, the father agreed with her. Nothing else was left for Ema to do. She was out of luck to talk her mother over, especially now, when such an important matter had to be solved which could make an impact on their daughter's future.

Mother took her time measuring Ema's bust, waist, arms, and legs in order to determine the length and the width of her new dress.

At dusk, all the pieces that previously had belonged to the mother's dress were cut and ironed. The mother measured the fabric with the centimeter ruler and marked the lines on it with a piece of white chalk. Then, she cut the fabric with the scissors along those lines.

Having closed herself in the bedroom, the woman worked until it got completely dark outside and in the room. Nobody disturbed her, and she worked diligently without even lifting her head. She was interrupted only when her husband entered the room and said that it was time to go to bed.

As soon as the mother woke up early in the morning, she instantly remembered this was Ema's dance Saturday morning. Therefore, no time could be wasted. Every minute was precious, since the dress was needed for the coming evening. Ema's mother understood that if she was unable to finish it by tonight, then there was no sense in sewing it at all.

This morning, she was up an hour earlier than usually. She hastily prepared modest breakfast. Before even her husband and Ema got up, she was absorbed in working on the dress.

The mother rushed hooking together the separate pieces of material, so that the fitting could be performed. She barely could keep up with her task. Nevertheless, she had to settle for whatever had been available, because Ema had to leave for her classes at the university. Therefore, the woman had to do the first fitting without being fully prepared.

As soon as her daughter returned home from school, she was in a big hurry to do the second fitting. This time, it was very thorough. Again, she drew lines with a chalk. Then, she marked the seams that had to be loosened up a bit or sewn in deeper.

She badly wanted for the garment to lay perfectly on their girl's figure. When all the smallest details had been taken care of and all the inaccuracies marked, the mother finally felt a relief.

The dress was finally finished. It was eight o'clock in the evening.

Ema's mother brought it to Ema and hung it on the half-opened door of her room. Ema was glad she did not have to try it on again. Those fittings seemed to be like some torture; she had to keep standing still for long time and let her mother fix all its seams and little details.

Ema was not overly concerned if the dress would fit her. However, she did not dare saying anything to the mother, because she was aware all the mother's efforts had been made just for her.

Nevertheless, as soon as Ema saw the dress, she did not need to be urged to put it on. She quickly pulled it over her head and carefully examined herself while twirling in front of the mirror.

The mother was watching her also while sitting on a chair. She was admiring the fruit of her labor. There was an expression of satisfaction on the woman's face. The work had been done so well that it was impossible to find even the slightest defect that needed to be fixed. The dress fitted perfectly the slender figure of the girl!

Ema was very happy about her new dress, and her face kept radiating with joy.

The mother also helped Ema with her hairdo which they had to change a few times. At last, the two of them left satisfied with the hairstyle, too.

When Ema began polishing her shoes, the mother asked, "What are you doing?!"

"What do you mean? I have to clean my shoes for tonight's dances."

"Are you going to wear those ugly shoes with your new dress?! I hope you're not going to wear them tonight."

"Yes, I'm going to wear them. Bronius doesn't know how to dance. He can ruin my good shoes by stepping on them. I promised to teach him dancing in the course of this evening. However, next time, I hope I'll be able to wear my new shoes."

"Don't even think of wearing those old shoes tonight! These ugly slippers could ruin your entire looks! Please, put on the new ones!"

"No, mom. I know what I'm doing."

"Papa, come here! Just look at your daughter!"

The tall father's figure appeared in the doorway.

"What..."

"Look at Ema…"

The father entered the room and placed a book he had been holding in his hand on the table. With astonishment in his face, he examined his daughter from her head to her toe.

"You look like some actress… True beauty! What can I say – the perfect dress. Your new hairdo suits you very well too."

Then he looked at his wife and said, "That was a great idea of yours to make the new dress for Ema. Otherwise, your old dress would have gone out of fashion while hanging in the wardrobe. Now, Ema can shine. I have no slightest doubt she will have a huge success at the dancing party tonight. I think she could conquer the heart of any guy."

"Father, just look at her shoes…"

"Really, the shoes could have been better… but you had to think about that earlier. There was enough time to take care of everything. After all, we were able scraping up some money to buy her new shoes. Oh well, you'll just have to dance with these tonight. But don't despair; there will probably be so many people at the dances that nobody will even notice your shoes."

"Paul, she has the new shoes!"

"Why do we bother then? Maybe they rub sore her feet… In that case, I also wouldn't recommend wearing them. How could someone dance with the shoes that are too small?"

"The new shoes don't hurt her feet at all. She is just saving them…"

"Well, there is no need to do just that. On the contrary, you should be in the best shape and looking immaculate from your head to your toes. Let those cavaliers be crazy about your!"

Surrounded by the undivided attention of her parents, she walked out the door for her first date with Bronius. It was eight thirty in the evening.

Ema was literally flying to the university. In her head, the most beautiful hopes and dreams interlaced. She had been cherishing them for a few weeks now, and she waited for this evening impatiently.

Ema was walking down the street without feeling ground under her feet. On her way, she dropped by her girlfriend's with whom she had arranged to go dancing together. Despite being still pretty early in the evening, it was already dark outside.

When both girls arrived at the university, it was a little after nine o'clock. Ema was not sure if Bronius had been able to leave his work earlier. She eagerly looked around, but he was nowhere to be seen.

Suddenly, a wave of disappointment mixed with anger gushed over her. However, she did not have to experience this strong feeling for long.

Lively music playing, Ema was dancing one dance after another, and Alfa was the one who asked her to dance most often.

He kept devouring her with his eyes. In fact, he had not left her alone during the breaks between the lectures lately, too. However, today he was especially tenacious and even intrusive.

It was well after ten o'clock, but Bronius had still not shown up. Ema kept dancing with Alfa in retaliation.

Finally, after she had almost given up her hope, he suddenly appeared. He was standing in the doorway as if being afraid to enter the hall.

As soon as Ema saw him, the color instantly flew into her cheeks. Again, she could not feel the ground under her feet. It seemed to her that she was not dancing but flying above the floor.

Their eyes met, when she was passing by. Bronius smiled at her while blushing at the same time. He nodded his head greeting her.

When the music ceased playing, Ema quickly pulled her hand out of Alfa's palm. Soon she found herself in a circle of her girlfriends, where she happily chattered and immediately forgave Bronius for the tardiness.

After the break, the music began playing again. Without waiting until anyone asks her to dance, Ema firmly walked across the entire ballroom floor and found Bronius in the crowd of the other students.

Meanwhile, the couples were pouring into the middle of the floor from all the corners of the room. Instantly, the ballroom was once again chock-full.

A little embarrassed, she stretched her hand out to Bronius and said in a trembling voice, "Good evening. The other day, we agreed I would be teaching you dancing tonight. I hope you have not changed your plans, since I still have the intention to fulfill my promise to you."

"Hello, Miss Ema. I really don't know how to dance. It may take you quite some time working with me on that. Maybe it's not even worth to begin..."

Bronius could not take his eyes off Ema. He was lost in admiration with her. This evening, she was especially beautiful. In addition, a very pleasant scent of French perfume was dispersing from her that the mother sprayed on her upon her leaving for dances.

Now, he was standing in front of her looking like some angel who suddenly had fallen from the sky on the ground.

Bronius had never danced or even held a girl in his arms. He was growing dizzy out of happiness. He had no power of will resisting such an unearthly beauty.

Ema seemed dressed so amazingly well, and the wonderful smell of perfume was coming from her. He was literally hypnotized by her presence.

On his way to the university, he had become engulfed in doubt about his earlier decision to learn dancing.

However, at this moment, it seemed as if all his doubts were melting away. He had no power resisting the wishes of Ema and only faithfully walked behind her.

They both stepped onto the dancing floor, and Ema raised her arms in anticipation for him to put his hand on her waist. Bronius appeared a little confused.

Noticing this, Ema got lost too. Looking down at the floor, she was still waiting for him to embrace her by the waist. In addition, she herself was becoming more excited just by feeling him breathing so close to her.

Suddenly, Alfa shot up in front of both of them as if out of the ground. He grabbed Ema's waist and turned her face towards his. Bronius could not come to terms with such insolence.

If one of his gymnasium friends did that to him, he would consider that to be a joke. However, in this case, he had no doubts about the intentions of his opponent.

The audacious Alfa's trick instantly dissipated Adomaitis's feelings of timidity that had kept him constrained just a few minutes ago. Therefore, he did not even notice when he quickly grabbed Alfa's arm and literally snatched the girl out of his embrace.

Both young men exchanged angry glances at each other, and Bronius spat out his words through his teeth with hatred, "Get out of the way! Nobody asked you to come here!"

"No girl should wait for a fool like you... Don't make her blush."

"It's none of your business. She may not need a jerk of ready sympathy..."

Being agitated and without thinking, Bronius placed his hand on Ema's waist. After treading on her foot, he turned her twice around and stopped.

Now, he realized Ema was right, because one had to know how to dance in order to be on the ballroom floor.

He uttered perplexed, "Ema, nothing good will come out of our dancing. Besides, I shouldn't have said anything to that impudent person. Now, he really won't retreat".

Bronius showed with the slight move of his head toward Alfa who was standing just a few steps away from them and smiling hypocritically. It was evident he was glad that his opponent had no luck with his dance steps. Alfa kept in close proximity to them so that he could ask Ema for a dance if Bronius could not manage dancing himself.

Bronius again turned the girl around several times while still stepping on her feet. Finally, his patient was exhausted. Losing his courage, he did not notice when his left arm drooped down and his right hand made itself free from Ema's little fingers.

Alfa, of course, immediately took advantage of the situation. He quickly like some acrobat ran up to them and took hold of Ema.

The same moment, both of them already were flying through the hall carried by the sounds of the music.

Bronius left standing alone like a scorched stake driven into the ground at the scene of the fire. His whole face turned red with vexation. He was angry being unable to defeat the opponent who seemed to be walking all over him. He started even feeling as if Ema herself had begun having an aversion for him.

Therefore, Bronius decided now was the appropriate time to remove himself and not even try to get between her and Alfa.

His feeling was only further strengthened seeing Ema's glowing face when she was flowing by together with his enemy. Bronius was burning with shame.

Without feeling ground under his feet, he started retreating backwards. Found himself behind the door or the sports hall, he decisively walked out into the street.

Cool breeze outside dried fast his sweaty forehead. For some time, Adomaitis kept walking without realizing where he was going and what had just happened a few minutes ago. Only now, he totally came back to his senses and "cooled off" completely.

However, now, doubt sank into his mind. He stopped on the pavement of the street feeling completely lost. Bronius was debating what to do next.

On one hand, he wanted to go back and be with Ema. On the other hand, he was overwhelmed with shame. Therefore, he did not dare to return, even though his soul reached out for her.

Being highly distressed, he went home. After drinking a couple of cups of strong, hot tea, he tried to get absorbed in notes of tomorrow's lectures. However, all kinds of anxious thoughts began flashing across his mind.

It was clearly no use of studying that night. Therefore, he put away his notebook, quickly undressed, and lay down in bed. Nevertheless, the failure at the dances kept haunting him and did not allow to sleep in peace.

He kept tossing for a long time. When he finally fell asleep, restless dreams did not let him having a good rest.

Only a beautiful, sunny morning revitalized his aching soul. Bronius washed his chest and face with cold water and started feeling himself again.

IN THE HOMELAND

Several days past the dances at the university, Bronius was still haunted by the memories about that evening. Those memories crushed his self-esteem.

Happiness that had started shining recently, seemed completely covered with clouds now. By unexpectedly crossing his path, Alfa ruined beautiful hopes that Bronius had been cherishing for months. If not for this villain, something good would had definitely come out of Bronius's first dance lesson.

Instead, Alfa had been triumphing now. After suffering humiliation and shame, Bronius had had no other choice but to withdraw and give preference to his enemy.

Surprisingly, once upon a time, both of them had been good childhood friends. Nevertheless, Alfa had trodden under foot their old friendship and became fierce enemies with Bronius.

As if it was not enough, both of them met at the university dances under such adverse circumstances. Alfa just kept taunting him in the presence of the girl Bronius had been in love with. He could not bear that.

Now, in his imagination, Bronius saw himself again in the ballroom, only this time, competing with Alfa who himself had just recently learned how to dance.

However, Bronius understood that Alfa had significant superiority in comparison to him. He already danced like a professional, and he was a leader at the university.

One political system changing another, Bronius had failed to adapt quickly to the new circumstances. Moreover, he distanced himself from the politics all together.

Being constantly run down by the new regime, he grew increasingly reserved. Then, a surprising, terrible blow hit his family with his father's arrest and disappearance. As if it was not enough, he himself was expelled from the university.

Being struck by the disasters, Bronius could never fully recover. Up to this day, all sorts of smaller setbacks, too, had been chasing him.

Thus, Bronius shunned himself away from other people. He got to the point where he was afraid of being mixed up even in slightest conflicts. A smallest shadow could shroud his already shaken reputation.

This time, however, he felt he would not succumb to the fear. Contrarily, he would fight to the last instead. However, his enemy was superior to him in the sense that he was able to dance.

Having these kinds of thoughts, Bronius retreated giving a positional advantage to the opponent, since he could compete neither in dancing nor in politics.

Moreover, he did not wish conforming to the current political system. The other way round, he was against it. Bronius looked soberly at all the political matters, and he did not want to agree selling his feelings to the invaders in exchange for an easier life. The price seemed just too high to pay. It went against Bronius's principles to derive his living from oppressing the other people. He didn't want the money covered with their tears and blood.

However, Alfa did not care a fig for all this. He just watched his own back and kept striving for his career. In addition to that, he was getting very close to the completion of the university, while Bronius's road to education had just begun.

Moreover, he did not even know whether he would be able to withstand all the obstacles awaiting him. He was not sure if he could have enough stamina and determination enduring all the humiliation and disdain until he finished the university.

Alfa carelessly treaded under foot their nation's sacred customs, too. At any cost, he strove to please the staff at the university. And he succeeded at that. He had been granted many privileges that he used without any scruples.

There was an enormous difference between the two of the young men.

Bronius's untarnished conscience dictated to him there was no way Alfa could not had seen what had been happening around. At least, the injustice against the Lithuanian nation that the Russian authorities had resorted to by enslaving it had been obvious to everyone else. Such a small country could not oppose the bloody dragon of the biggest country on the earth.

The "red dragon" seemed to despise everything that had been dear and precious to an ordinary Lithuanian. Obviously, that did not matter to Alfa, the person of the great ambition. He cared only about his personal goals which he cherished the most. He thought just about himself, and he refused hearing about others.

Alfa had been aware about massive deportations of Lithuanians to Siberia, since the Russian government had resorted to the most ruthless repressions imaginable. He knew well that all the people in Lithuania had been opposed to the politics of the invaders whom they terribly hated. In spite of that, he just spat upon their opinion.

Moreover, he understood that by kissing the invaders' butts, by kneeling to their feet, and by betraying his own nationals he would benefit highly.

Therefore, it was not surprising he actively assisted the Russian officials. Alfa was aware of Adomaitis's views, because both of them were good friends since their childhood. In the forties, when the Bolsheviks came to Lithuania, he himself had feared possible consequences to the country of Lithuania.

Nevertheless, starting with his high school years at the gymnasium, Alfa's apprehension manifested itself along with the treacherous adjoinment to the strong.

However, Bronius did not know that back then. He had still considered Alfa to be his good friend; their outlook on life had coincided for the most part.

Only after a few years passed by, Alfa's "demon" appeared in all its glory. He started acting against his own fellow citizens in hopes of having a better career.

Bronius no longer considered Alfa to be his friend. Rather, he began viewing him as an enemy, the tyrant, who would sell his neighbor for a slice of bread and betray his national without any pangs of conscience.

Seeing all the flaws of Alfa's character, Bronius began feeling hatred toward him. He harbored disdain in his heart because of Alfa's treason to the nation. Alfa's behavior at the dances added the personal side to the frustration.

Now Adomaitis viewed him as a personal enemy, since he constantly tried to weave all sorts of plots. It seemed to Bronius that he finally succeeded in his wrongdoings.

Bronius was sure that Alfa's intentions toward Ema were no good also. It had been long time he cherished the idea of seducing the girl and then leaving her, because she had never supported his political beliefs. He was acutely aware that she did not like the new system. She did not want to join the Komsomol. Alfa was frantic when he had learned she would not yield to any of his persuasions which did not allow him to control her.

However, things unexpectedly turned out to be the other way. Ema did not get into the trap that Alfa had set for her. Instead, she trapped him herself, even though she had no intention to attain such a goal.

Thus, Alfa himself lost his heart to her. After Bronius left the dances, he just would not leave her alone. He bored her to death with his intrusiveness. It seemed as if some spell had been cast on him.

Feeling desperate, Bronius could not find peace. And it was no wonder, since Ema had been the most beautiful girl in the Faculty of Medicine. If there was a beauty contest arranged, she would probably be the first in the entire university, too.

She looked especially beautiful at the past dances, where she drew attention of many guys. However, Alfa was the one who had succeeded spending the most time with Ema that evening. He could not forget the time when he was triumphantly spinning with Ema like a whirlwind through the entire hall in the vortex of dance.

However, his happiness was short lived. As soon as Ema became aware Bronius had left the dances, she herself left unnoticed shortly after.

She returned home much earlier than usually that night. Her mother's heart sensed something was wrong. She realized that her daughter's first date had failed.

Ema refused discussing anything, when the mother fixed her inquiring gaze on her daughter's face. For a while, there was silence between them.

Then, Ema went to her room and apathetically collapsed into an armchair without even taking off her raincoat.

She sat next to a small round table on one leg. The girl covered her face with her palms her elbows resting on the knees. She was afraid showing her mother the anguish of her heart.

Thus, she was sitting quietly; she did not sob. At the moment, she felt listless-minded and very lonesome.

It was so quiet around. After sitting this way alone for about fifteen minutes, she became increasingly sad and depressed.

Nevertheless, she could not bring herself to leave the room or even to modifying her posture. It seemed to her that it was easier staying numb rather than wandering around while sighing and moaning.

In addition, she could had drawn the mother's attention with such her behavior.

That evening, Ema did not wish hearing neither words of sympathy nor advice. Deep down in her heart, she wanted only to cry freely, lost in her grief. However, it appeared as if she was not entitled to do that either. Ema did not want to cause additional pain to her mother, even though she might experienced great relief after crying out her heartache.

No matter how quietly Ema held herself, the mother still felt that something was wrong with her. Carefully opening the door of the room, she quietly stole inside near the motionless daughter.

Ema was so deep in her world of thoughts that she did not hear the mother walk in. She gave a start only when she felt a hand on her shoulder. She quickly realized it was the touch of her mother, and she looked up with sadness in her eyes.

"Ema, child, what has gotten into you?" mother's voice trembled.

Ema did not have the strength or desire to explaining all last night's details and nuances. She just continued sitting the same stiff and indifferent.

"Ema, tell me at last what has happened!? Don't torment me."

"Mom, nothing bad happened. Don't worry. You better go to sleep. It's late already," uttered she without stirring her body which made the mother even more worried.

"Don't say that, dear. I can sense something is wrong. Share it with me, and you'll feel better. After all, you must know by now that I am like your best girlfriend who only means well. Two heads are better than one. I could give you good advice, since I am more experienced in life than you are. I worry probably more about you than you do about yourself."

Ema patiently listened to her mother's apprehension. She understood that she could not quiet her mother with just a few words now. It was obvious that the uncertainty was tormenting her. Most likely, all sorts of most terrible thoughts were flashing in the mind of the poor woman, and she could not be at peace with herself.

Ema took the mother's hand off her shoulder and squeezed it firmly in her palms. Looking at her with anguish, she still managed to smile when she uttered with an undertone of pain in her voice, "Mom, no matter how many times I will repeat the same, that nothing bad has happened to me, you will not believe me. Being in my current condition, it is very difficult for me to explain all the details. I love you. Therefore, I will tell you everything. I don't want you to worry. I love that guy. He makes me suffer, although, this is entirely not his fault. Nevertheless, you should not suffer together with me because of this. I feel that I must liberate you from my stress. You know that I do not hide anything from you. You have seen for yourself that I went dancing today in good faith, fostering the most beautiful hopes. However, another student crossed our path tonight. He separated us. Bronius got mad and walked out. I did the same after him. That is why I came home before dances had been over."

"Nobody has the power to keep you from the one you love. This is your adventure."

"Even if Bronius still loves me, it's probably not meant for me to date him. Laws of this new regime haunt everybody now. They don't value true love."

"I have never heard that the new regime would not allow people falling in love."

"Of course, no system has right to ban people falling in love. In any case, I mustn't obey any stupid prohibitions. However, there are some suspicious characters at the university who use their position to control other people. They make every effort to disturb the life of others. And if they fail carrying out their evil plans, then they resort to threats and intimidation. Such individuals often report on their victims hypocritically accusing them. That is what I am afraid of the most. I'm afraid this scum Alfa could invent some problem for me and Bronius."

"But what could he blame you for? After all, it would require some kind of proof, wouldn't it?"

"Mom, don't be naive. You shouldn't believe the liars. They have no conscience, so nothing is sacred to them. However, no repressions could make me disavow people that I love. The liars like Alfa only want to bring the others down to their knees. I will not allow anybody to do this to me! In the worst-case scenario, it will make me cease attending the dances. I must stay true to my principles. I have seen how Alfa hurt Bronius taking advantage of his family misfortune. This is such a scary world everywhere around us! You have no idea, mom, what dispirited atmosphere dominates at the University in general. It would be so wonderful if I could go away somewhere to another country. If that was possible, I would definitely do that without a moment's hesitation! At least, I might be able to study there without suffering any "masquerades". At the university, I can't run away from Alfa's electoral "comedies" and propagandas. I heard that we will have to work at unionized Kolkhozes this summer. I find it to be the irony of faith that the students have to work the land that had just been taken away from their parents and grandparents."

The mother interrupted her, "The best thing is not to resist their order. At least while you are still studying…"

Ema continued, "You are right. On one hand, it can create problems for me at the university, up to being expelled from it all together. On the other hand, what kind of worker I am anyway? What benefits I can provide the collective farm with? I have never done any earthwork. Why do they have to send the students for the summer work in the fields? We'll just trample everything down there. Students earn their vacation by studying hard their entire year. Instead, we will get tired more during our summer vacation than we do during our school year. I wish I could plug my ears and close my eyes in order not to know all this. I think I won't go dancing anymore, mother. I don't want Alfa using me. I cannot stand him! Now I understand why Bronius never attended the dances before. He also was the very first to leave home today. I think he will not come back there anymore. Neither will I. Of course, it's not easy for me giving up the only amusement I've had. Let Alfa have all the fun for himself."

After hearing out her daughter's complaint, the mother calmed down, since she had thought much more serious reasons had brought Ema home before the dancing had been over.

In fact, now she was glad this had happened. On one hand, she felt sorry because of her daughter's failed first date, for which both of them had been preparing with such joy. On the other hand, she thought it was still a little too early for her to think about a serious relationship.

The mother had been worried not knowing if Bronius had been a decent person. It had not occurred to her that if she knew Bronius, she wouldn't take everything so seriously.

She had been in constant fear that he could be some shifty charlatan, who had succeeded luring their only daughter. The mother was extremely afraid of anything bad happening to her only child.

She did not share her thoughts with Ema, even though, deep inside, she wanted to meet Bronius. She also understood she had no right to forbid her daughter seeing him. After all, he could become her husband! Therefore, the mother did not want making a mistake by ruining her daughter's future.

Nevertheless, now she was content because of the new turn of the circumstances, but she also was sad along with Ema for the outcome of her date.

The school holiday had been nearing to an end, and the girl had not managed getting to know Bronius closer.

Finally, both Ema and the mother calmed down after concluding that everything in life had its positive aspect.

Later, Ema's mother talked about this issue with her husband. However, he had a different opinion that was quite opposite to hers. He thought that Ema should choose her friend for life herself without anyone interfering. According to him, the only time when parents had the right to get involved in their daughter's heart matters was if the man turned out to be some bad person. Worrying in advance made no sense to him, especially when they had not met Bronius at all.

After learning her husband's opinion, mother decided not to bother him anymore about the subject of Ema's heart matters. She reasoned the time would be the best cure for their daughter.

Soon, the same old routine returned to their family. Ema regularly came home after her classes at the university. Also, she stopped attending school dances, just as she had promised.

True, Ema met Bronius a few times in the coatroom of the university and in the hallway. However, the conversation between the two of them turned out to be very official. Both of them only exchanged a few words. Bronius told her several modest jokes, and they separated.

They were very busy studying, because the exams had been nearing. Bronis was even more occupied than Ema. Lately, his workday had been double swamped with the chores. In the evenings, too, he had to prepare for tomorrow's lectures, various tests, and quizzes.

Thus, he lived day by day without lifting head from his school book until dawn. In the morning, having had little sleep, he went to work.

Bronius lost significant amount of weight due to such strenuous work. During the lecture at the university, he noticed his head started spinning. The other time, his eyes went dark. In spite of all this, he continued working hard.

One day at work, Bronius became so weak that he was literally carried outside. Even though he came back to himself shortly after, he felt like intoxicated all day long.

The incident reached the ears of Director. Few days later, he called Adomaitis to his office. Bronius was afraid. In his head, all kinds of thoughts started spinning before their meeting.

He could not think of any wrongdoing at work. However, he was very worried on the way to the director's office. When at the door, he could hear every beat of his heart. However, delay was not an option. No matter how much he wanted to avoid this visit, there was no other way than to go in.

Gripped by the fear, he knocked with a trembling hand on the tall oak-wood door and immediately heard a hollow man's voice, "Come in, please."

Adomaitis timidly, like some offender, opened the door slightly and quietly slipped inside. He stopped in the middle of a large room and greeted the director in a low voice. Then, instantly, he started sweating and growing red in his face as if he was standing not in the spacious office but in a bathhouse.

Looking at Director sitting behind a huge, fancy writing-desk, he suddenly became glad for a moment. He was thinking that even if this man scolded him, no one else would be able to hear or see anything. Therefore, he would not have to feel ashamed in the presence of the other employees.

"Sit down, please," lifting his eyes from papers, uttered Director. He reluctantly moved aside his documents that he had been studying attentively and fixed his inquiring gaze onto Adomaitis.

"Your secretary informed me you wanted to see me," perspiring even more, mumbled Bronius in a faltering voice.

"Yes," answered Director. He appeared looking tired and older that usually. "I wanted to chat with you. I would like to ask you how you like your new responsibilities at work. Quite a bit of time has passed, while you have been working in this position. How are you coping with it? Your job is really not the easy one…"

"I try as hard as I can, even though I might have not achieved the results you had expected from me yet…"

"As far as I know, department management is satisfied with your work. So am I. However, as I understand it… I think it's too hard for you to carry a double load. It requires too much energy."

"Of course, it's not easy to go to work after attending the lectures at the university. If not for the end of the semester, there would be no need for me studying so intensely. However, now, after coming home from work, I must do my homework for a few hours every night, also. Naturally, no one could handle this for a very long time. Four hours of sleep is never enough… However, the school year soon is over, and I will be able to concentrate on my job alone."

"I've heard you fell down in a faint during the work hours…"

"In spite of that, sir, I worked until the end of my shift that day, and the enterprise did not incur any losses because of me."

"I have called you to come here not to accuse you. I perfectly understand that you find it difficult carrying this double load. Therefore, I would like to help you. I'm not some kind of monster who can't understand the circumstances of my workers."

"Sir, you have already done so much good for me. I feel very grateful to you for that."

"It's okay. I've only done my duty, and I did it purely out of the humanitarian principles. Now, let's move onto my objective. This is why I have asked you to come here. As far as I know, you are studying medicine?" asked Director.

"Yes, sir. I do."

"I would like to offer you a job that suits more the specialty you have chosen. There has been a physician assistant's vacancy at the medical office of our enterprise. Of course, pay there is significantly lower, but the work itself is a lot easier and less stressful, too. You cannot even compare the work conditions to those at the department. I think the responsibilities there would meet more your heart's desire. In fact, the salary is not that small after all - seven hundred rubles. You could work there for a while, and if some other suitable position for you came up, I would be happy helping you again. You'll have an opportunity to put in practice the knowledge you have gained at the university. Our enterprise is big. The opportunities are limitless. I suggest you think about this offer and take advantage of it."

"Sir, there is no need for me to think about that. I agree, and I'm very grateful for the new job offer. I'm simply lacking the words to express my gratitude to you. Moreover, you have taken care of me as if I had been your real son. How could I not accept the offer?! The salary also should be enough... After all, I get a scholarship. Both together should make it nearly a thousand rubles a month."

"Well, then you can fill out an application, and, on the fifteenth of May, you can start working in your new position. In about a month, your classes at the university should end. After that, you could take an unpaid leave. Lately, you have become very thin... You look tired. I think you are due for some good rest. You need to take some time off to restore your health. If you have parents living out in the country, I would suggest you spend some time there, because your health is the most important asset. Studying in the field of medicine, you know this very well yourself. Therefore, if you think you can make it financially, I would let you go on the unpaid leave. Think about it and let me know. Now, I have to go back to my work," said Director. He put his eyeglasses back on and pulled the pile of papers closer to him.

Adomaitis did not even notice when he came to a big company yard. He drew fresh air into his lungs, and it suddenly felt so light on his heart. He did not have any desire going back to the plant, where the same bothersome equipment kept always buzzing in dim light.

Bronius did not wish to be in that dusty, stuffy environment. He slowly walked to the building wall, where tall shrubs by the window with the bars on it have already been unfolding their soft, gentle, green buds.

He sat down straight on the ground and leaned his back upon the trunk of the tree. Bronius lifted his eyes and looked at the spring sky growing blue through the thick branches of the lime-tree. Only now, he noticed that the buds have already burst.

He sat there for several minutes without thinking about anything, like a cat in the sun. He was enjoying the stillness of the moment.

He could hear hollow noises of the office machines coming from underneath the closed door of the shop. That woke him up from the blissful numbness.

Now, he had become fully aware of what had happened to him recently. In addition, he remembered he had not thanked the director properly upon leaving his office. He had just walked out overwhelmed with joy, and he had even forgotten to say thank you! However, Bronius realized that he could not fix his mistake right at this moment, and he felt a little disappointed.

Soon, Bronius took over his new responsibilities. He loved his new job; he performed all its new tasks very thoroughly and with the biggest enthusiasm. In fact, there was not that much to do. There were days when he had to sit through the entire work shift hours almost without moving a finger.

The summer had already started, and his classes at the University were already over. Adomaitis began dreaming about his vacation out in the country. He just needed to wait until a doctor of his company returned from vacation. Then, it was Bronius's turn utilizing his vacation together with the additional 'pay free' month that Director had promised him some time ago. There were nearly two months free of work or studying awaiting him. Therefore, Bronius was very anxious about the doctor's return to work in about three days.

Finally, the long awaited day came, when Bronius was sitting on a wooden bench and listening to the monotonous rumbling of the wheels over the sleepers' junction. He hungrily gazed at the rapidly changing landscapes through the window of the train.

His soul had longed for this moment during long winter months. Bronius's eyes kept soaking up the colors of the passing through greenery of the distant fields and trees, the blue of the sky.

The train unceasingly kept flying forward, further away from Vilnius. It felt a little sad leaving his city. However, the longing for his country land had been stronger. It seemed as if the whole eternity had passed since his last visit there.

In spite of visiting his mother last year, he spent most of the time lying in bed. In addition, his visit took place during the late fall, when the nature had been so unattractive. Wide country fields had been shrouded with such sadness that sometimes he wanted to cry just by looking through his parents' house window.

However, this particular day, the weather turned out to be amazingly beautiful! The sun was shining brightly. It appeared as if every creature and every plant had been enjoying the sunshine. Everything around was filled with life.

The same was happening to Adomaitis. He was full of anticipation of joy while rushing deeper into that refuge of gladness and warmth which had been eagerly waiting for him with the outstretched arms.

However, some kind of uneasiness still was nagging him. He was a bit sad because he had to leave the girl who had been so dear to him. While sitting in the train, he thought that he would not have a chance meeting with Ema for the rest of the summer, living in such a remote corner.

This was the only thing that currently bothered him. Otherwise, he would gladly stayed forever in his native countryside, where the memories were so sweet and so dear since his early childhood.

Clenching his teeth, he tried to convince himself that it was supposed to be this way. He reasoned that, most likely, he would not be able to continue seeing Ema in any case. Thus, there was a possibility this stay could serve him as the medicine in an attempt to forget her.

Long separation could reconcile people with their destiny and help forget their friendships with the significant others. Bronius came to a conclusion that, in solitude, it would be easier coping with the separation.

Plunged in his thoughts, Adomaitis did not feel when he got out of the train. It was still light around, since the days were longest and the nights were shortest during this time of the year. The sun was slowly setting down in western horizon.

He was walking fast along the road and not wasting his valuable time. Bronius wanted to make it as far as he could while it had been the day light. There was still the long walk waiting ahead of him.

He was thinking that nights had been bright and short lately, especially on the days when the sky was clear. On his way home, he kept looking at both sides of the road; he did not want to miss a thing. Each roadside tree seemed so familiar and precious.

Many of the trees appeared bigger than before, but there were also sprouts of the new ones. Previously, there had been none of the little ones growing along the road, or maybe he just did not notice them. He also saw several newly built farmsteads.

Bronius noticed even more changes on his way home. Namely, he kept seeing the houses with their windows boarded up. Did the residents of those homes leave in pursuit of happiness? Alternatively, maybe somebody just had forced them to leave.

In any case, it was clear that nobody had been taking care of those homesteads any longer. The backyards had been severely neglected and weed-grown. Cottages stood sad and needless, with no windows; the winds were howling in all sorts of voices inside of them. In addition, the tiles of the roofs had been so badly damaged by the storms that their tops were completely naked. Boards, like some ribs or skeletons, were protruding out through the hay joist ceilings in all directions, indicating that the hosts had long been gone.

Bronius passed quite a few such homes. It was pathetic just looking at them. Once upon a time, life had been in full swing there. Cheerful laughter of playing children could be heard.

Only God knew where previous residents of all those houses were now. Maybe, they had been exiled to some Arkhangelsk region; maybe, they had been struggling somewhere in the sands of the Kazakhstan, snatched from the arms of their native land and taken away somewhere by their ruthless subjugators.

It was sad seeing the deserted homesteads. Recently, Bronius had been a witness to the cruel deportations. Now, it seemed to him as if not the winds were howling and whizzing through the broken windows and the fallen doors, but the invisible souls of the people sunken in deep sorrow were moaning. They wept longing for their native homes. A lot of sweat had been shed here, but a lot of sadness and a lot of joy had been experienced here, too.

Every corner was familiar, dear, and precious to Bronius. While he was walking, it started rapidly getting dark, since the sun already had hidden itself behind the horizon.

Therefore, he picked up the pace even more. The black veil began covering the dome of heaven. Finally, it got totally dark but not for long, as a tip of the moon appeared on the east side. It was coming up fast from behind treetops of a distant forest. A moment later, the moon totally detached itself from the trees, and the full of the moon illuminated all around with its silver light.

Finally, a little plot, clinging to the earth, appeared in the distance. His parents' land was still far enough, so it was difficult to distinguish its boundaries.

As he kept walking closer, the contours of the homestead became more distinct.

When Bronius found himself right on the boundary of the property itself, which had been separating the field from the homestead, he could see a little quivering light through the trees.

For a few seconds, it would disappear in the night. Then, it would reappear again revealing a blurry image of the cottage quietly dozing under a cobweb of the branches of old apple-trees.

The flickering of the window light through the orchard trees riveted Bronius's gaze. It almost appeared like the burning of a candle-flame.

Bronius was standing on the native land and looking at the windows of his parents' wooden house.

It was obvious his mother was still awake. Several times, Bronius drew refreshing cool air deep into his lungs, and he instantly felt himself coming to life after his long and tiring walk. Even the air was healing at home.

He stood for a little while longer, and then he walked toward the house his unbuttoned chest put out forward. Gentle breeze pleasantly caressed his naked neck cooling his hot blood and drying the sweat.

Dismal appeared at this late hour of the night this rather shabby corner of the Aukstaitija region. However, at the same time, it was so precious and so dear to his heart. Each foot of the land here was familiar to him from the very childhood.

He walked guardedly in the dark, as if he was afraid to step on something. Sure enough, suddenly, some little frightened bird took wind just from under his feet. Scared Bronius gave a start.

Despite the fact that he was on his parents' land, he did not want to walk along the dirt road leading to the house. Instead, he chose the shortest path through the open field. Therefore, it was not surprising that he interfered with some more little birds' tranquil night's sleep.

At last, he found himself by a small gate, where tall birch trees had been growing with their branches drooping down to the very ground. Willow bushes were so overgrown that, in some places, their branches touched the little gate door itself.

He opened the creaky wooden door and stopped again fascinated. He was listening to the silence in the orchard, where the exuberant apple-trees with beehives beside their trunks were peacefully dozing in the fog. Clusters of the insects so useful to humans were also resting inside.

Bronius listened to the magic silence for a few seconds. Then, he closed the wooden gate behind him and walked into the mist. Opened window shutters shone white, but the light already was turned off. Apparently, the mother with grandmother went to bed.

Bronius looked around. Everything seemed to be in their own places like always. Even the bathhouse that Russian occupants had burned was newly rebuilt.

Bronius approached the door of the house. Without waiting any longer, he loudly knocked on it and lent his ear. The somber silence was reigning indoors and outdoors. Only somewhere in the distance, he could hear faint dog barking that disturbed the silence of the night. Then a cricket gave a whistle at the riverside, and everything fell silent again.

However, Bronius no longer wanted listening to the mysterious sounds of the nature. He gave another loud knock on the door.

After a while, he heard the front door crackling, and the familiar, deep mother's voice came out of the other side of it, "Who is there?"

"This is me, mother. Let me in."

"Jesus Christ," he could hear her voice behind the door again.

Without him even having a chance to answer, the door widely opened, and the mother appeared on the doorsteps stretching her arms out to hug the son.

"Why, Bronius, you didn't notify me about your arrival? I would have come to the train station to meet you," patter spilled the words the mother and kissed him on the cheek.

"Knowing how sensitive you are, I didn't want to cause you any troubles. If I had notified you about my visit, I would have only brought more worries to you. Instead, I've made a surprise for you. Isn't it better this way?"

"Not quite, sonny. It would be much more enjoyable for me taking you home myself. At least, I would know that I have done something good for you. Well, enough talking! One way or the other, I'm very pleased you have come. Why are we standing here? Let's go inside. By now, you probably are quite hungry. After all, you have had to overcome long distance on foot in the dark. Come in, son, I will quickly make something for you to snack on."

"Mom, don't you worry. I'm not a child any more. At my age, such trip is pure pleasure. I feel no fatigue. Quite the opposite - I liked walking along the native path in the moonlight. It was quite light for the most part of the walk. Summer nights aren't as dark as they are in fall."

Bronius walked into the house. When they entered a big family room, the mother turned on kerosene lamp. The bright light of it suddenly lighted up all the walls and ceilings in the room. Bronius began blinking fast.

In a few minutes, though, he got used to the bright light in the room. Here, in their family room, it felt like in some atrium. Several widely branched out flowers stood in the corner. Few of the branches, covered in thick green leaves, were leaning over a table touching the white tablecloth on it.

Soon, a pleasant smell of frying bacon dispersed across the room. Shortly after, the mother herself appeared in the doorway with a frying pan in her hand. Placing on the table a thick stand, she sat the hot frying-pan on the top of it.

The mother again went to the kitchen and quickly returned carrying bread and a pitcher with milk. She poured the milk into a cup and spurred the son, "Have a cup of milk. Eat the omelet while it's still hot."

Bronius had not been hungry yet, but he already felt relaxed at home. There was nothing to be shy about here. All big city pressures disappeared. Again, just as in his childhood, he felt as safe as houses.

Although reluctantly, he had a few sips of milk, and very soon the appetite came to him. He quickly consumed the late supper and washed the food down with the milk.

Now, he was feeling so full that he didn't even want to go to bed. Both of them sat for a good an hour and talked, talked… The mother kept asking him about his studies at the university, about his job, and, in general, about life in capital. And he told her everything in detail.

The woman was gazing at a gaunt son's body. He looked very tired. The thought flashed across her mind that it probably only appeared to her that way in the artificial light of the kerosene lamp.

Then another thought came to her that he could just be exhausted because of the long walk home on foot. She was expecting that, after a good night's sleep, she would see him looking much better and full of energy.

Not wanting to keep her son up any longer, she wished him "good night" and went to bed herself hoping that the weariness would surmount him too.

Bronius turned off the light and opened the window. Outside, silhouettes of the sleepy apple-trees black loomed in the orchard. Next to them, he could see the beehives, where diligent little bees rested after a hard day's work.

Bronius lay down on a bed made by his mother's caring hands. He pulled up the sheets to his chin and drew deeply into his lungs the cool air flowing inside through the widely opened window.

He was still wide-awake staring at the dark orchard, where the mysterious silence reigned. The view of the apple trees riveted his eyes hypnotized. Thus, he lay in bed for long time not being able to get asleep, no matter how hard he tried submerging into the kingdom of dreams.

His eyes got used to the dark, and the contours of the apple trees revealed themselves in all their glory. He felt at peace.

Bronius's eyes began closing, and he did not notice when he drifted asleep.

However, his sleep was uneasy. Despite of not waking up once, horrible dreams tormented him to the point, where he started moaning even in his sleep.

The mother was up together with the sunrise, and she had already been toiling in the kitchen. The rays of the rising sun illuminated the wooden floor, when she heard son's faint moaning. The woman stopped in the middle of the kitchen and lent her ear. Then, she heard another moan coming from the room, where her son was sleeping.

The mother silently walked into the room, where he was still lying asleep on his back. Now, in the day light, she saw his very gaunt face. His eyes were deep sunk into the sockets, and he had dark circles around them. On the bony chest, slowly and heavily heaving, rested his right hand. It also looked thin and bloodless. Through its skin, bluish, puffy veins were showing. It seemed as if his hand with all the five slightly curled inwards fingers was trying to embrace his chest and sooth his coming out pain.

The mother, seeing him so terribly skinny, grabbed her chin with her hand out of horror. She had to control herself, so that the painful moaning would not escape the bottom of her own chest. She was afraid it could wake up the son, whose sleep had already been troubled enough.

This very moment, standing next to her sleeping boy, she quietly took an oath making it a priority taking care of him. It seemed to her, that she needed giving all herself to him, because her life would lose meaning without Bronius. Now, her only consolation was Bronius. She was lovingly gazing at him . His face seemed pale because of hard life in the big city.

With difficult thoughts, she left the room. Then, she helped a shepherd driving cows out of the cowshed in order to send them to the grassy field.

She poured mash to pigs as well and returned into the house. This time, though, she could not hear any sounds coming out of Bronius's room. Apparently, now he was sound asleep.

She began peacefully toiling around the stove. There was nobody helping her. The grandmother had already grown so old that she was spending more time in bed than around the house.

Breakfast was ready. Now, the mother was only waiting for Bronius to get out of bed. She did not want to disturb his sleep by waking him up herself.

At last, Bronius got up. The day had been extremely beautiful. Everything around, was lit up by the sunrays. The see through streaks of light were playing and dancing in the orchard. They also penetrated the whole room which was now filled with the light. Fascinated Bronius was gazing at the small specks of dust dancing in the air.

Even after rising up so late in the morning, Bronius did not feel well rested. Quite the opposite, he felt as if, during the last night, he only got more exhausted.

Suddenly, though, he realized he was in his beloved homeland, and he gave a sigh of relief. An amazing vacation was awaiting him.

He went outside and drew a bucket of icy-cold water out of a well. Then he washed his face, chest, and arms. Now, he started feeling much better.

The grandmother got out of her bed to have breakfast together with Bronius and the mother. Knowing that her beloved grandson was home, the old woman cheered up so much; she even forgot that she could hardly stand on her feet anymore.

While at the table, all three of them got into conversation about approaching hay harvest. Bronius offered the mother his help haymaking.

Hearing this, the granny, infected with the enthusiasm, volunteered going together.

Many kind words were exchanged during this modest breakfast. They also had a few little glasses of delicious homemade wine that just further brightened the mood of all three of them.

After the breakfast, Bronius did not have anything to do. Therefore, he went to the riverside to get some suntan. He bathed in the river too.

Soon, lunchtime came. Upon returning home, he found cabbage soup with a big piece of boiled pork already waiting for him. All this had been prepared in his honor by the loving hands of his mother and the grandmother.

After eating, Bronius took a nap. Then, he had half a jug of milk and went to the riverside fishing.

After sitting on the bank nearly for three hours with a fishing rod in his hands, he caught only one little fish.

Nevertheless, Bronius returned home in a good mood. There, he again had a meal and drank some more milk, and he returned to the riverside.

The fishery had not been successful. Nevertheless, he continued sitting on the bank with his eyes fixed on the bob floating on the surface of the water until his mother came looking for him.

The sun had already been set behind the horizon, and everything around was submerged in dusk.

Precisely at that time, the fishes started frantically biting. Now, Bronius lost any desire going home. The mother also left sitting by his side. She watched him dropping minnows on the bank. One little fish after another would suddenly flash in the twilight and fall on the grass. The mother would take the fish off the hook and, through its mouth, she would thread it on to a thin, strong cord.

Only well after dark, Bronius with his mother returned to the house. They carried plenty of catch. About twenty wee silver fishes were sporting on the string.

The days were going by identical to each other. Every morning, well before the sunrise, Bronius went fishing. During the hottest part of the day, he would lie in a cool lumber-room reading books.

It had been a week that he had been staying at his parents' house. However, during this entire time, he had not crossed their property boundaries. Most of the time, though, he was spending at the riverside. He not only fished there, but he also bathed in the river several times a day. He loved basking in the sun, too.

Bronius had been delighted by his wonderful time off of work and school. He did not feel lonely at all. In fact, he was so pleased and so happy that he never even missed people whom he left in the city. Now, he did not want to associate with any friends, and he had entirely forgotten about everyone. Moreover, he did not even have any close friends.

Not having any male friends, Bronius began more often remembering Ema. Sometimes, she emerged in his mind in all her glory. The memories about her kept disturbing his quiet relaxation more and more often. At those moments, tender feelings would shroud his heart.

He tried to get rid of the longing. During the day, things would go well, since Bronius had opportunity to jump into the river and swim vigorously from one side of it to the other. He liked diving into a depth trying to reach the bottom until the longing went away.

In the evenings, he often took long walks in the orchard. Occasionally, he sat under an apple tree looking down at blades of the grasses, where tiny ants were crawling up and down. Namely then, sad thoughts came to his mind most often.

The secluded corner at his homeland could not offer numerous fun distractions as the life in the capital did. Few times, he got overwhelmed with boredom. Then, he killed time taking a nap.

However, even then, Bronius preferred staying in his homeland over the stay in the big city. He did not want anybody bothering him. Bronius knew he had no true friends who could give him sincere advice. There were only hypocrites and lickspittles around.

After making a mistake by choosing Alfa to be friends with, he had been afraid to get into a close relationship with others. Nevertheless, he'd understood that he could not completely isolate himself from society.

Then, Ema had unexpectedly emerged in his life. However, she made Bronius feel different; she had managed to capture his heart the moment he'd seen her.

Now, the thoughts about her would not leave him alone. At the same time, she appeared to him so unreachable. He often rationalized the best thing would be to forget about her. However, he had not succeeded at that.

Since the time Bronius re-entered the university, he often saw her in the hallway. Those meetings clearly contributed to a growing relationship between the two of them.

Now, Bronius was hoping this long separation would not affect their relationship in a negative way.

On the contrary, everything turned out to be just the opposite. This time, their separation not only precluded him from throwing her image out of his mind, but it forced him to think of her very highly.

Bronius, like some little boy, dreamed of having a magic keyhole through which he could get at least a glimpse of her. Sometimes those childish dreams made it easier on him. The other times, he would get overwhelmed with an uncontrollable desire to leave this fine homeland corner and go back to Vilnius. Often, in his imagination, he saw himself walking along deserted corridors of the university where he had been lucky to see Ema during their breaks between the lectures.

Even Bronius's mother noticed his depressed state. A couple of times, he walked around in the orchard and did not notice her laboring there. He just past by plunged in though. Another time, he wasn't listening to her when she tried to start a conversation. Finally, his behavior began to worry her.

The mother did not know how to awaken him from his stagnation. She could not believe this was the same once so fun to be around person with great sense of humor.

No matter how hard the mother tried to cheer her son up, it seemed as if nothing helped. In spite of that, the progress was happening in another area. Namely, over the last week spent at their home, his health greatly improved; he put on some weight. Now, Bronius also had a nice suntan.

The weather being hot, hay harvest started earlier than usually. The haymaking had been the first big job of the farmers' at the beginning of every year.

Getting close to the evening, the sun still hanging high above the horizon, the mother took her prepared in advance scythe out of a shed and went mowing grass in their field located behind the bathhouse.

This was their first day of the haying this year. She kept cutting one row after another.

Soon, the sun completely hid itself behind treetops far in the distance. Rising from the river mist spread to the meadow, where the woman kept turning a windrow after the windrow. Finally, the thick fog drowned the whole meadow, and the lonely haymaker was gone...

Now, one could only hear gentle strokes of the scythe cutting grass, and, at intervals, penetrating sounds of a whetstone up the surface of a steel sickle.

Those noises called Bronius's attention, when he was walking in the orchard. Realizing the mother already had started cutting the grass, he took another scythe from the shed without undue delay. With the scythe on his shoulder, Bronius walked like a real farmer into the field, where he soon disappeared into the fog as well.

Seeing his silhouette approaching through the fog, surprised mother asked, "Bronius, what do you think you are doing here?"

"As I promised, I have come to help you mowing the grass."

"By now, you've probably completely fallen out of the hard farm labor. I prefer to see you resting while you still have an opportunity to do just that."

"You are kidding, mother. Have you forgotten that I helped you mowing those meadows the year before the last year? In addition to that, I used to mow together with dad all the time. He had never complained about me troubling him. Don't tell me that I can't do this job. I could even compete with you. Then, we would find out which one of us is a better haymaker."

The mother did not want her son doing hard farm work. After all, that was not why she had sent him to a school in the capital. She had dreamed of a different future for her boy - the future where he would never have to shed his sweat while performing heavy physical labor.

Nevertheless, Bronius did not give in. He kept swinging his scythe and did not retreat a foot working behind the mother.

After making several rounds, large drops of sweat showed up on his forehead. In spite of that, he still kept abreast with her. An hour later, his entire linen shirt became damp and started sticking to his back. However, Bronius further continued laboring; he was driving himself forward in the meadow that had been warmed up by the sun now.

"Well, sonny, maybe we should take a break... We already have mown away a big chunk of the meadow. Perhaps you've got tired. Do your muscles hurt? Mine are already tense. You're not used to hard work. I think you'll really feel pains in the small of your back tomorrow."

"I might have pains tomorrow, but I should sleep well tonight. Like a little baby in a cradle..."

Mother and Bronius with their scythes over their shoulders walked home. Once in the orchard, Bronius handed his scythe to his mother. He went swimming in the river, since he had been so sweaty that even his hair was stuck together on his forehead.

He ripped his damp shirt off, ran all the way to the end of a wooden footbridge, and plopped right into the water. It was warm like tea.

Bronius did not want to get out of the river. The water was so nice, and it was much colder on the bank. Reluctantly, he finally had to come out of this fine bath prepared by the Mother Nature itself.

Standing on the grass, he immediately began shaking. Bronius, his teeth chattering, put the clothes on. Now, they were clinging to his wet body.

He ran fast along the riverside home. Only in the orchard, he stopped to catch his breath. Right after having crossed the threshold of the cottage, he smelled a delicious smell of fried bacon.

"Mom, what's for dinner?"

"I've fried the eggs for you. Come and eat."

When he sat down at a small kitchen table, the mother put the frying pan with the frizzling eggs onto a tray next to him. There had already been sitting a pitcher with milk on the table.

Bronius, with biggest appetite, started eating his supper. The mother was standing nearby watching with admiration her son eating.

He emptied more than half of the jug of the milk and said while stroking his stomach, "Boy, I've had enough."

"Good! Now, get to bed. It's late already."

Bronius, without having properly warmed up after the swimming, lay down into a ready-made bedding. He carefully covered himself up with the blanket. Now, he began slowly warming up and did not notice when he fell soundly asleep.

When Bronius awakened, it had already been broad daylight. Sitting in bed, he stretched his upper body. He noticed that his muscles were hurting, and not only the muscles of his arms but also the muscles of both sides of his torso, too.

Bronius rolled out of the bed and stretched more. He forced himself to perform a few exercises which made him feel better.

He opened a curtain and saw that the sun had already been high in the sky. He became ashamed. Before going to bed yesterday, he had planned to get up well before a sunrise. Secretly he expected he would come to the field first, even before his mother.

However, just the opposite happened - the mother alone had long been cutting a row after the row, while he had still been in his sweet sleep.

Without waiting any longer, Bronius took his scythe and walked to the meadow. As soon as he was getting ready to make his first stroke, the mother sprang up next to him and exclaimed, "Bronius, look what I've got for you!"

She walked him to the area that she had mowed earlier this morning and pulled out from under the grass a white handkerchief. When she unfolded it, Bronius saw a big piece of a fragrant honeycomb all filled with the sticky, golden wild honey.

"Taste it."

"It's not worth hurting the wild bees. We ourselves have so much honey at home that we could probably swim in it."

"That's not the point, son. I just remembered when your father, during the hay harvest season, used to bring you the honey of the wild bees, and you ate it with pleasure, even though we always had jugs full of honey at home..."

"Back then, mother, I'd just been occupied with my boyish fancies. I used to wait not as much for the honey as I'd waited for the father himself returning out of the field."

"You will always be a child to me regardless you want it or not."

"Am I really still a kid to you? Believe me, I could plough this soil. But I'm happy anyway to hear you say this. And this honey really reminds me of the father…"

Bronius took the honeycomb out of his mother's callous hands and started chewing on it. After finishing it all, he began mowing the grass. Thus, he kept one swath after another until treams of sweat started trickling down his cheeks, and his shirt got drenched through.

"I think we should go home, Bronius. It's enough for today. There is no reason to hurry, since the haying season has just started."

"But I've just come here… You better go home by yourself. I'll mow one more chunk of the meadow while you prepare breakfast."

After the mother left, Bronius rushed to cut down as much grass as he could. He was cutting the furrow after the furrow wiping away the sweaty forehead with a back of his sleeve.

He did not even notice when time for the breakfast came. Bronius heard his mother's deep voice coming from somewhere in the orchard calling him home. He realized it was time to go eat.

However, he decided to take a swim in the river first. He quickly ran to the footbridge, and the next moment he was already in the water. This time, it felt almost as cold as the water in their well. It always took an entire day for the sun to warm the river's water up.

This time, his bathing in the river did not last longer than a few minutes. During this time, he plunged into the water a couple of times and washed his face. Next moment, he was already picking his clothes off the grass.

After eating breakfast, Bronius with his mother did not go to the fields, where the sun had been scorching badly. Instead, he remained at home, where he sharpened his and the mother's scythes. In addition, he put in broken teeth into their rakes. After accomplishing all the household chores, he began preparing a cart to carry the hay.

Thus, he even did not notice, when lunchtime came. After a hearty meal, he went to a lumber-room and slept there a good couple hours. However, when he woke up, the same intense heat reigned outside. Therefore, Bronius with his mother had to remain inside.

Finally, an evening came, and the sun had already been descended low on the west side. Along with the sunset, the heat subsided as well. Therefore, Bronius took his scythe and went back to the field. Soon, the mother came there, too, and both of them got absorbed into the labor again.

Only well after dark, he jumped into the water that had already been warmed up by the sun during the day. Just like every evening, Bronius did not want coming out of the water.

After having late supper, he quickly fell asleep like an exhausted man. The next day, he woke up already well after broad daylight. Only this time, his muscles hurt even more. Not only he could hardly move, but also his sides ached when he tried to take a deep breath.

Nevertheless, prompted by his duty, he rolled out of bed and went to the meadow, where his mother had long been laboring alone.

This morning, mowing was more difficult, even though Bronius was not trying to compete with his mother. He only concentrated on accomplishing as much haying as he could. However, the scythe as if on purpose did not obey him today. Often, even on the level ground, it kept sinking into the soil.

After breakfast, Bronius with the mother took the rakes and went turning hay that had been drying in the summer heat for two days now. They were going to cart and take to a barn the part of hay which they had harvested yesterday. However, before doing that, they had to turn it over twice, in spite of the severe midday heat that was hanging in the field. It was difficult even to breathe, and Bronius's mouth completely dried out.

After lunchtime, the sun started scorching even harder. Despite that, both had to continue working, since every hour was precious. The hay was already completely dry, and it even had been piled up into stacks. The only thing left to do was to collect those ricks of hay and, using a pitchfork, load them onto the cart.

The mother suggested Bronius relaxed or had a swim. However, he did not listen, because he understood how precious their time was. Therefore, he did not cease working even for a minute.

Soon, in the distance, Bronius saw the grandmother passing through the orchard. In her hand, she was carrying a pitcher. The granny was walking bareheaded, and light breeze was gently tossing her gray hair. He did not mention to the toiling mother anything about having seen the grandma, since he was not aware if she was coming to them. He was absorbed in his work and did not notice when the grandmother showed up in the meadow.

Bronius lifted up his head only when he heard the mother's voice, "Look what granny has brought to us. Come, have some kvass." She raised the pitcher above her head in order to get her son's attention.

Bronius did not need to be urged. His mouth had been dry already for a long time. He wanted to drink so badly, that he could barely stand on his feet. He ran up to the mother, and, after grabbing the clay jug out of her hands, he began guzzling down dark brown liquid.

The kvass was cold and refreshing. While he was taking in big gulps of the kvass, it kept trickling through the corners of his mouth. Then it ran down the chin joining into a one thin stream in the middle. The little jet reached his wide-open chest and ran down to his waist, where his tightened belt captured it.

Without even taking a breath, he emptied half of the jug. Tearing his lips away from the edge of the pitcher, Bronius took a loud breath and wiped his lips and chin off with his sleeve.

"Great kvass! I feel like in a different world now; even my eyes have lightened up. Thank you very much, grandma, for the delicious drink."

After returning a pitcher, he fell on his back down onto the loose hay.

"You, Bronius, rest a little bit. Meanwhile, I'll go harness the horse to the cart. The time has come to take our hay to the barn. It had got so dry, like some gunpowder..."

After the mother left, Bronius exchanged a few words with the grandmother. Then, he resumed working.

The mother standing in the cart and holding the reins came galloping to the field. Now, the job got really under way! Bronius kept piling up the hay into the cart with the pitchfork, and the mother treaded it under her feet.

Soon, the first cart with the hay rolled away to the barn accompanied by all three of them. Then, two more carts, stacked high, followed. Even the grass cut yesterday evening and this morning, was already stacked into the cocks. The day was nearing to an end, but there still was some grass left to rake.

This evening, Bronius with his mother were so tired that they decided not to go mowing anymore. Although exhausted from work, Bronius still went to the river, where he was swimming for quite a while.

When he came home, the mother gave him a clean shirt to put on. The old one had been all wet from sweat.

Such intense labor lasted for three more days, and much sweat was shed during that time. Nevertheless, the hay harvest was coming to an end. The grasslands around the house had already been mowed. It remained only to dry the hay that still had not been taken to the barn.

Bronius with the mother figured out this would take them another few days, if they were lucky and the days happened to be the same clear and hot.

However, as ill luck would have it, the storm flew into a rage. No matter how hard Bronius with the mother rushed stacking the hay into the ricks, they felt powerless against the pranks of the Mother Nature.

It was pouring until midnight. Thunder shook terribly, denying people in their rest after a hard day in the fields.

Only after the midnight, thunderstorm stopped shaking the ground. The lightning, also, ceased splitting the night sky with its fiery stripes. All this was happening when Bronius, hardly being able to stand on his feet, finally lay down.

Next day was foggy. In the meadow, there was not much left to do. Bronius started feeling a little guilty without having any occupation at home.

However, soon, he found something to do in the storeroom. There, he got absorbed in organizing his old school books and notebooks dating back to his gymnasium years. He scanned through them, filled with beautiful handwriting in blue ink. They looked so old that even edges of some of the notebooks had already turned a little bit yellow. They also were diffusing some sort of ancient smell like old manuscripts did.

In the pile of the old notebooks, he stumbled onto one manuscript that grabbed his attention. Soon, he lay down with it in his hands on the bed. Lying on his back, he read it from the beginning to the end.

Holding already closed notebook on his chest, Bronius got absorbed in thought his gaze fixed on the ceiling that had been darkened from the old age.

He had written this abstract about five years ago. His imagination caught on memories from the past. He remembered how much he had suffered because of this work, and how many beautiful hopes he had put into it. He also recalled the time when he had been dreaming of writing a story, too. However, as years went by and the circumstances changed, that dream of his sank into the oblivion. Now, suddenly, the idea rushed into his mind to start working on his story!

It was raining relentlessly. Big heavy drops monotonously kept knocking onto the window glass. Although the day had been misty, it brought peace of mind and long needed rest after the hard fieldwork. This day was also significant because of the new idea that was reborn in his head.

The last few days of haying turned out to be very long due to unbearably hard physical labor while raking and hauling the hay virtually from dawn to dusk.

Because of the big rush to rake up all the hay before it started raining again, Bronius became so exhausted that he literally felt as if somebody beat him up. He had calluses on his palms, which hurt so badly that he could not hold anything in his hands. He could not even think about picking up a pitchfork again.

Only now, Bronius realized that such heavy manual fieldwork did not require much education. He understood that not only intelligent but uneducated people as well could perform this kind of work.

However, book writing was different from working in the fields, and not every graduate would be able to create a good story. Creative writing required not only higher calling but also countless hours of labor all year round. Of course, this kind of job could not squeeze out sweat or leave bloody calluses on one's hands. Nevertheless, it required much effort and time.

Bronius delved so deeply into his dreams that he forgot about his surroundings. For a short moment, he did not realize where he was. Therefore, when the door of the storeroom opened up loudly, he jumped frightened and sat down in bed.

The unexpected mother's appearance scared him. Without being able to utter a word, he fixed his gaze on the mother. The woman herself was embarrassed for her "bustling invasion", "What… have I frightened you, son?"

"It's okay, mom."

"I went to Adutiskis to find out some things. Last spring, the Kolkhoz had been formed there. You have no idea what kind of comedy is happening there now," mother uttered. She sat down onto the edge of the bed next to Bronius.

"What is going on there?"

"Maybe I will have turned into a clown myself soon… just like the other locals have."

"Are you trying to say that you, mom, plan to join the collective farm, too?" Bronius asked, surprised.

"I have no choice. One way or the other, they'll make us do that. You can't blow against the wind, sonny… Therefore, today, I myself have turned in an application to join the Kolkhoz."

"Are you serious, mother!?" still not being able to believe what he was hearing, Bronius exclaimed.

"Yes, of course! Do people joke when they write an official statement?"

"It is difficult to believe that these words actually are coming out of your mouth. As far as I remember, you yourself were the biggest opponent of this so-called new agricultural reform. With your own actions, you contradict your principles."

"Are you against my decision?" The silence for a while reigned between the two of them.

Then, Bronius said, "I just don't know what to say to you. This unexpected news simply stunned me. I would be afraid giving you any advice before going into the essence of this matter. Really, I don't know what to say…"

"It seems to me as if you are trying to overshoot on my question..."

"No, I just don't know how to answer. It appears to be the very responsible act. Moreover, my future could be affected by it, too... What I am trying to say is that joining a collective farm could provide me with some benefits. Now, my enemies won't be able to reproach me with the father's arrest. However, I have no right to give you advice while having my best interest in mind... You should think over everything well so that you make no mistake."

"Of course, son, I have already weighed all the options myself. Even before turning in my application, I also had a thought that it should play the positive role in connection to your career. Looks like our new situation is favorable for you... However, even this was not the main reason why I had decided taking such a drastic step. Of course, I am not happy about this land reform! On the contrary - I am against this kind of nonsense. I had been thinking for a long time, but I don't know if you want to hear about it. "

"Of course, mother, I want to hear about it, especially because it has something to do with me. Although, it hurts when foreigners despise our way of life. We are being forced to build some kind of new life that does not promise anything good, either."

"I thought much about that myself, son, and I could not make up my mind to take this step for long time. Ironically, I had been the greatest opponent to all those nonsense of the Russian invaders. Nevertheless, by not joining their collective farm, I would do even greater nonsense myself. First of all, I'm doing this for you. Second, I just don't want to destroy our small farm. After a year or so, I would still have to sell it. With this new order coming into place, I could not bear paying taxes. Perhaps, I would remain even owing some money to them. Then, my homestead would be confiscated. That's exactly what has already happened to some other farmers in our vicinity. The Russian government had started taking land from them first, because they'd had more land than I do. Now, you see where those farmers ended... They went begging with sacks flinging over their shoulders."

"Mom, I would not let you end up on the street," Bronius said.

However, she did not pay attention to his words and continued, "My farm is in its very prime. And it could stay this way, if I don't oppose this new order... Look, we have two cows now. Therefore, one cow I can give away to the collective farm myself, and the other cow – I could keep for myself. In fall, I will slaughter the pigs, and I'll sell the meat. We should have enough money to pay taxes. I also have my orchard that blesses us with fruit and honey. It ought to be enough of that for us both. After all, we never have been a white-handed people. We've been accustomed working hard from young age. Therefore, people like us, who are not lazy, always had enough and always will have. Simply, we urgently need to adapt to the new circumstances. Otherwise, we may suffer the same fate as many other farmers did. The entire county is going to perdition. Now, you know my outlook on the new land reform."

"When I listen to you, mom, everything you're trying to do sounds logical. However, we don't know what the future may bring; we have not lived under this new system yet."

"True, we haven't, but I already can see what's going on around us. For example, let's look at this newly put together collective farm in Adutiskis. I've just come from there. Local people make fun of the new government's arrangements in town. Team leaders keep driving the farmers to work in the collective farm. However, only a few of those farmers gather after lunch. Even then, they spend most of the time sitting around and wagging their tongues talking nonsense. In addition, many students from the city have been called to help with the farm work this summer. I counted about thirty of them working in the field today. It appeared as if they more trampled down the grasses in the field than did some appreciable work."

"I'm glad I haven't been sent to work for a collective farm this year," Bronius said.

"In spite of that, you have ended up working harder at home. Now, you have an opportunity to compare their work to the work of the farmers at their own farms. There are just two of us, but all our hay has already been dried out and brought into the barn. The collective farm can use many working hands. In addition, people are being forced to work on Sundays, too. The question arises - what is the problem? This is happening because people do not have interest in their work results, since they do not work for themselves."

Bronius interrupted her, "Another bad thing is that they are forced to work for the collective farm."

The mother went on, "It was funny even watching those poor students at work. Rain kept pouring down, and all the boys and girls with their soaked through shirts were cutting the grass… I felt sorry for them. The same applies to the locals - they work without any desire looking forward only for the evening to come. They don't care what the harvest will be. People always count only their own paydays. It shouldn't be this way. For example, we don't work when it rains cats and dogs. Neither do the other farmers who have been lucky still to own their land. Only the comedians, who had introduced this new order, keep others looking like fools in the fields. That is the reason why the hay rots in the fields of the collective farm. I'll tell you - nothing good will come out of that collective work."

"Do they make students work in the fields too?"

"Yes, the students have come in crowds already. In addition, not just the boys have arrived, but the girls as well. I heard they have even organized dances for the students every other evening. You could also go dancing with them. Do you remember the lame musician Rimsiokas from our village? He plays accordion at the dances there. Although having the disability, he at the same time, is a very good musician. Accordion just weeps in his hands. Or laughs… Even though God wronged him this way, He certainly spared him the talent. You should go and have some fun with those young people. Otherwise, you could get bored of sticking alone in the village for weeks."

"I don't have time for fun, mother."

"And what else is there for you to do? You deserve having some good time. You already helped me so much with the farm work."

"I have what to do. I've found my old writing that I would like to develop," he slapped the thick notebook over his opened palm.

"What is this, son?" Mother took the notebook out of his hand and read aloud the inscription on its cover, "Sy-nop-sis. What does this word mean?"

"This, mom, is the short essay that I'd written before preparing myself to write something bigger than that…"

"What are you trying to say, son? Are you going to write a book?" asked surprised mother.

"Yes, I am going to try. I had created this essay when I was still at school. I had put my hopes into it, I'd spent long, countless evenings until I filled up this entire notebook. During my years at the gymnasium, my friends had occupied most of my time, and, in general, I had very little experience in writing. No wonder, this synopsis had got somehow lost. Later on, I went through some mental shocks in relation to the dad's arrest. Thus, my work became completely forgotten. It has been laying on the shelf here for a few years now. As you can see, even the corners of the notebook have already turned yellow. Today, by some miracle, Fortune accidentally handed my writing to me over again. Therefore, I would like to expand and develop it further. I know I'm capable of carrying out this kind of work."

"But you, Bronius, have been studying medicine. What does your profession have in common with the specialty of the writer?"

"It has nothing in common... I've just liked writing since my school times. I have also written a number of rhymes and two poems. However, the occupation of our country by the Russian invaders and the father's arrest totally disturbed my "equilibrium". Changes in living conditions and struggle for the existence coerced me to forget this so pleasurable to me pursuit. It's too bad; I could have had a few books written by now. All my free time could have been spent usefully. But maybe, not all is lost. Perhaps, now, is the best time to do just that. Who knows – I could even bring some benefits to the public."

"Do what you can. Just don't neglect your studies at the university. You have been striving for it too hard, and you have struggled enough already."

Having said that, mother rose up and walked to the bookshelf, where her son's books and notebooks have been displayed. She took one of the notebooks and started turning its pages with her chapped from hard work fingers. For some time, she was standing and quietly reading the poetry written in his beautiful handwriting.

The rain stopped knocking on the roof. Outside the window, clouds dissipated, and the sun smiled. Its joyous rays lit up transparent verdure in the orchard. Diamonds of clear glittering dew landed on the luxuriant grass, the already blossomed out tree leaves, and the tops of the beehives.

When the mother left, he became melancholic. Not wanting to sit cooped up inside any longer, he put his notebook back on the shelf and went out to the yard.

The sun already started leaning towards the west, but it still was spreading intense warmth. He took a fishing rod out of the shed and walked through the orchard by the river. In the orchard, he again came across the mother.

She badly wanted him to put on some more weight during the holidays. Therefore, the woman had been circling around him lately and urging, from time to time, to eat something or drink some milk. She always let him have the tastiest morsel, as if he still was a little boy. Now too, seeing Bronius walking through the orchard, she offered, "Bronius, maybe you better have a snack first and then go fishing."

"Thank you, mom. I don't feel like eating at the moment. Maybe in an hour or so. If the fish isn't biting, I'll come myself and have some milk."

When at the river, Bronius cast the line, and, not even five minutes later, the bob went under the water. Bronius instantly jerked the fishing rod upwards. A small silver fish briefly flashed in the air and fell on the grass.

Soon afterwards, the second and the third fishes were pulled out of the water. The fishery has never been so successful. Bronius totally forgot he wanted to go home and have some milk.

The evening sun was hanging above the western horizon. However, its big fiery disk did not let the human eye to look at it without experiencing tension and pain.

Soon, the mother herself came to the riverside to remind Bronius to go home and drink some milk. However, fish was biting so frantically that Bronius did not want wasting his valuable time. He just kept pulling from the water one little fish after another. Fishing had never been so good in his entire life.

All the mother could do at this point was to stand on the bank watching him with amazement pulling the fishes as if someone had been hanging them onto the hook on the bottom of the river. The woman realized that, now, she by no means could palm off him to have a cup of milk. Therefore, she didn't even try.

Bronius returned home very late; it was already dark. He carried with him about forty silver fishes.

Next morning dawned very sunny. Therefore, work got under way immediately after breakfast. As soon as dew dried out, haystacks were shaken up and dry grass was turned over in swaths.

Around the midday, the sun began scorching so ruthlessly that they had to start carting the hay into the barn well after lunch.

Suddenly, the air filled up with a smell of approaching rain. On the left and on the right side of the sky, threatening clouds were gathering. That made the mother and Bronius spin even faster. Thus, the hay was brought into the barn that evening earlier than usually, and the remaining hay, that had not been quite dry yet, was loaded into ricks.

After finishing his work, Bronius as usually took a swim, came back home and had a snack, and returned to the riverside.

This time, though, he came there not with the fishing rod, but with the notebook in his hand. In this unspoiled corner of the nature, away from everybody, he immediately got absorbed in his reading. In the kingdom of his thoughts, Bronius himself felt like a fish in the water.

At home, the mother was engaged in her customary chores that people living in a village had never lacked. She rushed to feed pigs first; she wanted to make supper earlier this evening.

However, an unfamiliar girl unexpectedly showed up at their front door, and she interrupted the woman's routine.

The girl inquired if she could spend a night in her house. She was almost begging, "Please, let me sleep at your place tonight. It has been a few days now as I work in Adutiskis collective farm. During the day, we play around more than we work in the fields. But our dances after work deprive us of sleep. They end at ten o'clock, but students continue rioting and shouting until two or four o'clock in the morning. Then, we must get up at seven in the morning and go to work. I've hardly had any sleep. I just have no strength left. It would be nice to have some rest, at least for one night. Please, let me get some sleep, hostess. I could sleep even on the floor. I'm not asking for any food; I just need some sleep. Please, help me..."

"Don't you have a place to sleep at the collective farm?"

"We do, but it's impossible to fall asleep there. I get more tired than rested there. You can't imagine how noisy our students' crew is. As soon as the dancing ends, the boys start climbing through the windows into our rooms. They talk and laugh with the girls until the daybreak which makes it impossible to sleep. I can't get good rest while sleeping in my clothes, either.

Therefore, I have gathered myself to leave the collective farm and knock on the door of some generous local people. I promise I won't be of any trouble to you. In the morning, I'll get up and leave," begged the girl again.

"I don't know what to do with you now."

"Please, let me in; I promise not to disturb you."

"Okay, you can spend the night here, and you can eat supper here, too. Thank God, we have enough food in this house."

"Please, don't worry about the supper. We get some food at the collective farm. Actually, I've just had my supper there. I'm not hungry, I just want to sleep."

"Well, come inside. I was getting ready to cook now. How is the food at the collective farm? Is it any good?"

"The food there is not that great, but we don't starve there, either."

"Have a seat, and I'll make something to eat. My son is now at the river. He comes home hungry. He goes fishing every night. If you change your mind, you are welcome to eat with us."

When the woman mentioned her son, the girl felt somewhat uneasy. That was the very reason she had escaped from the collective farm; she ran away from the cavaliers bothering her. Recently, they had just been haunting her.

Now, however, she felt trapped, and it was already too late to change her determination. After begging so much and after finally having convinced the woman to let her stay, she could not leave.

A thought crossed the girl's mind that perhaps she was worried for no reason at all. After all, her son could turn out to be a decent guy.

The mother left her sitting in the room, where it was so beautiful and peaceful. There were many flowerpots around. The girl almost felt like sitting in a small atrium, since the whole room had been buried in the verdure and blossoms. In spite of being alone in the room, she did not dare looking around much.

"Are you bored sitting here alone?" the mother asked entering the room. "I walked to the river to call my son for supper. Soon, he will be here, and we can eat."

Soon, manly steps were heard in the hallway. Her torso stirred revealing that she was feeling uncomfortable. Nevertheless, she tried to control herself in front of her generous hostess. All tensed up, she listened as this woman's son walked into the hallway his steps already approaching the room, where both of them were sitting.

"Here he is. It's time to eat the supper, Bronius," the mother said.

She turned her face to the girl and added, "We also go to bed early, since we get very tired during the day working in our meadow."

The figure of the young man suddenly got rooted-frozen in the doorway. Unexpectedly seeing the girl, Bronius stopped dead in his tracks and was staring at her with his mouth opened.

For a few seconds, he was standing motionless unable to utter a word. The girl also jumped off the chair, and her face flared up like a live coal.

For a while, both of them were standing like stunned. The mother kept looking at her son and, then, at the girl not being able to understand what was happening.

At last, Bronius broke the silence, "Ema... Is it possible?! Maybe I am only dreaming..."

The girl did not answer being unsettled herself by this unexpected encounter. Ema, her hands clutched together close to her chest, was standing and gazing at Bronius.

Similarly, he also could not find what else to say. Both looked terribly puzzled.

Finally, the mother broke the uncomfortable silence, "It appears the two of you already know each other..."

"Yes, mom, I know her. Ema and I are studying at the same faculty. We have known each other for almost a year now."

Then, he looked at Ema and said, "But how has the fate thrust you over here? Maybe something bad has happened?"

"Ema has come to help the collective farm with the work in the fields. There are many students from Vilnius in our vicinity. How nice that you know each other! Well, ask your guest to sit down at the table. The supper is ready."

Soon, the mother returned carrying a tray with hot boiled potatoes, a homemade fried sausage, and scrambled eggs with bacon. After bringing plates with forks, she laid them out in front of everyone on the tablecloth.

When the food, smelling deliciously, started steaming on the table, the mother invited the grandmother too.

Lately, the old woman had been eating at the same table very seldom. It happened only on special occasions. Today was one of those occasions. When the mother told her that her grandson's classmate is at their house, she also wanted to eat together with the family. Everybody sat down, and Bronius asked, "Mom, would you treat us to some wine too?"

The mother did not need to be reminded a second time; soon, a bottle of the homemade wine was standing on the table. The grandmother was the first to pick up her glass. Lifting her glass, she encouraged, "Let's have a drink to health of our youth."

"Grandma, we should drink to your health. We have enough of health already"

"Dear, you need to listen to the old people. You still have your entire life ahead of you. Therefore, you will need your health. I have already received out of life everything I wanted over the full measure... So, to you, kids!"

The grandmother clinked glasses with Bronius first. Then, smiling to Ema, she did the same with her. After the old woman took a sip of the wine, the others followed.

"My mother made this wine. Do you like it, Ema?"

"Very tasty. To tell the truth, I'm not an expert of wine, but I can testify that this cherry drink is wonderful! Your mom did a great job."

"I am glad you like my mother's wine. Let's have a bite now. Maybe our food is not as good as it is at the first-class restaurant, but I can promise we won't be hungry either."

"Don't say that, Bronius. You mother's food is far better. You can't get the food like this at the restaurant. I have to admit, I haven't eaten such a tasty homemade meal for quite a while now."

The happy mother was piling up the food onto the girl's plate, "Ema, don't pay attention to what he is saying. Bronius knows he is at home. Therefore, he says whatever rushes into his head. I would like you to feel at ease with us. Make yourself at home. Usually, I cook different kinds of dishes for our guests. Of course, that requires more time to prepare them. However, I didn't expect having the guest coming this evening... We'll just have to share with you whatever we have on our table today. The only thing I can promise is that you won't go to bed hungry. The main thing in life is not the food, anyway, but it is peace... Also, trust in people..."

They were eating their modest supper, but, at the same time, it was also one of the most remarkable encounters in their lives.

The grandmother was the first to rise from the table. She apologized for having to leave. The old woman went to rest. Soon after, Ema also thanked Bronius's mother for the hearty, delicious meal, and she started walking towards the front door.

However, the mother stopped her saying, "Where are you going, dear?"

"I'll go back to the collective farm. I have troubled you enough already with my unexpected visit today. I didn't know that ..." the girl suddenly stopped short and turned red on her face.

"What didn't you know? Maybe you didn't like something? Then, I apologize," the mother said.

"Oh no, hostess! I don't even know how to thank you for such warm welcome. Nevertheless, I don't want to disturb your peace by staying overnight as well. I've decided to go back to the collective farm. I have got a bed there, and I can spend the night there, just as I usually do."

"Mother, she probably doesn't like it here with us. Then, I can see her to Adutiskis. There, probably is more fun. There are many young people there, too, while it is so quiet here... I have to admit we live like some hermits."

"But, Bronius, she literally begged me to spend the night here. She had said she would even sleep on the floor. I don't understand what has happened now. Why all of a sudden she changed her mind?"

"I was thinking... Anyhow, I don't want to cause you any trouble by staying the night."

"Don't worry about that, Ema. We have plenty of room to sleep. Even though we can't offer you 'a feather bed', you still can have a decent night's sleep. Mom, make her sleep in my bed, and I'll go to sleep in the storeroom. Let her have a good night's sleep in our home."

The mother pulled clean bedding out of a wardrobe. Then, she changed the sheets in Bronius's bed, so that Ema, at last, could go to sleep.

Bronius wished her sweet dreams and went to the storeroom himself. There, he could not get asleep for a long time. Ema's portrait was standing in his mind not letting him forget about her even for a minute. Bronius dreamed creating for Ema good conditions in his parents' house, so that she would never regret having spent time with him and his family. He decided to get up early in the morning, well before the sunrise, and go fishing. Namely at this time, during the very sunrise, the fish used to bite like crazy.

With such thoughts, Bronius fell into troubled sleep. He jumped out of bed several times fearing to sleep away the whole morning. Making sure it was still dark outside, he again closed his eyes and immediately fell back to sleep.

It was almost light around in the storeroom when he woke up. He jumped out of bed frightened thinking that he had slept through. Angry with himself, Bronius looked out the window. However, soon, he got convinced that it was still very early, and the sun had not risen yet. Now, it was the very time to go to the river. Without wasting a minute, he quickly dressed up and took out his fishing rod.

The sun had not shown itself yet, when he came to the riverside. However, the eastern horizon was already very enlightened which predicted the imminent beautiful sunrise.

Bronius cast the line. While sitting on the grass, he was thinking of Ema still sleeping in his bed. Somewhere close, a nightingale broke into singing. It was jugging so beautifully that Bronius could not get enough of it. Then, the disk of the red sun began raising its head out of behind the cloud. Now, it appeared as if the sounds of the birds were emanating not from interwoven branches of the willows towering above the water but they were coming from some Garden of the Eden. Bronius himself started feeling like in Heaven…

He pulled his fishing rod out of the water and put another worm onto the hook. Approximately half an hour elapsed, but the fish, as ill luck would have it, had not been biting at all. The float on the surface of the water was almost motionless. Sun had already changed its color into golden; it was detached from the horizon and climbing the sky.

However, he had not caught a single fish yet. It appeared as if the fish were mocking the impatient angler. The time was flying fast, but there still was no fish. Out of tension, tiny drops of sweat appeared on Bronius's forehead. He already buried his hope bringing home some fresh fish.

However, the float suddenly plunged under the surface of the slowly moving water. Bronius quickly jumped on his feet and jerked the rod. All trembling with the excitement, he began slowly pulling his catch toward himself. He felt that the fish of a considerable size was fighting for his life on the other end. However, that which he saw coming out of the water he could never expect to catch. After the considerable time of struggle, he finally dragged the stubborn fish out on the bank. Although for a while it did not want to yield itself a prisoner to the fisherman, the beautiful fish finally wore itself out fighting with him.

The fish was huge, weighing about one and a half kilograms. Never in his entire life, had Bronius succeeded in catching such a huge fish by using only his fishing rod! Now, he was in a great spirits...

He also pulled out a couple more small fishes. Now, he knew he would be able to treat his beautiful guest to a nice breakfast.

Bronius still could not believe such good luck was smiling at him, and it came by itself straight into his home... Now, he had only to properly welcome it. Being sunk in his beautiful dreams, he caught three more medium size fishes and some more small ones. Then, he decided it should be enough for this morning's breakfast. Therefore, Bronius wasted no more time and went home.

When he walked into the kitchen, he found both the mother and Ema already up. Greeting them, he laid the fishes on the small table there. The kitchen itself was as little as a pocket. Therefore, with the three people being inside, it did not leave much room for the mother to turn around in order to prepare the meal.

Bronius was already going to leave, when the mother said, "I was thinking that you, Bronius, are still asleep. Yesterday, you told me that you wouldn't go fishing."

"Right, I did not plan on going fishing, but today I thought it would be nice to treat Ema to a fresh fish. In the city, you won't find such fish even with a candle in the daylight. However, we have plenty of it here, in the village. I only mustn't be lazy, and we can eat it to our hearts' content every day."

"I can help the hostess clean the fish," volunteered Ema.

"Well, you can if you want. They say a meal prepared by the cook tastes better. Bronius, an apron is hanging on the wall over there. Give it to Ema; this way, her dress will stay clean."

After tying up the mother's apron around her waist, Ema began deftly scraping the scales. Soon, the silver fishes were sitting on the plate without the heads or the intestines. It only remained for the mother to place them onto the pan and to fry.

Meanwhile, Bronius invited Ema outside so that she could wash her hands. He placed a large metal bowl on the stool and filled half of it with water.

The water was so icy that Ema's hands got numb with cold. However, she did not say anything to Bronius. She just washed them and took a towel out of his hands.

After breakfast, she cordially thanked the mother for the food and the place to sleep. Mother seeing the girl off through the doorstep, invited her to come again to their home in the evening. She also added that as long as the student work lasted at the collective farm, Ema was welcome to sleep in their house every night.

Feeling very grateful, Ema promised to come back after the fieldwork in the evening. All radiant with joy, she walked along the gravel road that led out of the homestead, when Bronius caught up with her and volunteered to accompany her to Adutiskis. His heart was filled with joy, too, since it was obvious that Ema enjoyed her stay last night. In addition, his mother appeared to be well disposed towards her.

Bronius with Ema was walking slowly; they did not lack a conversation. She told him in detail how she had entreated Bronius's mother to allow her to spend the night in their home. His mother had appeared to be a strict person. Ema said that she had almost lost her hope for the overnight stay.

Bronius in return told Ema how hard his mother had been laboring at their farm. Since the father was no longer with her, the burden of the entire farm rested on her shoulders alone. That, of course, required from her many efforts and much endurance. He thought that had been the reason why she'd appeared so stern to Ema. He added that in reality she had been a good-natured person.

Thus, having a chat, both of them did not even notice when they came to Adutiskis village. Bronius would have gladly continued walking with Ema further.

However, Ema suddenly changed the subject. Now, she told him that Alfa had come to the collective farm together with the rest of the students, and that he just would not leave her alone... She said that recently he bored her with his talks so much that she had to bring herself to run away from him.

Before saying goodbye, Bronius announced that he would eagerly be waiting for her to come in the evening again.

Ema still tried to convince Bronius it was inappropriate to take an advantage of his mother's kindness. She also mentioned that people around them might think something bad about their relationship. Therefore, they could talk rot about the two of them...

However, Bronius did not submit to her. He did not part with Ema until she promised to come again.

Bronius returned home to help his mother rake up the remaining hay. The day was very warm, and the work was not particularly difficult, because there was not much grass left to cart to the barn. As the result of this, they finished working much earlier than usually.

Since there was not much left to do now, time for Bronius started dragging very slowly. Therefore, he decided to go to Adutiskis and wait for Ema there so that they could come home together.

Soon, he found himself walking on a road to Adutiskis. Rural fields were extending far ahead and bushes stretching on both sides of the road. Bronius kept looking around to see if there were any students working in the fields.

However, he could not see the soul alive, even though the workday had not been over yet. On the contrary - just at this time of the day, the action usually took place in full swing.

Since the meadows were empty, Bronius realized that Ema, too, was free for the day. It aroused speculation why, then, she had not come to their home yet. Restless thoughts kept spinning in his head.

Hiding in the bushes, he started looking at the nearby buildings. Although Bronius lived not too far away from Adutiskis, he had hardly had any acquaintances there. He only had known a few people of old age. As about young people, he could not remember any of them. Most of them had been just kids at that time when he had left to Vilnius in pursuit of his education. Now, many people in Adutiskis changed so much that he could hardly recognize anybody.

Bronius wished Alfa was not there with the rest of the students. Then, he could walk inside of these buildings and look for Ema until he found her. He was also wondering about Alfa's relation to her, since she had complained about him not leaving her alone.

Was Alfa weaving some kind of plot? Did he actually love her, or did he just want to seduce her?

In any case, Bronius's instinct told him that anything could be expected from Alfa. Bronius badly wanted to protect Ema. He decided to warn her to be very careful, and he was anxious to do this as soon as possible. Today...

Bronius decided not to leave until he found Ema. He got in to a dense bush and sat down onto a thick willow branch. Then, he slightly parted the branches in front of him and watched the students who went in and out of the wooden buildings. Bronius did not know which building Ema was staying in, but he decided to sit and wait for her anyway.

Somewhere in the yard, he could hear children yelling. Then, lively laughter filled the air.

Adomaitis already reconciled with the fact that he would have to spend time in the bush until dark. However, suddenly, Ema appeared on the road. He immediately recognized her dress.

Ema was walking fast. Occasionally, she kept running a few steps forward. A couple times, she turned to look back. Then, she continued rushing ahead.

She was nearing fast. Soon, she past the place where Bronius was sitting in his willow hideout. Now, Bronius came out of his lurking-place and stepped on to the road. Ahead, the colorful dress of quickly walking Ema was twinkling cheerfully. She was no longer looking back over her shoulder.

Bronius loudly exclaimed, "Ema!"

The masculine voice struck her like a lightning. She stopped frightened, and, only after a few seconds, she slowly turned her head back as if she was afraid to see some beast.

The instant she saw Bronius, an expression of the fear on her face was replaced with a bright smile. Her lips opened up widely revealing her pearly white teeth.

"You are sweeping as if somebody is chasing you."

"You have scared me! Did you fall out of the sky?"

"Not really. I have come from those bushes. I've been sitting there for more than an hour now. I was afraid to miss you," in good spirits spoke Bronius walking toward her.

"I didn't want Alfa to see me. He had not been retreating from me a step. Today he even reproved me for yesterday's disappearance. He just kept questioning me where I had been. As it is, I have to keep it secret, so he wouldn't know where to find me. I try to associate with him as little as possible. Let's hurry. I'm afraid someone can see us together."

"It's not safe for a girl to walk alone. It's better to walk together with someone."

"I'm not afraid of Alfa. I simply cannot stand him. I'm aware of his intentions. Namely because of that, I find him even more repellent."

"It's good to hear you know his plans. I myself wanted to talk to you about it so that you wouldn't get involved with him. But now, since you know that already, I feel relieved."

"That is why I was in such a hurry. I don't want anyone seeing me with you together. Then, Alfa would start tangling up all sorts of intrigues. Best thing is for him to never find out that you're here, also, and that this is your homeland. Or, he would just be barking like a dog all the time."

"I understand, and I completely agree with your opinion. So we can speed up to make it faster. Give me your hand."

After grabbing Ema's hand, Bronius first broke into a run. Therefore, she had no other choice but to run along with him. Thus, both of them were running on the dusty rural road until they got out of breath. Finally, the two of them stopped laughing merrily.

When Bronius and Ema found themselves at home, the sun was already hanging low over the western horizon. Soon, it totally hid itself behind the forest-belt. The mother greeted them cheerfully. Again, just like yesterday, she offered to eat supper. She wished her son gained more weight before his return to Vilnius.

"Please, don't worry about me. I'm not hungry. But thank you," out of courtesy refused Ema.

"Then, mom, I won't eat too."

"See, Ema, because of you, Bronius will stay hungry too."

Hearing his mother's rebuke, Ema turned red with shame.

"Don't pay attention, Ema. Mother was just joking. Weren't you, mom?"

"Of course, I was joking. I just wanted you to have some milk. Here, I have brought the fresh milk right from under the cow. It's still warm. I have also baked bread this morning; it is so delicious with the milk."

"Ema, we need to listen to Mother. Mom, bring the bread; we'll eat it."

Each of them ate a slice of the homemade bread washing it down with the milk that really was still warm.

"Well, let's go to the orchard now, Ema. I will show you my mother's assets."

"Not my assets, Bronius, but your own assets," hearing this, corrected him the mother.

"Yours, mom. I am just a guest here."

"Bronius, stop insulting your old mother. You are my asset. Everything here is yours."

"I'm giving up. Be it as you wish..."

Bronius took out the girl into the quiet orchard. The evening was extremely beautiful. A big red disk of the sun was hanging above the horizon."

Looking at the drowsy sun, wrapped in a transparent mist, Bronius's eyes did not hurt as they used to when he looked at it during the daytime.

Even here, in the orchard, they could feel some kind of stuffiness. It seemed as if a storm was approaching. Bronius with Ema slowly crossed a sleepy kingdom of the apple trees on their way to the riverside.

They sat down on a steep precipice, lowered their legs over its edge, and admired the sunset. For a while, there was silence between the two of them, but Bronius interrupted it, "Somewhere in the distance, it must be raining hard. Maybe it's even lightning and flashing."

"What makes you think that?"

"Do you see how calm is the surface of the water in the inlet? If the storm wasn't approaching, you could see fish once in a while disturb the surface of the water. Sometimes, you could even hear the splashes when they jump out of the water. When the water is so calm, the fish don't bite. Therefore, it's better not to even waste your time trying to catch it. But let me tell you - the water now is as warm as tea. I often swim in the evenings after the sun is set, and it's a pure pleasure. It feels just like being in a bathtub. In fact, it's usually more cold on the bank than it is in the water. Then, I run home as fast as I can, and I get under covers in my bed. I sleep like a baby. It's an awesome feeling! If I was alone, I would take a swim now, too. Let's go, I will show you our wooden footbridge. It's over there, hiding behind those bushes. I like jumping off the footbridge straight into the river. I'd knocked together a small springboard out of the planks, too, last year. We can get onto the little bridge to check if the water in the river is warm right now."

Soon, they found themselves on the footbridge. Ema sat down onto the edge of it and immersed her legs down to the mid-calf into the water.

It was quiet, warm, and beautiful around them. The water was also incredibly warm. Ema gave a little cry out of satisfaction and started dangling her feet in the pleasant current.

"Really, the water is so warm. Like a tea. I envy you this wonderful place. It feels like paradise here! I love this river with its clean water and your mother's old apple-tree orchard with the beehives. Look over there, on the other side of the river! See those tall white birch trees looking like guards that protect this beautiful, remote corner of the nature. It's a true gift from God to your family. And those branches of the willow trees are so nicely leaning over the water. You are lucky being able to enjoy this beauty!"

"You, Ema, haven't had a chance to see the entire splendor of this corner yet. You need to come here very early in the morning, when the sun has not risen. Then, you could hear nightingales trilling in those willows, and you could see white mist rising up from the water like from some kind of huge boiling cauldron. The fog, then, covers leaves of the trees and the grasses on the ground; it forms dew. These willows are more spectacular early in the morning than they are now. It seems as if their droopy branches are crying, and the tears sparkle in the sun like some diamonds."

Both were enjoying the surroundings.

Bronius pointed with his hand at the river and said, "Look at the surface of the water! You can already see the fine mist beginning to rise. Only in the mornings, it stays much thicker. Everything then appears so mysteriously... Now, it's beginning to grow dark; soon, this entire view will disappear under the veil of the night. Even my shirt has turned cool from this moisture in the air. I think we should go back to the orchard. It should be warmer under the trees. I made a bench this morning under those big cherry trees. I would like to show it to you. We can even sit on it for a while. It's healthy to breath some fresh air before sleep. The air is so clean here that it could probably alone sustain a human being; no food is necessary."

Bronius helped Ema get up off the bridge. Still holding her little fingers in his trembling hand, he helped her to climb the steep slope. Only then, he released her hand.

It was much darker under the trees in the orchard. However, they still could distinguish the beehives dozing under the widespread apple trees. Diligent little bees were sweet asleep. When passing the fruit trees, Ema wanted to sit down under one of them on the grass. Nevertheless, she did not dare to offer that to Bronius, and she only walked obediently next to him.

Suddenly, the eastern side of the sky was lit up. Such an unexpected flash scared Ema. She stopped and asked Bronius, "Did you see the glimpse in the sky just now?! Or, maybe it just appeared to me?"

"I also noticed. It was the lightning, but it's still very far away, somewhere beyond the horizon."

"Why didn't we hear a thunder then?"

"The clouds probably have still not fully formed themselves. Or, maybe because it's so far away, we couldn't hear anything. Here again, there was some glow in the sky!"

"I've seen it. For some reason, I'm getting scared. It may be dangerous to stay here under the trees..."

"Are you really scared?"

"I am, but at the same time, I find those kinds of events of the nature to be exciting."

"I also like when the lightning flashes so gently at night... But if you are afraid, then perhaps it's better for us to go home. It would be selfish of me to force you to watch this performance of God..."

"I'm not so much afraid as I am amazed that we can't hear the thunder when it has been lightning so intensely. Usually, each flash is being accompanied by sound that shakes the ground. I have to admit I like watching summer storms. We can stay outside a little longer. The air now is so fresh. Probably it has been saturated with ozone. Also, I don't want to miss such an amazing natural phenomenon. Besides, I'm not alone. If the lightning hits me, you won't leave me, will you?"

"Of course, I would not leave you. You are my guest. Therefore, I must take care of you. However, I don't think this storm will require great sacrifices... In such a beautiful corner of the nature, we shouldn't think of anything else but about delight of the mysterious surroundings..."

Thus, chatting away, they came to the other side of the orchard, where two large birch trees had been shooting up into the sky. Next to them, a few willow bushes were leaning over the fence and hiding the entire orchard from the eyes of the passersby. Further away, old cherry trees stood spreading widely their gnarly branches. Under one of them, there was the nice little bench newly hammered together. It was very quiet there, and a scent of resin, mixed with a smell of the earth, could be felt in the air. It was coming from nearby standing pine trees.

"Well, we have come. Please, be seated, Ema. I have made this bench this morning especially for you. I think this is the most beautiful place in the orchard. I was keen on you being able to sit on it and admire the trees around."

While the two of them were sitting on the bench, the lightning flashed again. This time, it was so bright that everything around was lit up, and for a moment, it became as light as during the daytime.

"Yes, it's very romantic here."

"I'm very happy you like the place I've prepared for you."

"I'm also very grateful to you for making the efforts to impress me."

"I've named this bench after you – the Ema's Bench. It will always remind me of you..."

"Bronius, I have such thoughts going through my mind at this moment... but I don't know if I should say it loudly. I'm afraid you will laugh at me..."

"Ema, even if you said something funny now, I wouldn't dare to laugh."

"Bronius, do you remember the time when you told me that you love me? Was it true, or you said it just to tease me? Or, maybe, you were only joking?"

"Yes, that was the truth... I have never joked with you."

"And what about now - do you still love me? Just don't lie to me, because it's very important to me..."

"Of course, I love you, even though this boiling lava of love is like some unerupted volcano... It only warms my body without being able to pour out itself onto the surface and be united with another love in order to turn into one big passion..."

"Bronius, please forgive my frankness, but I don't believe you. I don't believe that you love me. When a guy loves a girl, he tries to meet with her as often as he can; he always wants to be together. Even if there were no occasions for those meetings, he would still try to find them himself. However, you, Bronius, had acted just the opposite - you had never attempted to meet with me. Sometimes, you had even avoided me. I already have some experience in this area. For example, I know for sure that Alfa rally loves me. In the beginning, I could not understand his intentions. Maybe then, his plans had only been to seduce me, to play with my feelings, and to end his romance with me. However, he himself fell head over heels in love with me!'

Ema ceased talking, and a deadly silence reigned between them.

Since Bronius was not saying a word, Ema continued, "Now, he is so in love with me that he does not leave me alone. Like some ghost, he literally keeps on haunting me. I have no strength to get rid of him. Just thinking about him disturbs me. However, the worst part is that he does not pay attention to my wishes; he keeps bothering me all the time. I think he acts like this because his feelings govern him, but not he governs his feelings. Because of his behavior, I assume that he is love with me. It is said that actions speak louder than words. However, you act differently towards me. I noticed you don't make any efforts to develop a relationship with me. Why should I believe your words but not your actions?"

Suddenly, another lightning flashed across the sky. Again, the entire orchard was lit up and, for a split second, it was freed from the darkness of the night. This made Ema fall silent.

Bronius did not say a word, too. Despite that, the silence was interrupted by the distant loud thunder which forced both of them to pick up their ears. Then, too, neither one of them uttered a word.

This moment offered a good opportunity to break the silence between them, but their open talk apparently affected both of them equally, and no storm could shake them now out of their stagnation.

Nevertheless, this awkward silence had to end... Desperately searching for words to say, Bronius finally uttered, "Ema, I don't understand why you have to dig in other peoples' feelings... Can you be sensitive to another person's pain? Anybody can draw conclusions like that. You will not understand my feelings..."

Instead of hearing her verbal response, Bronius saw tears coming down Ema's cheeks. Not being able to withstand the pain, she hid her face in her palms and burst into tears.

Bronius never expected such her reaction. He jumped off the bench and knelt down on his knee entreating, "Ema, darling, forgive me, please. I didn't think my words could offend you so badly. I had no intention causing you pain. Please calm down for God's sake. I'll never express my opinion anymore. Instead, I will try adapt to your situation. Moreover, I won't talk about any love affairs at all!"

It took a while for Ema to recover her composure. She just kept sniveling, while Bronius was trying to comfort her in any way he could. Finally, she wiped the tears away with a corner of the skirt of her dress and began tidying her disheveled hair.

Then, she said in a dispirited voice, "Bronius, I would like to know the truth. Namely, what do you think about me? I won't get mad at you, even if you admit that you have spoken those nice words not because of being in love... but just because you wished to act like a philanderer... I would like you to be sincere with me; I would like to know the truth."

"I can repeat the same to you again. My feelings toward you have not changed... Even if I had to die on a scaffold tomorrow, I couldn't renounce my words, because I've spoken the truth. I simply could not say anything different. If you want, I can repeat the same again, even if I had to do this a thousand times more. In fact, I would be very pleased to say that to you over and over again. I would like you to know that the first time I had seen you in that corridor, under those hapless circumstances, you had brought light into my life, just like a little star... No, like the sun! I could even hardly look at you without my eyes hurting... Every living being needs the sun, even though neither one of us can bare looking at it with the naked eyes. I'm the same way - I did not dare staring at you. In addition, I'd been afraid to pester you. Therefore, I had tried to be content with those rare occasions meeting you just for a short while at the University between our lectures. Already then, I had been secretly in love with you. You brought a new phase into my life. My inner world became much better, filled with exciting new feelings. If you wish to know the truth, then it won't be an exaggeration for me to say that I not only love you... I adore you! If I could express my feelings better, I would do it with no hesitation. You are the most precious person in my life now. I hope I'm not bothering you too much with my dithyrambs... Look - the sky has lightened up again... In a minute, the thunder will start rumbling. I like listening to the thunder. It feels as if the largest rocks ride over the clouds somewhere in the skies."

"Bronius, would you like to hear my opinion on this subject?"

"I don't know..."

"How come?" asked Ema surprised. Her mood improved significantly while listening to Bronius's confession.

"Because I already know your opinion about me... Once, you had already expressed it to me by saying that you had hated me. I had believed your words then. This had been another reason why I'd not bothered you..."

"Bronius don't say that. I beg you..."

"Ema, you don't need to beg. Just ask me, and I will be your obedient servant..."

"Bronius, who needs such resounding phrases? Are you taunting me?"

"I already told you I never taunted you, and I am not going to do that now, either. But I'm not angry with you. Quite the contrary, I even enjoy listening to you no matter what you say."

Once again, there was the flash of the lightning, and, after a few seconds, the loud thunder shook the ground under their feet.

"Ema, are you cold? Take my jacket. Put it on, and you'll be warm." Without waiting for her reply, he took off his jacket and covered Ema's shoulders.

"Bronius, I would like to say something very important to you, but just thinking of telling you that gets me gripped with fear..."

"If this is something bad, then better don't say it..."

"No, Bronius, I must tell you this. I believe you, and I don't want to hide anything from you. You should know it, even though it's scary for me to say that..."

"Ema, for God's sake, say it! What is tormenting you so much? Can I help you in any way?"

"Bronius... I..." she was in no time to utter the words that almost slipped out of her lips, because another deafening thunder hit along with the lightning that illuminated the entire orchard with blinding light.

Immediately after that, the thunder kept threatening with the terrible rumbling right above their heads. Suddenly, cool breeze started blowing which predicted a rapidly coming storm.

"Bronius, let's go home. I'm afraid..."

"Ema, you wanted to tell me something very important..."

"If you, Bronius, haven't understood anything yet, then maybe I'll tell you this next time, when an opportunity comes along... Let's go home now!"

Bronius did not need to be urged anymore. Without saying a word, he got up, and soon the two of them found themselves in the front yard. The lightning with the thundering had not ceased until they reached the house. When in the yard, Bronius felt an enormously big, heavy drop of water fall on his back. It got right through his shirt. Bronius felt it melting on his skin.

Nevertheless, the rain did not get them. Only after they walked under the roof of the glass porch, the hail of the falling far-between huge drops was heard loudly hitting the soil.

As soon as they walked into the room, the huge storm already was raging in the yard making loud, startling noises.

"Where have you, Bronius, been gone so long? I already wanted to go looking for you. While the storm is raving, don't lay down to sleep. Son, get a pitcher with milk out of the cupboard and drink some of it with Ema."

"Ema, maybe you are scared... I will turn on the light," offered Bronius.

"It's not necessary. We can see everything anyway, since the lightning keeps flashing. But why can't we go to sleep?"

"You see, Ema, in the village, the lightning can ignite homes and farm outbuildings. Then, we could burn down together with the entire house. Most people in the country don't sleep during the lightning storms. In the city, people are probably delighted with this natural phenomenon. Out in the country, though, we are very afraid of the thunderstorms. In our village, all the locals are religious. According to them, God is in control of those kinds of natural events that He uses to punish some of us. When the storm like that rages, many people fall down on the floor in their cottages. On their knees, they beg for God's mercy. I'm sure our granny is also saying prayers now. She is probably asking the Lord to make this God's scourge pass by without punishing our family... This is why my mother warned us to stay up until the storm passes away."

"Bronius, would you please bring the girl some milk," asked the mother again.

The guy obediently went to the kitchen and returned carrying the brown clay jug. After filling up the glasses, he encouraged, "Drink milk, Ema."

"I don't really want milk. Maybe just a little... Such light food definitely can't hurt."

"As for me, I can eat anything. In fact, I feel worse if I lie down hungry. Then, I can't get asleep at all."

Both of them were sitting at the table and sipping the milk. Bronius fascinated watched the lightening illuminate the room and Ema in it. He observed her anxious facial expression. He saw how she, from time to time, cast her glance at the window, then at him, and then at the pitcher sitting in front of them.

The two of them were sitting in silence. A conversation between them suddenly had ended. However, neither Bronius nor Ema tried to resume it.

Every time the lightning flashed, Bronius could see Ema's motionless interlocked fingers pressing down against the edge of the table.

Here again, another short flash of lightning blinded both of them for a split second. Bronius did not even feel when he put his hand on Ema's hands.

Her fingers slightly gave a start, but she did not pull her hands from under his large palm. The new flash followed, and Bronius saw a frightened look on Ema's face. Her big, beautiful eyes were gazing straight at his, at such close proximity. It was the short, but at the same time, very precious moment that would remain in both of their memories forever.

"Bronius, don't... Now, that you know my views, you are allowing yourself a little too much..."

"Ema, I don't have any bad intentions... I held your hand only to encourage you; I got an impression you are scared being in the dark."

"I'm not afraid of the thunderstorm. Living in the city, I used to feast my eyes on it. When in the village, I don't feel fear, too, especially when you are next to me. I hope you wouldn't forsake me if some danger threatened me."

"Of course, I would not forsake you. There is no need to even think this way. This storm won't bring anything bad to our homestead. Nothing to worry about... I just want to ask you for one thing - promise me that you will come to spend every night at our house after your work at the collective farm. My mother and I will try to make you feel at home here. I promise you will not be disappointed. I'll show you more of beautiful places around. I want you to know that it's possible to find nice sites out in the country, too, especially at this time of a year."

"Bronius, I have not experienced anything exciting during my few days' stay in Adutiskis. In addition, I started feeling a lot of rejection toward Alfa. Even beautiful surroundings of the nature couldn't make me happy there. Can you believe, the first night already, some bugs had attacked me?! I had not had a wink of sleep after my long trip from Vilnius to the collective farm. I remember the first morning in the fields very vividly. There, I had to face a very unusual work for me, since I had never mowed grass, tedded it, or cocked hay in my entire life. So suddenly, this exhausting physical labor tumbled over me. Maybe it wouldn't be as bad if I, at least, could have normal rest at night there. It would be easier to handle the hard fieldwork during the day. Those sleepless nights had worn me out. As if it hadn't been enough, Alfa began poisoning my life there. He just wouldn't retreat a step from me. Last time, he questioned me; he wanted to know where I had disappeared after work. I don't know what will happen tomorrow. Will I be able to get rid of him? I can't handle that any longer. Therefore, I had run away from there in hopes of finding a more humane accommodation where I could get some rest, at least, during the night."

"And you ended up at my parents' house... It could be Fate," Bronius said.

"I think it had been written in the stars for me to end up in this amazingly beautiful corner of the nature, where I met your generous mother. Yesterday, I had a good night's sleep; I slept like a baby. I have to admit I have never seen such a beautiful place. Your homeland is the true paradise. I can assure you that my stay at your mother's will remain in my memory for a lifetime! How can I forget the magnificent sunset that we had opportunity witnessing this evening before the storm? And the rising mist from the water... The whole cove looked like some giant pot, where the water was about to burst boiling and bubbling! How could I not remember the quiet place by the willows at the river or 'my bench' in your orchard? And the orchard itself with the dozing silhouettes of the apple-trees with the sleepy bee hives underneath of them. That will always remain in my imagination. However, the thing that surprises me the most is that even though I had not wanted to come to the village, now, I am happy to have discovered how beautiful it is here. It seems I would never tire of living at your mother's house."

"I am very happy you like it in my homeland, and I'm very grateful for the nice words you've said about my birth place. It is the most precious place to me in the world. Nevertheless, you still haven't seen everything it has to offer. But leave it to me; I will make sure you have a good time staying with us. Believe me - you will have much more wonderful memories accumulated about this beautiful corner of the nature before you leave back to the city. Well, looks like the storm has ended. I will open the window; it's so stuffy in the room."

As soon as Bronius widely opened the window, the stream of damp cool air moved inside the room taking together in aroma of the orchard. Outside the window, the rain was still murmuring gently.

Occasionally, the thunder still disturbed the rain. The lightning, time from time, flashed across the night sky, even though it was not as bright anymore. Its illumination rather beckoned through the open window than it scared.

"Ema, tomorrow is Saturday. We usually take a bath in our bathhouse every Saturday. We bathe so that we could be as clean as crystal on Sunday. You are welcome to take the bath there, too."

"I don't know. You should be tired of me by now…"

"Don't say that, Ema. I would never get tired of you, even if you lived here all the time. Looks like the storm is over. Now, we can go to sleep. You will have to go to work at the collective farm tomorrow morning. You must get good rest, even though you don't have much time for that, since it will be dawning in a few hours."

Bronius poured two glasses of milk. He handed one of them to Ema, the other he emptied himself and loudly set it onto the table. "Well, good night, Ema. Sweet dreams."

"I'm wishing you the same, Bronius. Where are you going to sleep? Maybe you are not comfortable there. So, you can take the pillow. I don't need two pillows. Do you even have a blanket? You can take this one. I won't get cold. It's warm in this room."

"I will sleep in the storeroom. It's cozy there. In general, I love spending time there. There is my library in that storeroom where I often read books. True, the bed there is not as soft as this one. Your bed has springs and mine just has the straw instead of a mattress. But it's not that bad at all lying on it. I also have a pillow and a blanket. They are just like yours, made of wool. The only difference is that your blanket has been purchased at the store and mine is homemade. Therefore, I have everything I need. Tomorrow, I will show you my storage room."

Once more, he wished good night to Ema and walked out of the room.

Next day, Bronius got up well before a sunrise and went out fishing. While in the beginning the fishery was not very successful, he still caught four small and two big fishes.

At home, the mother alone cleaned them out, and she still had a little time left to fry the fish for breakfast. After everybody ate, Ema left for work, and Bronius accompanied her again. Only this time, he did not walk with her all the way to the village.

When parting with Ema, Bronius told her that he would come again and wait for her by the same roadside bushes as before. However, Ema flatly refused, "Bronius, I will not come to spend the night at your house any more... Really, I don't want to make a nuisance of myself."

"Ema, why are you saying this?! I don't understand you. Tell me for God's sake, what's the matter? Maybe you are mad at me, because I put my hand on yours... yesterday. I really can't see any other reason. Talk to me so that there is no misunderstanding between you and me. Otherwise, you'll just needlessly think bad thoughts all day long at work."

"No, nothing bad happened. I just think that it's better for me not to go to your house anymore."

"Why? I won't leave you alone until you explain me why you no longer wish to come to our house."

"Okay. I will tell you, even though it's not easy for me to say that. Bronius, I think your mother doesn't want me coming to your house anymore. Her behavior this morning gave me some clues. She acted strangely when I was leaving this morning. I had thanked her for the breakfast and said her good bye. However, she did not answer me, and she didn't even look at me... So now, you know... Please don't insist on me coming to your house anymore."

"Well, what if she treated you differently? Do you think it would make difference if she herself invited you to come after work? Would you honor her wish, then?"

"I would."

"Ema, I believe you. You're so sensitive. I don't justify my mother's behavior. Nevertheless, I would like to tell you some things about this extraordinary woman. She had suffered much in her life. Even now, a big load of worries weigh down on her shoulders. It's not easy to maintain the farm of that size for a woman alone. Nevertheless, she does a great job! Everywhere inside and outside of our house, exemplary order prevails. That requires much of her strength and stamina. I sometimes think my mother has two souls living in her body - the feminine and the masculine. Her masculine side helps her to perform toughest chores. This way, her masculine side manifests itself. Indeed, she is so strong physically that not every man could perform physical work as she does. Of course, her sturdily built body testifies about that. The feminine side of her cuts its way through with the maternity feelings. I can catch something incredibly gentle in her character, too. I'm saying this not just because she is my mother. Ema, if you had an opportunity to talk to people in our vicinity about my mother, they could also confirm the same to you. Forgive her, Ema. I am asking you to forgive her because she had endured so much in her life. You already know that my dad had been arrested, and that we have no knowledge where he is. Moreover, she had also suffered because of me being expelled from the university. Only because of my mother's efforts, I've been able to attend the classes again. My mom is only a little over forty years old, but she is already grey-haired. Please, don't get mad at her..."

"Bronius, I am not mad at your mother, and I don't have anything to forgive her, since she has not done anything bad to me. Still... I'm begging you... Please, don't ask me coming to your house anymore."

"I don't know how to respond to you. At least, I would like to thank you for not being angry with my mother, and I'll take care of all the rest myself..."

He gently squeezed her hand before saying goodbye and left.

Ema was walking the opposite direction her heart overflowing with tears. She still hoped that Bronius and her continue seeing each other. However, now that she refused coming to their home, her hope began dyeing out and doubt started creeping into her heart.

Saddened Bronius returned to the homestead and went straight to the storage room. He wanted to concentrate on his thoughts before starting a conversation with his mother.

As soon as he lay down, the door quietly opened up, and the mother walked in herself. Bronius sat up straight. He did not expect her visit. He was planning to talk with her himself first, but she as usually surpassed him.

The mother approached Bronius's bed and sat down on its edge. She was silent for some time which made him a little concerned. At last, she said, "Bronius, I have come here to talk to you..."

"I myself wanted to talk to you, mom... If you didn't show up here, I would have come to you myself."

"I believe you have something to share with me, and I'll be glad to listen to you. But since I have come to you myself, you'll have to hear me out first... After that, you can lay out your own business to me. Does it sound like a good plan to you?"

"Okay, mom."

"Then listen. Even if you committed same wrongdoing against me or some misconduct against others, I would forgive you. At this point in your life, it may be difficult for you to understand this. It's a maternity feeling which governs every woman. I am just a weak person. Therefore, it is difficult for me to resist the nature. However, I think the Mother Nature endows every person. I would like to share my view concerning this matter. Son, I have made this long introduction for a reason. I want you to know my outlook on life."

"I don't understand what you mean by all this. Why do we need this philosophy? We've had enough time grasping each other's characters already. I think, we can understand each other without any resounding phrases. Without any explanations, I realize that no mother could repudiate her child even if her child started walking the life astray. But that's not the main thing I'm trying to get across to you. What I would like to say is that I have never had a thought committing an offence against you or anyone else. I don't break laws and I don't do immoral things. I am sure that I will keep within the law until the rest of my life. Moreover, I know that I would strive for all goodness and sow it myself. I always try to eradicate any root of evil. You, mom, have nothing to worry about."

"I'm glad to hear such noble words coming from your lips. But as we already agreed in the beginning, I wanted to tell you something else. So let me come to my main objective. Of course, we both support the principle of goodness. However, now, I would like to tell you something very important."

"Mom, you are frightening me... Listening to you, I feel as if I have done some crime. Can you, at last, get to the point?! What did you want to tell me? I would like to learn what concerns you so much."

"Okay, son. I will tell you why I've had no peace for the last couple of days now... But you also have to tell me the truth."

"I always tell you the truth. Therefore, this time, I promise to do the same."

"How long have you known this girl?"

"Soon, it will be a year as we have known each other."

"Do you know her intentions toward you?"

"Yes, I know."

"Does she know your intentions in relation to her?"

"Yes, but I have promised myself to root her out of my heart and of my mind. Mom, you can rest assured that I will do the right thing."

"You, son, are talking like some villain!" The woman got up and fixed her bitter gaze on him. Then, quite unexpectedly, she slapped him on the cheek.

Bronius, astonished by this surprise attack, suddenly felt ringing in his ears, and he instantly gave a lurch to the side.

The mother turned away from him and walked to the window. She looked out to the orchard for a while. Outside, a gentle breeze was joyfully tousling the leaves of the apple trees that were shining in the sunrays. They had still been a little wet from yesterday's rain.

"Mom, I would like you to explain me what this kind of your behavior means. I don't see how I could deserve having this slap in my face."

"As far as I understand, you are going to leave this girl. Or maybe, I have misunderstood something?"

"I told that I have to pluck her out of my heart. What else is left for me to do?"

"Then, I've understood everything correctly... I can't believe I have raised such a villain. You have turned into a real dragon, who no longer needs his mother's breast milk. Now, he thirsts for blood."

"Mom, stop throwing such harsh words at me! That sounds like a challenge. And not the righteous one..." Bronius said in husky voice.

He jumped off the bed feeling offended to death. In a few big steps, he ran to the door. Then, he suddenly stopped and put both his hands over his head.

The mother was still gazing at him with an angry expression on her face. At any other time, seeing his mother so angry, Bronius would definitely get concerned. However, at this moment, he could not concentrate on her feelings.

"This is what my beloved son acts like when he takes off his mask... I had not slept many nights, and I had shed much sweat to make your life easier."

"For Christ's sake, stop moralizing me, mother! It's not my fault that I've been given a birth. Am I to blame that the nature has given me the ability to feel?! Because of that, now I go through the agony over this girl... Haven't you experienced the first love yourself? By now, you should know the taste of love. We are all alike! I received those tender feelings with your breast milk in my childhood. Yes, I am grown-up now, but this is not true that I thirst for blood or that I have turned in to some dreadful dragon that feeds off innocent souls."

"Bronius let me tell you... You would experience even more suffering if you seduced her or dishonored her veil of virginity."

The mother appeared to be regaining her balance. She almost completely calmed down, and she again sat down onto the edge of the bed.

"Mom, I don't understand what you want from me. Why are you saying things like that? What is the point of all this rhetoric? And what this has to do with Ema?! This is not my fault that I fell in love with her... I love this girl with all my heard, with all my soul, and with all my being! The problem is that she does not love me. This is not easy for me to deal with at the moment. On top of that, you came here to blame me for nothing! What have I done wrong?! Perhaps my only fault is that you have given me a heart that radiates humanly feelings..."

Bronius walked to the mother sitting on his bed, fell on his knees, and with tears in his eyes continued, "Take my heart and tell it what it must feel from now on... I am too weak-willed, and I can't help but try to tame Ema... I have to admit that I love her; I can't help it... You've given me my heart, and you can take it away from me. Even after that, she would remain in my soul forever. Both you and her can do with me whatever you wish. The only thing I would like to say, mom, is that you should have not treated Ema so harshly this morning. Practically, you were the one who turned her away. She liked being with us here. She was able to rest in our house, but you ignored her this morning, and she got offended. I think she won't come to stay with us anymore... If I had foreseen that happening, I would have left to Vilnius. Then, she could stay in our house. Have you noticed how fragile she is? She can't handle difficult earthwork. You are a very strong woman both physically and spiritually. In addition, you are used to the farm work, but don't think that everyone is the same way."

"Son, forgive me for accusing you falsely," mother laid Bronius's head in her lap and started gently stroking his hair. "I was terribly afraid you could seduce this girl and, then, leave her... I didn't want anything bad to happen right in our home. Therefore, I was determined to prevent it. My fear made me worry not only because of your future, but also because of her future as well. So, I dropped a hint to her this morning... Apparently, she also loves you. Sensing that, I was afraid that you could take advantage of her weakness. I did not believe you could resist your feelings. I felt sorry for the girl, so I decided to scare her off... In spite of that, I like her. Moreover, I think you are suited for each other, like a pair of shoes. Therefore, I'd be very happy if you loved her as deeply as she loves you. Do you know her parents' occupation? I can tell she is a city girl, since no such delicate girls could be found in our vicinity. Local girls are muscular and exhilarating with health."

"I don't know where her parents work. I only know that they live in Vilnius. It appears they are highly cultured people. Once, I heard Ema's conversation with her girlfriends. They wanted to celebrate some occasion, and they asked Ema to let them use her room at her parents' flat. Probably they have a big flat. Nevertheless, she refused, since her father had been working on some translation at that time, and she did not want to interfere. That implied to me he is an educated person. As about Ema, I can only tell that I used to see her almost every day at the university. Occasionally, we talked. I know she is not seeing anyone; lately she hasn't even been going to the dances. She had told me once that she hates me... That's all I know about her..."

"You can believe your mother, the old crow; I have much more experience in life than you do. Once upon a time, I also was young like Ema. Therefore, I can tell just by observing her behavior that she loves you. I have no doubt about it! I just want to ask you one thing - don't get tempted to disgrace her virginity prematurely. Loving you, she could hardly resist the temptation herself. Don't become a bad, dark shadow in her life. Before between two people can be anything else, they have to be friends first and always! Ema should find in you a loving soul and a source of comfort. For now, quit tormenting yourself, because she loves you dearly, and she will come to you... Well, son, get up now," saying this, the mother kissed him on the back of his head and rose up herself.

"No, mother, she won't come... I know this for sure."

"Well, you don't need to come to such conclusions in advance. We shall see what we shall see! Then, you will admit yourself that I was right. It seems to me, you should get back down to Earth from your Elysium. Better yet, go and heat up a bathhouse. After all, today is Saturday. We must wash off all the mud that our bodies have "encrusted" with during the last week's hard work. In a meanwhile, I'll go to the meadow and shake a few remaining stacks of the dry grass. It should make another cart or two of hay for us."

"Mom, you better do your chores at home; I will shake the hay myself, and, then, I'll heat the bath too."

Feeling relieved, Bronius walked out to the field, where he started loosening the remaining hay. Upon coming home, he ate early lunch and went to the bathhouse, where he filled up the stove with the firewood and lighted it up.

Then, he took a pitchfork again and walked back to the field. Only this time, he loaded the already turned over hay into the cart.

In about a couple of hours, the mother came to help him, also. This way, the last hay was stacked up high into the wooden cart. Finally, the cart of hay rocking from one side to the other was towed away by the horse to the barn. Only a flat open field with monotonously humming bees in it was left behind them.

Bronius helped the mother turn out the hay and stack it under the roof. The last job of that year hay harvest was accomplished, and Bronius, tired but happy, walked to the bathhouse.

However, the mother's chores had not been over yet. She unharnessed the horse. Then, sitting on his back, she rode off to a pasture.

When Bronius walked in to the bathhouse, the fire in the stove had been nearly died out. He again filled the stove with the wood and firmly whiffed live coals.

After that, the dry logs quickly flared up. Thick smoke started wreathing into all directions and out of the bathhouse. Soon, Bronius had to run outside himself.

He walked onto the footbridge, sat down on the edge of it, and dipped his both feet into the cool water.

Meanwhile, the mother tied up the horse to the tree, where the animal started nibbling grass. She herself walked to Adutiskis on foot.

When in the village, she did not need to inquire where students had been staying. She had already been there a few days ago. Therefore, she knew where the girls were staying.

She walked right into a big shabby wooden building. After passing a long, dusty corridor, she knocked on the only door there, at the very end of the corridor.

There was no answer. The mother waited a few seconds, and she pressed down the door handle. The first thing that caught her eyes was numerous rows of metal narrow beds placed in the middle of an enormously huge room. Everywhere around, there were students sitting on the chairs lined along the walls. They looked dirty and tired. Apparently, they had just come from the fields.

Ema, seeing this strict woman so suddenly sprung up in the doorway, began trembling with fear.

The mother looked around and noticed Ema. She approached the girl, took her by the hand, and softly said, "Come with me, Ema."

Ema could not find strength to resist this strong-willed woman. She rose up obediently and walked with her.

Immediately, out of the blue, Alfa shot up from somewhere in the middle of the room and blocked their way. Ema's entire slim figure began quivering again. He had discovered her disappearing from the collective farm two evenings in a row now, and he warned her not to leave again.

"Let her go! She can't leave these premises!"

"Please, don't give me any orders!" Bronius's mother paid him back angrily.

"That's right! It is an order! I am responsible for this work crew, and everybody must listen to me."

"I won't listen to you. Your responsibility is to help farmers gather harvest during the summer months but not to act like some grand chief. You are too young to reproach me so impudently. As about Ema, she comes to work on a daily basis. Right?! However, after work, she has right to spend a night at my house. She is my relative. From now on, she will stay in my house every single night. I don't care if you like it or not. Now, get out of my way, or I'll tread you underfoot like a warm."

Ema's little, delicate fingers just crackled while being squeezed in the woman's firm hand, callous from hard work.

"I'm telling you - let Ema go! Please, leave!"

His impertinent behavior made the mother very angry. She did not know in what way Ema had been associated with this rude guy standing in front of them his chest forward, but she didn't even want to know that. Moreover, there was no way for her to retreat now.

The most important thing to the mother was to know if Ema loved her son. After learning that Bronius was in love with Ema, the mother considered it to be a good reason to fight for their happiness.

Since Alfa did not step aside, she pushed him away with all her might herself. After receiving the unexpected blow, he lost his control; he involuntarily made a few steps backwards and fell on one of the beds standing behind him. If not for the bed, he would had fallen all his length onto the wooden floor. The students were standing around and observing the entire scene.

"This is called violence..." snorted Alfa while getting up with difficulty.

"Then you can go and complain about me to your authorities. However, I want you to know that if you bar Ema's way to my house once more, then I will complain about you! I can turn you to an office of the university. If that's not enough, then I will go higher. Do you understand that?! Now, get out of my sight!"

Both Ema and the mother walked out of this big ugly room with dirty opaque windows.

After they got outside, the mother still did not release Ema's hand as if being afraid that she could escape from her.

"Ema, forgive me please for this incident. I don't know myself how it has happened."

"That's okay, mistress. I am not angry with you; I don't have any reason to be mad at you. Quite the reverse, I am very grateful for everything you have done for me. You don't have to apologize for anything."

Finally, when both of them were walking on the road away from Adutiskis, the woman released Ema's hand. There was nothing to be afraid of. Bronius's mother decided now was a perfect time to talk from the heart with this girl.

Therefore, she said, "Ema, could you frankly answer a few of my questions?"

"Sure, mistress."

"Don't call me mistress, please… Such salutation does not suite me, the person from the village. Ema, I don't want to trouble you, but I really need to have an open and honest talk with you. Bronius and I already discussed this subject. Therefore, I know his view. Now, I would also like to hear your opinion on this matter. I'm asking you to be sincere with me. Would you share your thoughts about your personal matters that affect my son as well? If you don't wish talking about that, I won't force you."

"I will, miss…" stopped short Ema without finishing her sentence.

"Ema, do you love Bronius?"

Ema did not expect hearing such straightforward question. She got so lost that she even ceased walking. Turning red on her face, she lowered her eyes to the ground. However, soon, she contained herself after experiencing the unexpected turn of their conversation and glanced at her strict interlocutress, who had her penetrating look fixed on Ema.

The mother's stare was hard for Ema to bear. The tension was hanging in the air as if between some rabbit and a python.

"Okay, you don't have to answer my question. I can answer it myself for you. Yes, you do love him…"

Now, Ema was confused even more. She threw herself to the side as if trying to get free from a mouth of a monster. It seemed to her as if the mother was drilling her with her fiery eyes like some predatory dragon wishing to destroy her. Ema could no longer withstand the tension.

She was ready to turn around and run back to the collective farm, but the mother held her back, "Ema, you can't go back there!"

The girl knew well that the mother was right. She took a few steps toward the woman submissively. Now, she was standing her arms hanging down next to her sides, looking helpless.

"You don't have to respond to my questions. Everything is clear to me already. I'm asking just because I thought we already agreed on having our open talk."

Ema still did not say anything.

Then, mother continued, "I can tell that you are a faint-hearted person. Because of your lack of firmness, you will find it difficult coping with calamities in your life. You won't be able to defend yourself from the hard blows. You could even become a victim of a saucy guy like the one who blocked our way out of the collective farm building today. Moreover, through your weakness, you could perhaps marry a person you don't really love. You might lose the one and only, the real beloved man of yours just because of your lack of courage. Both Bronius and you are equally idle, and this kind of behavior can quickly ruin the love that unites you both. I am disappointed just by watching you so easily burying your love..."

"I will answer your question. Let me gather my thoughts and collect myself... please. I was going to tell this to Bronius yesterday myself. But he didn't take my efforts seriously. My opinion about him probably does not interest him because he has not asked me about it even once. Meanwhile, the rude guy you have just met today at the collective farm does not retreat from me a step. However, his love seems somewhat trite to me. I have nothing to say to him... As about Bronius, I would like talking to him. Only he doesn't wish to listen to me..."

"Then you can tell that to me. I will hear you out..."

Ema again glanced at her interlocutress's face. Casting down her eyes, she quietly said in a hollow voice, "I love..." The girl briefly lapsed into silence.

Then, an entire flow of words poured out of her lips. It seemed as if that one word, which had come out of her mouth with such difficulty, at last, gave a start to the open, free conversation.

"No, take it back! I not only love him; I'm crazy about him..." holding her interlocked hands on her chest, she cast her pleading look at the mother. "I even don't know how to put that in to words... I love him with all my heart, all my mind, and with all my might..."

The girl fell silent.

"That was exactly what I wanted to hear... I don't have any more questions for you. I want you to know that Bronius has exactly the same feelings about you... Your love for each other is beautiful. You have nothing to be ashamed of; others could only envy the love like yours... You should cherish those feelings until your old age."

Both the mother and Ema walked talking until they reached the homestead. The mother asked her to wait inside the house until her return.

Meanwhile, the mother walked to the bathhouse. Bronius, had already finished his bathing and he was cleaning after himself.

The mother asked, "Could you please bring me an empty glass from the house? I want to get a drink of water out of the well."

"There is a glass over there, on the table in the yard. It's clean, you can use it."

"Bring me one more, please. I will pour some water to you, too."

"Mom, I'm not thirsty. There are also at least four glasses on the windowsill in the bathhouse."

"You used them to drink kvass; they are all dirty. Don't be lazy; bring me a glass please."

"Okay, I will."

Bronius was utterly surprised, when he saw Ema sitting at the table and smiling at him... Shortly after, the mother walked inside.

"Well, who was right? You said she wouldn't come here... Do you remember what my answer was then? I said to you that if she loves you, she will come. And here she is..."

"Mom, don't make Ema blush. Maybe she doesn't want to know we were talking about her..."

The mother quickly removed herself leaving them alone. She didn't want to interfere. Hanging about in the yard for a few minutes, the woman could not find any immediate, pressing chores, and she came back inside.

There, she saw both Bronius and Ema sitting in the same exact poses she had seen them before she'd left.

"Why are you acting as if you were caught doing something wrong? Looks like you are not happy about this meeting..."

"Don't say that, mom."

"Bronius, go and heat up a bathhouse for our guest. Ema also needs to take a bath. After working in the fields, she probably has become covered with dust."

"What?" asked the guy as if he was woken up from the torpidity.

"I'm telling you, Bronius, go get the bathhouse ready."

"Mother, the bath stove is still hot. You can take a bath right now."

The woman covered the grandmother's shoulders with a big woollen wrap and took her along with Ema out to the bathhouse.

The girl walked next to the two women, one of which was so old that she could hardly move herself. Luckily, Bronius's mother was holding the grandma. As Bronius had rightly pointed out yesterday, the mother could be very gentle. Ema happily walked along them and, in her heart, she quietly admired Bronius's family.

A perfect order reigned in the bathhouse. Everything around, was squeaky clean. Even the small entrance-room had been nicely polished. In addition, there were some fresh straws stretched out under a sheet for them to lie and recover after whipping with a brushwood in the hot steam bath.

The mother asked, "Ema, would you like me to give you a bath just the way they did in old days traditionally?"

"Sure!" enthusiastically agreed the girl.

"Then, let's get to work!"

The mother poured a big bowl full of water and asked Ema to wet her entire body. Meanwhile, she poured water on the grandma and soaped her skin with a sponge.

Then, Ema's turn came, and the mother soaped her entire body from her head to her toes. The mother asked the girl to lie down onto a wooden bench that had been covered with a big linen sheet. The woman carefully poured water onto big, hot stones. Instantly, loud fizzle was heard, and clouds made of steam dispersed into all directions. Quickly after, the air around was filled with heat.

Ema found it difficult to breath this hot wave of air coming towards her, and she lifted her head.

"Be patient, I will give you a quick brushwood bath."

Mother vigorously but gently whipped her body with the brushwood. Ema's skin, while burning in the heat, now, was also starting to itch. Woman continued birching her while sometimes rubbing her soft skin and turning her body from one side to the other.

Thus, she whipped Ema's entire body from her head to her feet. Wiping away with her palm wet leaves that adhered to the girl's skin together with foam of the soap already turned gray, the mother pulled the large bowl with the water closer towards both of them. She carefully washed Ema's body with the clean water. The traditional ancient bathing procedure was over, and Ema was allowed to get up.

"Now, go to the front-room and lie down for a few minutes onto the straw mattress. There, you'll cool down quickly. Now, I'll birch and bathe myself."

When Ema got up off the bench, it was impossible not to admire her healthy, beautiful body. Youth itself, mixed with milk and roses, was spurting out of her. Mother could not resist a temptation, and she gently slapped the girl on her round pink back. She said, "Don't think of getting into the river right away, or you will get pneumonia!"

Pouring more water onto the rocks, the woman dipped her besom, made of the branches of a birch tree, into the water and began hitting herself on the back. Soon, her body turned deep red. It appeared as if a small stream of blood could squirt out if someone gave a scratch on her skin with a needle. Such muscular and healthy was her body.

After opening the door all the way to the front room, the mother was ready to take a swim in the river in order to cool herself down. However, she stopped in the doorway puzzled. She saw Ema lying on the straw bed her face hidden into the blanket. The first thought that came to the woman's head was that she probably had not been feeling well after the bath.

The mother bent down to check on the girl. She asked, "How do you feel, dear? Lift up your head and you should start feeling better right away."

When she looked at Ema, she noticed tears in her eyes.

"Good Lord! What has happened to you? Have you got overheated? You aren't used to this kind of bathing, are you?"

Kneeling down on her knees, the mother started stroking her hair. Ema sat down in the bed and looked at the woman with her reddened from tears eyes. She said in a sorrowful voice, "You washed me so well, and I did not even thank you. I feel bad because I had been stupid enough to talk down about you to Bronius. Now, I would like to apologize you for that. I feel very thankful to you and I have no words to express my gratitude for everything you have done for me."

"You were beginning to frighten me, honey. I thought the bath made you sick."

She sat down next to Ema and embraced her through her shoulders. For a while, she was calming the girl down by talking gently to her and calling her nice names. Ema was ashamed that she had been so fearful of this kind-hearted woman and that she'd dared to blurt out about it to Bronius.

As soon as Ema got back to herself, the mother rose up. Her body was still hot after the bath like a big piece of meat just pulled out of a pot of soup.

"I'll go and dive into the cold water."

"Aren't you afraid getting pneumonia?"

"Over the years, I have made myself fit. Therefore, I'm not afraid of diseases. They are afraid of me."

She walked out the bathhouse door and got on to the footbridge. With no hesitation, she jumped in to the cold water.

When the three women returned home, Bronius was nowhere to be found. The mother said that time to make supper had come and asked Ema to find Bronius. She was going to make him pick some vegetables in their garden.

First, Ema went to the storeroom and knocked on its door. There was no answer, and she timidly opened the door herself. He wasn't there.

Then, Ema headed to the orchard, where she found Bronius sitting on their bench.

The mother had not been in time to prepare supper; she wanted to feed animals first. She always started with the pigs. The poor things were hungry and were already shrieking so loudly that it could be heard inside the house.

Bronius helped the mother to clean up. Then, he went to the garden and gathered a bunch of tall beet leaves that he chopped finely along with boiled potatoes. He poured some rye flour over the vegetables and added some warm water over the top of the mixture. The feed was now ready.

Bronius filled up two buckets full with the hogwash and carried them to the animals.

The pigs received their food shrieking as if they were already being slaughtered. The animals rushed to the stall wall. They climbed with their forefeet onto the top board nailed horizontally.

Bronius snapped a few of the pigs onto their backs with a willow twig that had been kept leaning on to the wall solely for the purpose of the quieting those fidgets down.

Then, he walked back into the house, where he made another bucket of swill for two little piglets as well. Only this time, he poured milk instead of the water over the potatoes.

Meanwhile, a shepherd drove cows home from the field, and an entire yard picked up a smell of milk.

Bronius had to supply some water to the cows also. The red-haired animals were thirsty. Each of them drank two full buckets of water.

After that, the mother milked the cows filling up a full bucket of the frothy milk. Then, she penned the cows into a cattle-shed.

Now, there were not only the cows mooing in the shed. The sheep was bleating there also.

However, soon, all the animals calmed down. Being satisfied, they started drowsing. Just roosting hens were still quietly clucking as if talking among themselves.

Outside, dusk was beginning to settle in, and all the living things finally quieted down, but not the people. At home, the family gathered at the table loaded with food. In addition, two bottles of homemade wine were brought in.

The supper began. Ema was seated at the table. The mother covered her shoulders with a woollen shawl so that the girl could not catch cold after the bath. Above the table, a kerosene lamp was hanging and brightly lighting up the earthly blessings on the table and an entire room, too.

The grandma was brought in and seated next to Bronius. The young shepherd was sitting next to the mother's seat that had still been empty. Everybody was very hungry and impatiently looked forward to the hostess herself join the rest of them.

However, she still kept carrying dishes and placing them onto the table. Finally, the mother sat down. She filled cups with the delicious homemade drink and encouraged, "Well, let's raise the glasses to our health."

The shepherd was the first to pick up his wine glass. Poor boy rarely had an opportunity treating himself to this kind of food, because guests rarely came to Adomaitis's house.

True, he had been a herdsman in another family before. However, during a feast or if some guest dropped in there, a host with a hostess did not bother to invite him to the table.

Adomaitiene, though, always seated her shepherd at their family table allowing him to eat together with them. In return, he always sought to give thanks back to the hostess doing his utmost by diligently fulfilling her requirements regarding the animal care.

The mother glanced at the shepherd and smiled. The boy only now noticing he was the first to pick up his wine glass. He blushed with shame and sat it back onto the table.

Nevertheless, the mother encouraged him, "Why, Algiukas, have you put the glass down? Once you've raised it, you can only put it down after it's empty. Behave like a real man."

After another incitement to have a drink, everybody lifted their glasses. Even the grandmother kept her pace with the rest of them. Emptying half of her glass, the old woman placed it down with her trembling hand.

It was a long, nice diner, and everyone's mood was very uplifting. However, the shepherd seemed to be the happiest among them all, since for the first time in his life, he was able to sit at the same table with the guest of the family.

Only well after dark, the dinner ended. Even then, nobody rose up; they remained sitting on their chairs while talking about their daily affairs.

Bronius was the only one wishing the talks would run out soon, so that Ema and him finally could have some time alone.

Therefore, as soon as the mother took the granny to bed, he seized the opportunity and invited the girl to leave, "Ema, let's go for a walk in the orchard. It would be nice to have a breath of fresh air before sleep. You won't have such opportunity when you are back in Vilnius."

"Oh no, I will not let you go outside," objected the mother when she overheard their conversation after walking back into the room. "After the bath, you can catch cold. Now, the best thing would be to go to sleep, especially because we have had some wine. Tomorrow, you will have the whole day for yourself. Then, you'll be able to associate with each other to your hearts' content. However, now, it is better to go to sleep. The best medicine after the bath is bed! Believe me, I've had many years of experience in this area."

"Okay, mom. We probably should go to bed, so that we don't get ill tomorrow."

Soon, the mother picked up the remaining food off the table. Everyone left. Only the shepherd did not want to leave the table. In spite of not participating in the family members' conversation, he listened to everybody's talking with the utmost interest. Now, the mother had to make repeated requests in order to send him to bed.

Bronius went to his storeroom. The night finally landed in the homestead putting to sleep its dwellers. Ema was lying in bed trying to drive the sleep away. She was remembering the wonderful events of the day. True, in the morning, she had suffered the unpleasant incident at the collective farm, but the rest of the day was truly remarkable! Now, she was reliving in her head every moment and every little detail of the day. Nevertheless, the sleep kept creeping up on her, and happy Ema fell sound asleep.

She slept so well that she did not even dream anything. The first thing she saw when she opened her eyes in the morning was sunrays streaming into the room. They were playing cheerfully on the nicely washed wooden floor that had been painted dark brown. A pleasant smell of cooking food was felt in the room. It gave her an appetite, but she did not dare to get up. Therefore, she continued lying lazily and enjoying clean bedding.

Again, she closed her eyes and continued dozing. Through the thin walls made out of boards that had been glued over with colored paper, she could hear even faintest rustling.

The mother was rattling dishes in the kitchen. After a few minutes, she could hear a sound of her heavy steps. Then, a voice of the grandma joined her. A little later, Bronius walked in to the kitchen. His nice manly voice made Ema's heart beat faster.

Secretly she wished that he came in to her room to wake her up. Her expectation did not disappoint her. In a few minutes, she heard his mother say, "Bronius maybe you should go and wake Ema up. The girl has overslept. People always are in sweet sleep after a bath. Therefore, it's not surprising that her young constitution needs to have good rest also. However, it's time for her to wake up. Later on, she will be able to take a nap through most intense heat of the day. Go, Bronius, don't delay."

"Maybe, mom, we shouldn't wake her up. Let her sleep to her heart's content. Today is Sunday. No need to hurry anywhere."

"I understand, but breakfast is almost ready, and it doesn't taste good when it's cold."

"Okay, if you say so."

Without any more excuses, Bronius left the kitchen. He gently knocked a few times on the door of the room where Ema was lying. However, she did not answer. She pretended to be sleeping...

He knocked again. Only this time, he did it louder. She still did not answer. Ema, with her eyes closed, did not give a stir. She was waiting for Bronius, the guy who would make her heart beat faster every time she saw him, to come in.

Ema heard a squeak of the carefully tilted door. She opened slightly her one eye and saw Bronius stealing into the room on his tiptoes.

He approached the bed. Leaning forward, he was looking at her for a while. Ema held her breath and waited until he would shake her by her shoulder.

Instead, she felt a gentle tickling on her forehead. She realized that Bronius was tousling her hair. However, she decided not to show him she was awake.

Then, she felt a very tender touch over a quilt and heard soft whispering. Nevertheless, Ema continued to lie motionless. Only after a third try, she lazily cracked open her eyelids. Feigning she was startled to see him walk in unexpectedly, Ema pulled the blanket over her head.

Bronius said, "Ema, forgive me please for breaking into your room while you were sleeping. My mother sent me to wake you up. She has already fixed us breakfast."

Ema slowly pulled off the blanket of her head and looked at Bronius gratefully. She uttered in a sleepy voice, "I'm sorry I'm still in bed. After yesterday's bath, I slept like killed. It seems as if the first time in my life, I had such good night's rest. I didn't even have any dreams."

As soon as Bronius left the room, Ema got out of bed and quickly dressed.

Bronius poured half of a bowl of water outside, brought out a bar of soap, and called Ema, "Ema, you can wash your face. Cold water will wake you up right away. After the breakfast, we could go for a walk in the forest or I could show you our beautiful Blessed Mary Virgin Skaplierine's Church. Another option we have is to harness a horse and go for a drive on the rural roads in our vicinity. Which one would you like to do?"

"Unfortunately, Bronius, I must go back to the collective farm."

"What are you going to do there?! I thought today is your day off."

"Don't you see what this new Soviet system is all about? Alfa conceived to turn Sundays into workdays at the collective farm. I think he is trying to show the new government how diligently activists from the university are willing to work for it."

"That's not right! Is it not enough to work six days per week?! Students who labor conscientiously could do all the work without sacrificing the Sundays. There should be at least one day a week for entertainment and rest."

"What can I do, Bronius, about this? I am their slave. Therefore, we all at the collective farm must fulfill their plans. However, I don't think we are going to work a full day today. Most likely, we will be done earlier than on any other regular workday."

Both of them came back to the house and found breakfast already steaming on the table. Ema ate it with relish and got ready to leave for work in Adutiskis.

Bronius again accompanied her there. They separated at the same place where the road had been overgrown with the thick bushes on its both sides. Passed that section of the dirt road, about two hundred meters further, there was a wooden sign "Adutiskis" on the left side of it.

Bronius knew Ema did not want anyone seeing them together. She had been afraid that Alfa's fury would prompt him to play some mean tricks.

Being afraid to be late for work, Ema separated with Bronius and hurried to the premises of the collective farm.

There, she found other girls already eating breakfast. A few hands started waving in the air; the girls were inviting Ema to join them at the table.

Since she had still been full after she'd eaten with Bronius's family, she could hardly think about the food.

After the breakfast, all the students with the scythes and rakes in their hands gathered in the field.

Ema noticed Alfa there, but he didn't greet her. Just by looking at his face, she could tell that he was trying to tame the anger. Even a thick, blue vein on the side of his neck was throbbing, and it appeared as if his rage could pour out at any moment now.

Ema was afraid of the unnecessary conflict flaring up right in front of the entire crew of the students.

A couple of hours passed by, and she was used to this kind of atmosphere. She began to justify herself in her mind by thinking that she'd done nothing wrong. Therefore, she thought, she had nothing to fear. Nevertheless, Ema tried staying in the same place where the biggest group of the other girls was working.

An enthusiasm of the students soon started dying out, since none of them wished to bake in the sun. There were no local farmers working in the fields besides them.

Local farmers opposed the new order that required them working on Sundays. All of them were Roman Catholics, and their religion did not allow them to work on the seventh day of the week. In spite of being occupied by the Russian government, the locals still dared to follow their old traditions. Customarily, they always went to church on Sundays, but not to work.

After lunch, the students were forced to get back to the field. However, again, their energy started running out less than an hour later. The sun was burning so ruthlessly, that a few of them got a headache.

Therefore, a few girls and boys were lying down under the bushes their rakes thrown to the sides,.

Even an ideology of the Young Communist League, which had been disseminated through books and hammered in all other possible ways into the students' heads, was not able to restore their lost strength in the midday heat.

They could no longer obey their Komsomol organizer Alfa's orders, either. It seemed he spent more time chasing lazy-bones students wondering in the field than he spent working. It was getting obvious that under these circumstances he himself got tired of his pointless enthusiasm. The situation was beginning to look funny. Moreover, it had not proved to be of any benefit to the farming.

In the early afternoon, the students with the rakes and scythes over their shoulders were already walking on the gravel road back to the town of Adutiskis. Alfa caught up with Ema and uttered in an angry manner without looking at her, "We are going to have an open meeting of members of the Young Communist League tonight. Everyone's participation is mandatory. We will be discussing how to improve our productivity."

"I work not any less that others do. You can't reproach me with negligence."

"I don't know that yet. It's not enough to praise yourself... We should ask what the other students think about your work. Your bragging about yourself is worth nothing!"

"I'm not trying to brag. Our team leader himself pointed out a few times that I am an exemplary worker. I hope you have also heard that from others. Of course, if there is nothing wrong with your hearing... Today, I have seen quite a few of you lying idly under the bushes during the most part of the day. You yourself invited me to lie down together. In spite of that, I continued working."

"The team leader most likely just joked around, and you already have drawn a conclusion that you are one of the best workers."

"Well, even if I'm not one of the best workers here, then I'm not the worst one, either. Please, don't chase after me trying to reproach me. I noticed that you had been seeking a chance to pick on me before, too. I work all day long just like any other student does. I would like to ask you not to disturb me at least after the work hours. I am in title to spend my leisure the way I want to. You are also free to do whatever you want; you can even walk on your head… I don't care what you do after work."

"Today, you can't go to your relatives; you must be at the mandatory meeting at the collective farm. In addition, you should join our Young Communist League as soon as possible and start taking an active part in it."

"I know better what course to take in my life. I don't need any consultants in this sphere. Any person matures for his decision-making himself. Nobody can force me joining any organization! Please, remember that I'm not going to join your league just because you want me to do that."

"If you intend to continue your studies at the University, you will have to join it…"

"Alfa, you won't achieve anything by intimidating me. I hope you are not a violent person…"

"Think as you please, but I would advise you to be smarter than that. At least, I mean well, and that is why I keep constantly treading on your feet… You just don't seem to understand that I am taking care of your future…"

"I would appreciate you more if you left me alone and let me worry about my future."

"Ema, time has come when you can't make it on your own. We, the members of the Komsomol, follow a slogan 'all for one, and one for all'. This is one of the principals of the present government, and we have to reconcile ourselves to its politics. Our government knows what to do, and ordinary people like you and me don't have right to weigh if it makes right or wrong decisions."

"If we are not allowed to think, then why are we even discussing this subject now?'

"Don't be whimsical, Ema. In any case, you'll have to join the Komsomol. You will have to throw all these silly fantasies out of your head; I will make sure you get on the right track…"

"Thank you for your concern! Looks like I no longer need a father and a mother. Just one little thing... I doubt in your abilities. You yourself can't make living out of your scholarship alone. How would you be able to help others?"

"I have only one year left to study. After that, I will be independent. Then, I could support not only myself, but you as well..."

"Well, looks like I still have a year to be under the guardianship of my parents... Therefore, you have no right to tell me what to do. I don't need the cavalier who can't manage his own life. Goodbye!"

Ema waved at Alfa and broke into a run. Without stopping once, she passed all her classmates and left everyone far behind. Thus, she was the first to reach Adutiskis.

Nobody was following her when she was walking fast on a dusty rural road Jakeliai village direction. The sky was blue, the sun was shining cheerfully, and a breeze was tousling gently bushes growing on both sides of the road.

Under their cover, Ema reached the other side of the Adutiskis town where a ditch overgrown with thick willow trees was going right across the road. As soon as she walked to this part of the gravel road, Bronius unexpectedly crawled out of his hiding place.

"Oh my God, Bronius, you've scared me!"

"Why are you running as if somebody has been chasing after you?"

"Nobody is chasing me, but there is no guaranty that it can't happen... I had to trick Alfa in order to run away from him. Even then, I was afraid he would soon realize I'd left and start running after me. Bronius, we should hurry because he might notice something. I don't want him to find out you have come here."

"If you say so; we can hasten."

Both of them started running down the road. Soon, they were far away from Adutiskis, where neither Alfa's eyes could see them nor his ears could hear them.

"Ema, let's eat first. Then, we could go for a walk in the forest. This morning, I found a beautiful place with many wild strawberries growing there. I wanted to gather some for you myself, but then, I decided to take you there instead. You'll have some rest after the hard work at the collective farm."

"I'm not too tired. However, I would love having a walk in the forest."

As soon as both of them sat down at the table, the mother brought supper. However, Ema still could not relax. She said, "I'm afraid of Alfa. He might have already followed me here. He can cause us only grief."

"Ema, this is just in your head…"

"Bronius, don't you know him by now? Anything can be expected from this person."

"I have known him for many years now, but I don't believe he would be running in the fields and looking for you."

"I think just the opposite. He managed to organize the workday on Sunday. In addition, he gathered all the students for the meeting after work the same work-Sunday. Therefore, I would not be surprised if he came here looking for me, too. Even now, for some reason, I have a bad feeling… I'll step outside to look."

"Wait, Ema. I'll go there myself and check."

Bronius got up from the table and walked out to the yard.

Upon returning he said, "Your prediction was right. I just saw Alfa with my own eyes. He is walking on our road. I'm sure he is coming here."

"I told you… Maybe I should hide myself?"

"Eat, Ema, and don't be afraid of anything. I will not allow anybody bossing us around in our own home! We'll see what he has to say…"

In about fifteen minutes, the steps could be heard on the porch. The mother, without waiting until this uninvited guest walks in to their house, rose up from the table and hurried out to the front door to meet Alfa herself. He had already been standing at the doorsteps of their house.

"I have come here looking for Ema," he said firmly without greeting the woman.

"Has anybody invited you to come here? I thought I had made myself clear to you yesterday in the morning…"

"I need to talk to Ema; I'm responsible for her."

"Get out of my house! Otherwise, you'll have to answer for your impudence."

"What do you mean?! Are you threatening me?"

"Understand the way you wish! Go away unfledged youth!"

"I'll have to complain about your behavior to the Chairman of the collective farm. You interfere with out students' work. They have been sent by Vilnius University to help the farmers."

"Complain to anybody you wish - even to the God Almighty Himself! I will report on you myself to the Chairman of our entire district! I will put it in writing that you came to my home to intimidate my family! Don't try getting inside by force or you'll leave from here with the bloody nose! And nobody will be able to accuse me for that."

"I'm not trying to get inside of your house by force. I'm asking you in a friendly manner to let me talk to Ema. A very important matter brought me into your home."

"I will ask Ema if she wants to talk with you…"

Soon, on the porch Ema showed up herself. She seemed to be lost; she looked at the Secretary of the Komsomol with the fear in her eyes.

"Ema, I would like talking with you face to face…" uttered upset Alfa.

"I don't want to talk to you. What do you want from me? Why have you come here; why don't you leave this family in peace? You should be ashamed of yourself for being such a nuisance."

"I've come to ask if you are coming to the collective farm meeting tonight."

"I'm not… I have nothing to do there! You can discuss your business without me."

"Your attendance is mandatory, because we'll be discussing your conduct as well."

"I have no idea why, but go ahead and discuss it without me," she turned around and left.

"Ema, wait. You will be sorry… I will remind you that!" shouted Alfa after her.

"Enough those threats already. The visit is over…" under her nose muttered Ema.

There was nothing else for Alfa left to do but to leave. Bronius with Ema also left the house and went to the forest that was not very far away from their homestead. They were walking slowly on the road and talking about the sudden appearance of Alfa, and after about half an hour, Bronius and Ema found a refuge in the forest.

"Ema, look how many wild strawberries are here!"

"Where? I don't see them," looking around through the scarce trees she asked.

"Don't look on the trees... Wild strawberries don't grow there. Look to the left on the ground behind that little ravine over there."

"Oh yes, I see one! And here is another one. Oh, look how many are in this spot!" Ema, overwhelmed with joy, pointed with her finger that direction.

They jumped over the small ditch and found themselves on a little fill of the soil, where they both squatted down and began picking the berries. There were so many of them. It seemed as if full grass around had been strewn with the red beads.

Those wild strawberries were very ripe, sweet, and utterly delicious. Ema by the handful kept putting the fragrant, beautiful berries into her mouth. She was fascinated to learn about them at the same time while picking. Earlier, she had thought that the wild strawberries, just like black currants, grow on bushes. However, here, they simply cuddled down to the ground, enveloped in the grasses. The dew had not even withered from some of the berries during the course of the day. They also felt cool and refreshing when in her mouth.

"Bronius, lets pick some berries for your mother. I have already eaten plenty of them."

"Sure. You pick for my mother, and I will pick for the grandma. Okay?"

"Great! But what are we going to pick them into?" Ema asked. "We have brought no dish with us."

"I have an idea, Ema! We'll pick them into my handkerchief, and then, we'll divide them at home."

Bronius tied up all four corners of his handkerchief into the knots. Thus, the nice basket was created. After an hour or so, it has been filled over its full measure with the berries.

There was still early in the evening, and they did not want to go home. Therefore, both of them walked a little longer in the forest. Only when the sun hung over the western horizon, Bronius and Ema came back home carrying the beautiful red berries with them.

Seeing the handkerchief-basket, the mother marveled at the big, ripe wild strawberries. She put a few of them in her mouth and took the rest to the grandmother. The grandma also tasted the wild strawberries and asked to give the rest of them to Bronius with Ema.

Bronius, refusing of the dainty, grabbed Ema's hand, and they both ran outside laughing.

Soon, they were at the river. The sun was getting ready to cross down over the horizon line.

"Ema, if you just knew how warm the water is! Would you like to take a swim in it?"

"I would, but I don't have a swimming suite. However, it's not a big loss, since it is not that warm late in the evenings."

Bronius said, "It always makes me wonder that, while it is cool on the bank, the water in the river is as warm as tea. Lets' get on to the footbridge and I'll show you."

Ema sat down on the edge of the wooden bridge and submerged her both legs into the water. Then, she began dangling them in the slow warm stream.

"You are right! The water is amazingly warm. It's too bad I don't have the swimming suite. Otherwise, I would definitely become tempted to take a swim."

"Swim, Ema! I will go to the orchard and wait for you there. Don't miss on such an opportunity! You won't regret it for sure! You'll remember this bathing forever."

"You are so good at persuading… You have talked me into that. I'm sure I will never forget your wonderful homeland! Nevertheless, I don't want to separate with you, and I don't want you to sit alone and bored in the orchard, either."

"Don't worry about me, Ema. I'll be very happy to know you are having fun. I come to this place every evening and do the same."

Without waiting for her to say anything, Bronius got up off the bridge, where he had been sitting next to her his legs also down in the water.

In a second, he was already standing on the bank.

Making sure nobody was watching, she promptly threw down her clothes, ran to the very end of the footbridge, and jumped in to the river.

The water in that place was reaching up to her armpits. Few meters away from her, wide leaves of the water lilies were floating on the surface. Ema was not afraid of the depth, since her father had taught her how to swim in her early childhood.

She was not in a hurry to swim further away from the bank. Instead, she was holding onto the board of the wooden bridge with her fingers. Ema submersed herself into the water all the way up to her neck, since she had no clothes on.

She stood for a few minutes looking around. Then, she uttered a cry, "Bronius, come here! I'm already in the water!"

"Swim, have fun Ema! I will not interfere!" shouted back Bronius.

"I want you swimming too! Come on! The water is so warm, like in the bathtub!"

Bronius did not need to be asked again. Immediately, he walked on to the bridge. He saw Ema smacking with her palm the surface of the water and screaming with joy her face looking up to the sky. She did not even notice when her white round shoulders emerged out of the water. Her tight breasts also appeared in the clear water. The shape of her body kept changing with every ripple on the top of the water.

Ashamed Bronius turned his reddened face away. He did not know what to do...

He turned his head away. However, he realized it wasn't nice talking with her this way. When Bronius looked at Ema again, she came out of the water even more.

Overwhelmed with the ecstasy of joy, she did not feel her nipples popping out of the water!

Bronius, trying to save the situation, sat down on the footbridge. Then, her view was even closer. He became utterly lost and could not say a word. Tiny drops of cold sweat appeared on his forehead.

"Bronius, why aren't you talking to me? Are you going to have a swim?"

"I don't know, Ema. I don't want to embarrass you..." Bronius, gasping for air, could hardly talk.

Ema swam to the bridge and grasped the edge of its wooden board with her fingers.

"Get in to the water!"

She pushed hard with her feet against a supporting pole of the bridge under the water and swam into the middle of the bay.

Bronius undressed and slipped in to the water that cooled off his passion right away. He immediately followed Ema who was already on the other side of the bay.

For a long time, they bathed there swimming back and forth. Ema did not want to get out of the water; it was so nice and warm.

Finally, Bronius succeeded in convincing her to get out of it. He looked away while she was dressing up. Soon, the two of them vanished into the darkness of the orchard.

Ema was walking her teeth chattering out of cold. She could feel the chill, especially right after coming out of the warm water. Bronius threw his jacket over Ema's shoulders and brought her home.

He did not turn on the light and asked her to get in to bed right away. Ema did not want to separate with Bronius, but the circumstances forced her to obey.

Next day after breakfast, he as usually accompanied Ema to Adutiskis. Then, he returned home and spent all day in the room writing a story. Despite the mother coming there and trying to talk him in to going by the river and doing his writing in the fresh air, Bronius remained unyielding. He knew well that as soon as he came outside, he would be admiring scenery instead of writing.

Bronius was determined to achieve his aim. He wanted to devote himself completely to his literary work that he had started years ago.

Thus, Bronius his head bent over the notebook sat until the mother came to invite him for lunch.

When the sun turned to the west side, he was very anxious to go back to Adutiskis meeting Ema. Upon reaching the town, he again got in to his hiding place and observed the road, where his dream girl was just about to show up. Lately, he had been thinking of her day and night.

This time, he did not have to stay long in the willow bushes. Soon, he recognized the slim Ema's figure quickly moving towards him.

She was also anxious to see the one who had not left her mind even for one minute during the day.

As soon as Ema passed the place where the bushes on both sides of the road were growing, she heard steps behind her. She looked back and saw Bronius. There was longing in her eyes, and a bright smile was playing in her lips.

"I knew I will meet you here. How long have you been waiting?" Ema asked.

"Not long, probably just half an hour. How was your day? Have you got tired at work?"

"No one got tired today, since we did not work at all until lunch. Instead, we had a meeting in the morning. During that meeting, we discussed yesterday's meeting... All the members were fighting like some baiting dogs. The weather today was so beautiful. I think we should had taken advantage of the sunny day. We could had work with all our might. Instead, we spent half of the day jabbering to no purpose. That kind of help does not do much good for the collective farm. Even farmers say that students don't take seriously their work at the collective farm; they make fun of farming. Even making us work on Sundays couldn't help with productivity."

"What did they decide to do about this situation at the end of the meeting?" Bronius asked.

"I'll tell you. So, we only wagered our tongues during all the meeting. One person blamed the other, and it seemed there was no end to it. However, the funniest thing was that everybody unanimously was against Alfa. A few students even attacked him like some angry dogs. Then, he kept blaming others in return. He accused me, too. However, after a few students stuck up for me, he had to leave me alone so that he could defend himself. The best part, though, was the culmination of the meeting. Namely, we decided that our work at the collective farm is over and, on Wednesday, we are all going home! All the students are sick of working at the collective farm. I think even the farmers themselves are tired of us. We are not used to do the agricultural work; we only cause a lot of noise in the village at night. And even while at work, we only trample down the fields. Bronius, you can't imagine how happy I am that I won't have to listen to Alfa's dithyrambs any more. Soon, I will be in my parents' quiet flat free to take a rest whenever I want to, free to read books, go to the movies, shows, and concerts. How wonderful! It feels as if I have not seen a movie for an eternity. I would like to dress up again or spend some time in a nice public park, or take a walk in Gediminas Boulevard. City people are more polite. Here, if the girls lie down, the boys without getting any permission crawl into our room through the windows and don't let us sleep. They are such jerks!"

"Ema, didn't you like at my mother's, too?" Bronius asked in a worried undertone.

"Oh no, Bronius. Your place is a paradise in comparison to the doss-house of the collective farm. I have never seen such a fine corner of the nature in my entire life. As far as the collective farm work goes, all the students voted against it unanimously. All my girlfriends are waiting for the coming Wednesday like for some salvation. As about me personally, Alfa makes me nervous the most, and that is the main reason why I would like to break away from the collective farm as soon as possible."

"Then, you don't have to wait for very long... Only one day left which means that you only have to suffer through tomorrow. After that, there is your Wednesday."

Thus, having a chat they came home. It was still an early evening, and Bronius suggested, "Ema I promised to show you my library. Would you like to look at it now? We still have some time before the mother makes supper."

"I would love to," happily agreed Ema. "I love books, and I love people who love books... As a rule, they themselves have many books. They distinguish themselves from the rest of us by having broad views on life. As a rule of thumb, it is easier to associate with them, too, since they are more cultured."

Bronius was the first to walk up to the door that he, like a real gentleman, opened for Ema. In the cozy room, there were shelves covering the entire wall from the ceiling to the floor and through the whole length of the wall. There were many books standing and, in some places, laying stacked in piles on those shelves. In addition, Ema could see a great number of newspapers, magazines, notebooks, and some papers rolled into tubes.

Next to the window, a small round table covered with a vinyl tablecloth was standing. A little bottle of dark ink with a penholder was sitting on it. In the corner of the room, there was a carefully made single bed with a steel metal frame on the front and back of it.

Bronius pointed at the opened notebook laying on the table where he had been writing the story all day long, and he said, "Now you can see what the so called village storeroom library looks like. My father left me most of these books and manuscripts. He, in turn, had inherited them from my grandfather, his father. I am proud to say that my grandfather was the most enlightened person in the vicinity during his time. He could not only read, but he had also been the only one literate person in his entire village."

"You are lucky to have had such a wonderful grandfather," Ema said.

"Neighbors had been often coming to him. Someone needed his help writing a petition, the other person - a complaint or a letter. People in the village had called him 'our village teacher'. My grandma told me that he had also taught grammar to children in the village during the times of the Czar. My father loved books. He, too, added a great number of new books to this library. I tried to do the same after I'd received it from him. In this room, you can see the collection of the books of the three generations."

"I have never expected that someone in the village could have so many books! Not every educated person living in the city could boast about such a big personal library," said amazed Ema.

"Here is a chronicle that my grandfather had written. Do you want to look at it? It's very interesting. Here, many important events of his time have been depicted in detail. They all had happened before the year 1865. Around that time, my grandpa had started writing this chronicle. When he died, my father carried on with his work, and after my father was arrested, I started adding my notes in there. However, when I was expelled from the University, I became so apathetic that I had no desire to do anything. Now, I'm ashamed to admit that I've forgotten about this family relic all together. The last time I held this chronicle in my hands, was a few years ago. Then, I described in writing my father's arrest. In addition, I wrote about the circumstances of the other people I had known who had disappeared, too. I still have quite a few things that I would like to share with others."

Ema listened to him fascinated.

"Now, you are serving as my witness…" Bronius raised his right hand and with a serious expression on his face continued, "I swear I will continue working on this chronicle that my grandfather had started until I am able to hold a pen in my hand. As you can see, my grandpa had made the very first note in the year 1864. Further, he very comprehensively portrayed an uprising of the 1863. His tale about a late Governor of Vilnius by the surname Muravjovas has been stuck in my memory. The man had been so inhumanly brutal that residents of the city had named him "the little czar-blood-sucker". Here are forty-three notebooks with one hundred pages in each of them. Therefore, every notebook has no more and no less than fifty sheets filled in full. My grandfather had written the twenty-eight of them, my father - fourteen, and I wrote only one. However, even this one is still not completed. Shame on me! However, I promise to write some more in it about most important events from my past even before this vacation is over. Maybe this enables me to finish writing the one and only my notebook so far. I have already made a list of some dates and events in order not to forget anything that is worth mentioning. Ema, would you like to look through some of these notebooks now?"

"I would love to. I just don't want to trouble you unwrapping them. Some of them are tied together so nicely."

"If you wish to take a peep inside, I can unwrap them. That won't take much time."

Bronius undid the knot of the string that the notebooks have been wrapped with and took the first one off the top. It was all yellow because of its old age. The cover page was so faded that it was difficult to even recognize what color it had been in the first place.

Ema carefully was holding in her hands this precious relic of Bronius's family. Upon opening the cover of the notebook, she saw a neatly written year in a large print and considerably discolored ink. The corners of the cover have become very fray. Then, the beautiful handwriting in black ink inside caught her attention.

"Ema, would you like me to read you a little bit from this notebook? My grandfather wrote here in Dzukai dialect, but I can translate it to you as I go."

"I would love to hear what your grandparents' language sounded in olden times. However, if it's difficult to understanding it, then go ahead and translate it for me."

Bronius started reading the very first page, "It was the year of one thousand eight hundred sixty three, when an entire land of the country of Lithuania had been soaked with blood of its people who had wished to cast off the yoke of the slavery. People have been pouring in to churches for many weeks now. Somebody would get inside of the priest's pulpit and speak so nicely in front of the crowd that many folks would fall into tears while listening to the speech. Often, the speaker would ask people to join rebels or, at least, help them in any way they could. In addition, during days of bazaar, such speakers often jumped onto carts or carriages and begged for help. They told the crowd about Russian officials' ways of exploiting them. Meanwhile, a few men walked around in the market collecting donations for support of insurgents. Some folks at the bazaar were throwing money into the hats used for the collection of it. One person would throw in a copper coin, the other - even a golden ruble. The coins kept clanking, while the speaker was making his heartbreaking speech. Threats of Russians getting it hot were felt in the air. The speaker accused them of drinking and eating poor locals' food. Indeed, they have been thriving on hard work of the masses. However, the folks were getting nothing in return for their pains; they have encountered only hardship and misery. Our local people have been working so hard that they had no time to take a breath. As soon as some Russian officer showed up in the market place, the speaker instantly disappeared from the cart without even finishing his emotional speech. It was unclear where the individuals collecting the money vanished after him. Without being able to get more donations, they jogged away and hid themselves in the crowd like some scared pups. During regular days of the week, when there was no church and no bazaar, the agitators went straight to huts of ordinary people. In their homes, they told the same sad stories how Russians have been exploiting them…"

"How interesting! I just can't tear myself away. Your grandfather portrayed that in such simple words, but at the same time, we are able to learn some history about our native land. I wish I could read all these notebooks from the start till the end. Probably, I would find out more truth through reading them then I would from reading some school history textbooks... Many authors try to pull their books as if on their own boot-tree. However, your grandfather wrote this story only for himself and his family which means that this source is trusted, and we should accept it as such. There is no doubt in my mind it is as pure as a crystal!"

Ema took another notebook and started turning one page after anoher. Then, she topped and began avidly reading. She could not help it but admire every sentence in it.

"Ema, you've got so absorbed into this chronicle... What is it about?"

"It's so interesting! I can't stop reading. I would like to read all your notebooks. Now, I feel bad that I have to leave... Even if I wanted, I would not be able to look through all of your writings in one evening. I would love to get acquainted with the rest of the books in your remarkable library."

"If you decided to look through every manuscript and every book, then even a month of time would not be enough for that. I still haven't showed you essays that I had written during my school years. I have ten of them. Would you like to look at those too? That would give you a chance to get acquainted with my literary style."

"Did you write essays, also? Of course, I would like to learn your style."

"I wrote essays while attending the gymnasium. However, now, I started writing a story. If you would like, I can show you my work."

"Okay, but aren't you afraid of criticism? However, I heard that the constructive criticism can help the writers, too. It enables them to strive for perfection."

"Ema, I don't consider myself to be a writer. I write only during my leisure so that I wouldn't idle my time away. Therefore, when I finish this story, I will write a second one and the third..."

"I think you have talent for writing! Show me those essays."

Bronius rummaged between the notebooks in the pile that had been neatly stacked on the top shelf, and he pulled out one notebook. First, he turned over several its pages himself and, then, he handed the notebook to Ema.

"You can look through this one. I think this writing is pretty good."

Ema put the chronicle aside and, now, she started reading the notebook. Bronius sat down next to her at the small table and waited impatiently to hear her opinion.

Ema continued reading. He was anxious to find out what impression the creative work of his green youth made on her so far. However, Ema kept reading without even lifting her head.

At last, Bronius lost his patience and asked, ""Well, what is your opinion about my writing style, or maybe you just want to continue reading the stuff I wrote there?"

"Bronius, wait a little bit; have patience. I have barely come to the middle of it. When I'm done reading it, I will get an idea of your style, and then, I'll give you my opinion."

"Keep reading. I will not interfere."

Ema, again, got absorbed into the notebook, and Bronius started looking through another notebook. From time to time, he would glance at Ema sitting by his side. He was paying particular attention to the expression of her face. He knew well it would give him the best clue of her impression about his writing.

Despite observing her face, he had difficulty understanding what thoughts had been going through Ema's mind. When only a few pages were left to read, the mother unexpectedly opened the door and called both of them to come eat supper.

In a big hurry, Ema finished reading. She put the notebook on the table and still did not say a word.

"Well, what do you think?"

"Bronius, let's go and have supper now, or your mother might get offended. The food can get cold. We could discuss your essay in detail after we eat. The only thing I can tell you right now is that your writing is very good."

Both of them got up from the table. Soon, they were already sitting at another table. After the supper, Bronius and Ema went for a walk in the orchard, where they sat down on the bench under the cherry tree. It was the same place where they sat a few days ago.

They talked long and sincerely. The nightfall had long covered the orchard, but their conversation still did not cease. Bronius asked her about a matter that had been bothering him, "Ema, on the way home from Adutiskis, you told me that you'll be happy to leave to Vilnius on Wednesday. I hope you won't be surprised to learn that, this time, I can't share your happiness, because it goes against my wishes... What I mean by saying this is that it feels so wonderful being next to you! I have been waiting impatiently for the evenings to come so I could spend my time with you. When you are gone, I will miss you tremendously. During the past week, I got attached to you. I wish you loved me at least as half as strong as I love you, even though I understand that nobody can force the other person to love... But still..."

"Bronius, you know already that I love you..."

"Are you sure? Or you're just saying this out of pity for me?"

"Bronius, if you only knew how much I love you and how precious you are to me! I would be happy to be with you even if I had to live with you in a tent... However, our circumstances make us to accommodate ourselves to changes. First, our parting time was coming in any case. Second, I don't want Alfa finding out that this is your homeland. Your mother told him I'm her relative... If he ever learns this was not true, he could harm our reputation at the university... Therefore, for the sake of peace, it's worth to sacrifice our time here. I prefer to stay away from this Satan as far as possible! I just want you to know that, in Vilnius, I will love you not any less than I love you now. I promise..."

Being overwhelmed with joy, Bronius grabbed Ema sitting next to him by the waist and began slowly pulling her to himself. Their faces kept drawing nearer... A little bit frightened, she quietly whispered, "Bronius don't... it's dangerous... Somebody can spot us..."

He no longer could hear his sweetheart's supplication. Giving himself up to his passion, he clutched her mouth with his hot lips preventing her from saying anything... Unaware of what was happening around, he was submerged into closeness of the most precious girl in the world while holding her tide in his arms.

At last, Ema freed herself from his embrace. She sprang up to her feet and ran to the willow tree, where she pressed herself to its trunk as if asking for an intercession. Her heart was melting with joy, but at the same time, she was feeling some uneasiness.

Coming to his senses, he walked up to Ema and started apologizing to her in a trembling voice, "Ema, forgive me please. I had no strength to resist the temptation; my love for you is endless…"

Ema twined around his neck with her bare arms and tenderly kissed him on the lips. The moment she was about to step back, Bronius wound his strong arms around her slim waist and, again, both of them got absorbed in a passionate kiss.

Ema's arms remained around Bronius's neck even after both of them got satiated with the kiss. These had been the happiest moments in each of their lives! Love like this could happen to someone only once in a lifetime.

This time, they lingered in the orchard much longer than any other time before. Both of them told many beautiful words to each other.

Only well after midnight, Bronius with Ema came home, where he kissed her a couple more times and wished her sweet dreams before parting for the night. Then, he reluctantly went to his storeroom.

The one and the other fell soundly asleep only at the dawn. However, just like before, as soon as Bronius woke up, he at once came to her room. Ema opened her eyes, and he again started ardently kissing her.

He knew today was their last day… Tomorrow, she was leaving. Therefore, both of them were enjoying every minute of their happiness. They no longer had any doubts in one another. After all, they had already heard from each other's lips a declaration of love that would remain forever in their memory.

Finally, Bronius left the room allowing Ema to dress up and went to the kitchen. The mother was almost done cooking breakfast at the stove. Delicious smell of the frying pancakes was dispersing through the air which gave Bronius an appetite. Nevertheless, he tried not to show his mouth was watering.

When Ema left to Adutiskis, the day without her seemed to Bronius incredibly long. It even seemed as if the time stopped completely.

Every ten minutes, he kept looking at his watch waiting impatiently for the time to go meeting his girl.

However, there was more than an hour left just until lunchtime. After the lunch, at least four more hours had to pass before him leaving to meet Ema.

A couple of times, he sat down at the writing table in the storeroom and tried to continue writing his story.

However, nothing productive came out of him; he just could not concentrate on his thoughts.

Then, Bronius tried to add some more dates together with the description into the chronicle, since he had remembered some events worth to be mentioned. However, those efforts also went to pot.

At last, Bronius got into the river hoping that maybe this could refresh him and he will be able to concentrate on his writings. Nevertheless, memories of yesterday kept rushing into his head. Again, Bronius tried to concentrate on his writing, but as soon as he sat down at the table, Ema's picture emerged in his mind. Exciting memories mixed up in his thinking, and they totally ejected his creative thoughts.

Despite how slowly the time was passing by, lunch came. After eating, Bronius with much difficulty pushed forward another three hours. Then, he finally lost his patience and left the house to meet Ema.

However, now, he had to sit in his old lurking-place next to the road much longer than usually, since he had left the house the whole an hour earlier.

When, at last, he saw Ema running toward him on the road, his heart started beating as if he had not seen her for ages. Missing each other tremendously, they embraced heartily.

Next morning, she did not need to go to work at the collective farm any longer, because it was Wednesday, the day of her departure. She told her girlfriends at the collective farm that she would see them at the train station upon leaving.

That was exactly what happened, but only after the biggest meal at Bronius's house, which had been arranged especially for her. The farewell departure lasted almost half of the day.

Mother herself harnessed a horse to a cart; she prepared her present for the girl - a couple of jugs of honey. Ema tried to refuse taking it from her, the woman of a noble heart who had become so precious to her in such short amount of time. In spite of that, the mother did not take Ema's "no" for an answer.

Soon after, the three of them got into the cart and rolled out of the yard. Even the grandmother, leaning onto her cane, came out to the veranda to see off Bronius's girlfriend. He could not take Ema to the train station himself, because Ema was afraid of Alfa seeing them together.

Therefore, he drove with the mother and Ema in the cart only for a couple of kilometers. Then, he reluctantly said good-bye to his girl.

He stood on the road for a long time painfully looking at the carriage taking away his sweetheart. Ema, too, was looking back at Bronius and waving at him with a handkerchief. In her mind, she was sending thousands of kisses to her beloved.

For the last time, Ema's white handkerchief flashed in the distance, and the carriage disappeared among the trees and bushes. Bronius his head down, but his heart full of love, came home where he impatiently waited for his mother to return from the train station.

When Ema with the mother arrived at the train station, they found a bunch of students already waiting for the coming train there.

Alfa noticed Ema right away, but he did not even greet her. He had still been furious, even though he was more angry at the mother than at Ema. He was sure this woman was to blame for the past incident at the collective farm.

Since Alfa could not take his vengeance right there and then, in front of everybody, he tried to keep himself content by ignoring both of them. He demonstratively turned away. The rest of the time while waiting for the train, he walked among the students all inflated with pride like a turkey cock, and Ema with the mother quietly scoffed at him behind his back.

Ema wanted to bid farewell to Bronius's mother, but the woman insisted on waiting until the train arrived to the station. Besides Alfa reproaching Ema, the mother was worried about missing the train, since it stopped at their station only once a day. Therefore, it often used to be overcrowded, and not all of the passengers could get into its carriages being already crammed with people. In addition, Ema had a huge wicker basket filled with honey and other earthly blessings. In case the train came too full, the mother was ready to take her precious guest back to her homestead.

Thus, another hour passed by. Several girls with boys from the university walked up to the cart where Ema and the mother were sitting. A couple of them even jumped into the cart and sat down next to them, while the others were standing by to the cart.

All of them were talking and joking for some time, when suddenly, a sharp whistle of the steam engine broke out. Thick smoke also appeared wreathing over the rail and into the blue sky.

The racket in an instant died down, and everybody fixed their eyes onto the rail track, where the black locomotive was coming from around the turn. The railway engine, loudly hissing and puffing from far away, was significantly reducing its speed. Soon, it came to a complete stop.

Ema's girlfriends had already bought her a ticket beforehand, so she did not need to jostle at the cash-window herself. As soon as the train stopped, Ema with the other girls quickly ran up to one of the train carriages allotted for passengers. Without much difficulty, she boarded the train. Ema did not even have to drag inside her heavy basket with the food; her friends carried it in for her.

Ema was not looking for a place to sit down. Instead, she got right away to the window and tried to open it. After her attempt failed, she simply waved through the dusty window glass at Bronius's mother standing on the platform.

The engine driver gave a signal, and the train slowly gave a start. Then, it began moving faster. Pretty soon, the little village train station with the mother in it vanished out of her range of vision.

Ema stepped back from the window, and her girlfriends invited her to sit down on the bench between them. They already had occupied their seats and saved one for Ema as well.

After a lively four-hour trip, the train arrived to Vilnius. All the students spilled out of the train onto the platform. Alfa came up to Ema and offered his help carrying her big, heavy basket. However, she pulled it out from his hand and, without saying a word, walked toward a first driver in line waiting for his passengers.

As soon as Ema walked into her home, her mother came to the door to meet her. She exclaimed, "Father, come here! Ema has arrived from the collective farm. My dear, you have lost so much weight! Probably they did not feed you well there. Did they keep you underfed?"

The father came from adjacent room and took his glasses off. Radiating with joy, he said, "You, Ema, have a beautiful tan! Looks like you've just arrived from some resort."

"What do you mean? Look how thin she has become! Just bones and skin are left of her," Ema's mother disagreed. She took the basket from Ema's hands and asked, "What have you brought here that is so heavy?"

"These are the gifts for you and daddy."

"Gifts?" Surprised mother set heavy basket onto a chair and started pulling stuff out of it. She kept placing on the table one thing after another. "This is smoked country bacon." Mother opened brown paper on the side of the bacon and smelled it. Right away, its pleasant scent escaped and dispersed into the air.

"This is country sausage," the mother smelled and put it on the table together with the other products. "What are in these jugs? They are so heavy as if they have been filled with some lead."

"You can open one. Daddy look, here is the honey!"

"I see… But where have you got all this? You couldn't possibly buy everything, because you did not have enough money to purchase all this stuff. But maybe you had been paid well for your hard work at the collective farm?"

"We, daddy, we have earned exactly two zeros during those ten days working in the fields. Of course, I could not have bought anything for that! A very generous woman gave all this to me. Do you remember when mom had made me a dress for the dance, when I had had a date with one boy? Our date had not worked out then…"

"Yes, but what that date has to do with all these earthly blessings?"

"I had miraculously met the same youth in the village! Moreover, I stayed at his mother's house for six days! Upon my departure, she took me to the train station with her horse-carriage herself. She was the one who gave me this basket full of food. I refused to take it, but she was implacable. Therefore, I brought it with me here."

Ema told her parents about her work at the collective farm and about her stay at Bronius's homestead. She described everything in detail while they were drinking tea with jam that she had brought from the village with the rest of the stuff.

Her father and mother were captivated by the story of how she had ended up at the Adomaitis' family. She recounted her beautiful memories without missing to mention about the beauty of Bronius's homestead, the warm evenings and cool mornings there, and the fog on the river.

Also, she did not forget to tell about her bathing in the country bathhouse and her fine supper with the wine that followed it. Her parents were just happily nodding their heads. They could not have enough of Bronius's wonderful family. Without having even seen the boy, her mom and dad fully approved their daughter's choice.

THE BLACKMAIL

Bronius was sad after his separation with Ema. He kept seeing her in his dreams almost every night, and even during daytime, she would not leave his mind for a minute.

Despite enjoying his stay at home, Bronius still wanted to go back to the city. Counting days, he impatiently waited for his long vacation to end. Even the summer weather could not make him happy any longer. A few times, he even caught himself dreaming about long evenings of upcoming autumn.

He realized that being back in Vilnius he would be able to see Ema every day. He knew both of them would be attending movies and shows, walking in the parks.

Of course, there was no such a beautiful orchard in the city as in his homeland. He also understood that he will not have an opportunity to sit on grass with a fishing rod in his hands and listen to silence or birds singing while admiring a stunning sunrise or sunset.

In spite of this, Bronius felt he could gladly refuse from all those pleasures so that he could only be in his beloved city, where life had been in full swing like in some agitated anthill.

During this time of the year, the sun used to heat up stones and walls of the ancient buildings, where they would not completely cool down even late at night. In Vilnius, the air often became so stuffy that people were ready to run away any minute from that dusty, hot, and noisy environment to some peaceful corner of the nature.

Not surprisingly, everyone who had similar opportunity as Bronius did took advantage of it during the summertime. They wanted to escape from the dirty, noisy capital to the wide, green fields, where there was no dust, where nature breathed freely and welcomed everyone to do the same.

Ema's departure obscured Bronius's holidays. However, now, he knew she loved him and that they were meant to be together. He did not give much preference to their environment as long as she was near.

The only thing that reassured him, gave him strength and patience was her letters, which Ema regularly kept sending him once a week. Those letters gave Bronius hope for their bright future.

After Ema had left, he tried to sit down at the table and continue writing the story that he had started earlier. However, every time, he got up with no more than only half of the page written down.

Those interlacing thoughts about Ema did not let him concentrate on his writing. They worked their way penetrating deep into his subconscious and hindered his creativity.

However, soon, Ema herself saved the situation by writing another letter to him. She wrote that she had been missing him, but at the same time, she'd been glad he was now able to continue working on his grandfather's chronicle. Further, she expressed her hope to be able to read this story when he got back to Vilnius.

After reading Ema's letter, Bronius plunged into thoughts. In two weeks following her departure, he had not written one word! Beginning to feel anxious, Bronius puzzled over what he could show her upon his return to Vilnius; he had written only a few pages of the chronicle as well. That could only set Ema laughing and make him look like a hopeless liar.

Feeling ashamed and distressed, Bronius immediately sat down at the table in his storeroom, where he had lately spent many hours in vain without being able to write anything worthy.

This time, however, he was determined not to give into tempting thoughts. Again, nothing good came out this time.

After supper, Bronius came to the riverside distressed, with aching heart. He sat down on the footbridge and immersed his feet into the cool water. The same thoughts about Ema were buzzing in his head.

Nevertheless, a new, fresh idea suddenly flashed through his mind! One thought in particular kept jumping in his head which prompted him to decide that he should write about the very thing that had been so tiresomely thrusting into his mind during the last few days. Then, some other wonderful and uplifting thoughts started circling in his mind, too. It felt as if veil of loneliness had been lifted and a heavy lid to another, the brighter, world had been opened. All he needed to do now was to capture his thoughts on the paper.

Suddenly everything became so clear and simple. Not even five minutes later, he made his final decision to transfer a goal he had set for himself into reality.

With the new exciting thoughts, he got up off the wooden bridge. In a few big steps, Bronius climbed a steep river slope. However, he did not head for home. Instead, he went to 'their' bench. To be exact, that was 'Ema's bench', because Bronius himself had named it this way right after putting it together.

Bronius leaned back his arms thrown out widely to the sides and resting on the top board of the wooden back of the bench. He lifted his head up and gazed at the tops of the standing nearby trees.

However, he did not stay there for long. Having drawn into his lungs enough strength from the nature, he got up and walked home.

As soon as Bronius entered the storeroom, he found a clean notebook and started writing in it. Soon, a word after a word, a line after a line started flowing down the white page. Thus, half of the notebook was filled in.

In the beginning, he had to spend some time scratching his head, trying to figure out how to express his thoughts in better and nicer manner, or in a more interesting way.

As the sun was going down, his mother came to the storeroom carrying a pitcher.

"Bronius, I've brought you some fresh milk. In fact, it's still warm."

"Mom, I'm tired of milk. I would rather have something cold," asked Bronius pushing away the notebook.

"Would you like me to bring you some cold kvass from the cellar?"

"I would love it! Thank you, mom."

When the mother came back with the kvass, Bronius drank two full cups of it right away.

"It's very refreshing. Nevertheless, it is almost too cold for me."

"We have a great cellar. Your dad built the walls and the floors of it entirely out of stones. No wonder it is so cool there. Maybe I will leave you, Bronius, this pitcher with milk, too. You can drink some of it before going to bed. Milk is more nourishing than kvass."

"Take milk, but leave the kvass," Bronius asked.

As soon as the mother left, he, again, got absorbed into his writing that, now, was going without a hitch.

Thus, he sat writing until the midnight, and he filled his notebook almost to its last page. Bronius went to bed after his eyes had been tiresomely shutting for a while and his whole body was almost fainting from a desire to get some sleep.

In the morning, he got up early and worked intensely all day long, even though he would rather went fishing and swimming. Nevertheless, he just kept pushing forward. He had known that he had a worthy pursuit that fully occupied his entire leisure.

Every evening, he came to Ema's corner as well, where he liked to spend some time dreaming about the beautiful evenings he had spent here together with her.

Bronius almost neglected the rest of his chores around the house. He just kept writing without ceasing during the days and, very often, even during the nights. On those nights, he would fall asleep only when the dawn was breaking. Then, he would inevitably sink into a kingdom of dreams for a few hours. After having spent a lot of time working the previous night, Bronius sometimes tried to have a swim in the river the next day. On those days, he also caught up with his sleep by taking a couple of hours of nap during the daytime.

Nevertheless, approaching rye harvest interrupted his routine. Now, Bronius had to help his mother make all the arrangements to reap the harvest. After working in the field, he no longer could spend time writing. A few times, he tried to work on his book. However, as soon as he sat down at the table, fatigue chained him and, then, sleep surmounted him.

Bronius kept toiling and moiling, and he did not even notice when an entire week passed by. Then, the time to cut summer grain had come. He had to help his mother bring the harvest into the barn which demanded a couple more days of very strenuous labor.

Half of the summer grains had already been harvested, and Bronius decided that Mother alone could manage to finish the rest of the fieldwork.

Therefore, he instantly returned to his abandoned writing and totally devoted himself to it.

One eventide, he came out of the storeroom to have a breath of the fresh air, and he met his mother in the yard coming out of the fields. She had been so tired that she could hardly drag her feet, and she had a great deal of work left for her to do that evening at home. She still needed to milk the cows and feed the swine.

While exchanging a few words with his mother, Bronius became a little bit ashamed of himself seeing her so worn-out. However, he had to finish the story for Ema until his return to the city. Therefore, he again came to the 'Ema's corner' in the orchard where he resumed his writing until it started growing dark.

When Bronius returned home, he found his mother still running back and forth in a hurry to finish her household chores. As soon as she saw him walking in, she said, "Wait a moment, Bronius. I will make supper for you."

At last, all the work around the house was done. She poured a big bowl of water for herself and washed her hands and face with a big bar of soap. Then, she combed her tousled hair and sat down next to the son at the kitchen table.

This was the first time Bronius noticed how young and beautiful she still was. In spite of being tired, she was flourishing with health and inexhaustible energy.

He was listening to her talking. Bronius was gazing at her slightly tired eyes that needed only good night's sleep to put the spark back in.

"Well, son, I have kept you half way hungry almost all day long. Forgive me, please. It has been such a beautiful day. During a busy season like this, every day is worth more than gold. At least, it is according to an old folks' saying."

"Don't worry, mother. I probably have eaten more today than you have. Rather, I should apologize to you for not helping with the fieldwork, since I have been occupied with my own business. I could had postponed my personal work until the later time. I have heard another folks' proverb, 'it is said that even rocks move during the harvest time'. However, you couldn't say that about me, since I had stagnated the whole day in the storeroom…"

"You have already helped me a lot! I can assert you this year the harvest season has gone without much trouble for me. The most important thing is that the main and most difficult chores have been finished, and I certainly can manage all the rest myself. Would you, Bronius, go to the henhouse and bring me some eggs. I have forgotten about the hens. I will prepare nice supper for you."

Bronius took the matches and went to the hencoop. It was completely dark inside, and all the hens had been nodding on their perches. Nevertheless, as soon as he struck a match, the birds suddenly came to life. Right away, they started talking between themselves; all Bronius could hear around was the loud unaccustomed clucking.

When he returned from the hencoop with a full basket of eggs, sputtering sapwood had been burning cheerfully in the kitchen. The splinters of the wood had been piled between two bricks that had been standing on the top of the old iron stove. The mother sat a big frying pan onto the top of those bricks. There were already pieces of bacon showing white in it.

Bronius put the basket filled with eggs on the table. Soon, the frizzling of the frying pig fat was heard. The mother allowed the bacon to brown good, and she beat in ten eggs. In a moment, the sizzling pan with fried bacon and eggs was sitting on the kitchen table where Bronius with the grandmother had been waiting for the mother to give them a sign to start eating.

"Well, let's start eating," she said.

She picked up her fork first. Then, she let its teeth sink into a greasy piece of bacon. The rest of the family followed her example.

All three of them emptied the entire pan of eggs, and the mother poured a cup of milk for Bronius and another one for Grandma so that they could wash the food down. She herself took a pitcher with the remaining milk in it into her hands and started drinking straight out of it. Then, she stood the pitcher back onto the table.

The supper was over, and the women parted to separate corners of the house.

Bronius went to the storeroom, but he did not want to resume working on his writing. Instead, he lay down. Very soon, he fell into troubled sleep. Strange dreams kept bothering him all night long. He woke up a few times and drank some kvass out of a glass jar that had been standing nearby on his writing table. He fell asleep again and slept peacefully until the morning. Bronius got up and went to the fields.

He worked very strenuously until the rest of the week. The earthwork had nearly been finished, and the harvest had been brought into the barn. There was left only to thresh flax.

In a few days, all the rest of the chores were done as well, except smallest ones that did not require any hurry. The mother was also facing an approaching potato harvest.

Bronius started getting ready to go back to Vilnius. Now, in a big hurry, he kept writing nonstop. He wanted to finish not only his story but his grandfather's chronicle as well during the last days of his visit at home. Each day, he sat leaning over his notebook not only during the daytime, but late at night as well.

One evening, when he was busy finishing the last chapter, Mother came in. She had noticed a light in the window of the storeroom. As soon as she walked in, she saw her son concentrated upon his work.

"Bronius, what are you doing here? Is it not enough daytime for that? Go to sleep."

"Ma, I don't disturb you when you work."

"But, son, it is unhealthy for you to be sitting all night long without any sleep. Is it not enough the daytime for writing your book?!"

"Well, probably it is not enough if I'm sitting at night. I must finish this story before leaving to Vilnius."

"Then you shouldn't had worked with me in the fields. You could had been writing during the days, and, now, you wouldn't have to sit during the nights."

"Don't torment yourself so much. Few more days - and I will have finished my book! I'm going to sleep already. You do the same, mama."

When the mother left, Bronius indeed lay down. He did not dare write at nighttime anymore; he knew that she would be watching him from now on. In addition, he did not want to cause her any pain.

Until the very last day of his vacation, Bronius had been writing the story that, unfortunately, he still was unable to finish. He just could not come up with a meaningful ending.

The day he had been impatiently waiting for had arrived, and Bronius was already sitting in the carriage with two big suitcases full of county food that mother had stuffed in. She took him to the local train station. Next thing, he was sitting in the train that carried him away to Vilnius.

When he arrived, there was an unexpected surprise awaiting for him at the train station in the capital. Dragging his big trunks which seemed so heavy as if crammed with bricks, he spotted Ema in the crowd of people. She was with difficulty working her way toward Bronius fighting the stream of people that had just spilled out of the train and was trying to take her together the opposite direction. Therefore, she could hardly stand on her feet, let alone move forward.

Bronius allowed the stream of the people carry him until he found himself next to Ema, whose face was radiating with joy.

"Hi, Ema. What a surprise! Have you come here to meet somebody?"

"Hello, Bronius! You've guessed right. I really came here to meet someone special…"

"In this kind of crush, it's easy to miss that someone. Whom are you meeting? Maybe I can help you finding that person. Is it a man or a woman?"

"He is a man."

"What does he look like?"

"He is good looking. Ha ha ha… I have come here to meet you…"

"Me?! Are you serious?"

"Of course, I'm serious. I came here yesterday, too."

"Ema, sweetheart, you didn't need to go through all this trouble. Anyway, how did you even find out that I'm arriving today?"

"Hello… a week ago, you had written to me yourself that you were going to come to Vilnius yesterday. And that is why I came to meet you yesterday. But, of course, I didn't see you here. In the beginning, I thought that I hadn't noticed you in the crowd. But it wasn't any trouble for me to come here. On the contrary, it was rather a pleasure. I had waited for your arrival so much that I had started counting days and even hours just before it."

"I also have been waiting for this day to come as for a salvation. Ema, let's hurry out of here, or this stream of people will take us the wrong way."

Soon, both of them found themselves in the square located in front of the train station, where Bronius was going to hire a driver. However, they had spent too much time talking on the platform, and all of the drivers had already been snatched away by the other passengers.

Bronius had to content himself with hiring a two-wheeled handcart, which they followed on foot. The cart was being pulled by a service person. Ema was walking by Bronius's side. When all three of them reached an entrance of Bronius's yard, he paid the driver for the service and asked Ema to come to his flat and visit with him for a while.

However, Ema refused, since it had already been getting late in the evening and she did not feel like going to the strange place. Bronius did not want to say goodbye to her yet. Therefore, he asked her to wait in the yard while he quickly took his suitcases upstairs and came back to her.

Upon seeing Bronius, his landlady had tried asking some questions about his vacation, but Bronius only apologized to the old woman and said someone had been waiting for him outside. Then, he left immediately.

"Well, where are we going, Ema?"

"Wherever you want to, Bronius."

"We can go to the cinema or to Bernardinai Gardens."

"Let's better go to the Gardens. I have already seen all this week's movies. There is not even one good movie out there."

Soon, they came to this big, old city Bernardinai Square full of mature trees. Both of them sat down straight on the grass at a bank of the narrow capital river Vilnele.

Ema and Bronius shared their warm and still very fresh memories about the evenings they had spent in Bronius's homestead by the river. One major difference between the two places was that there they could listen to the birds singing and fish splashing on the surface of the water. Sometimes it used to be so quiet that they almost could hear the silence. The river at his countryside carried its waters quietly.

Here, they could hear loud murmuring of the shallow but swift branch of the main Vilnius river by the name Neris. In addition, they could also hear a monotonous noise in the background, so typical to any big city.

Even after dark, they remained sitting on the Vilnele River bank for a long time, and there was no end to their talk.

Nevertheless, the time had come for them to part. Bronius saw Ema till her home, where they spent another half an hour talking, only this time, by the wicket-gate of her yard.

Now, both of them kept meeting every evening and spending their time until dark.

Soon, September came, and Bronius had to return to his work and resume attending the classes at the university as well. Therefore, Bronius with Ema were able to meet only for a short while, most often on their way home from the classes. Only on Sundays, they had an opportunity to stay together longer. On Sundays, they would go to movies or to a theatre. Sometimes, they went to the Bernardinai Park or took a walk in some other city square.

However, even those pleasures soon ended, since weather got cold, and it rained heavily almost every day. Once in a whole, though, they still managed to find some place to talk for a short while in the middle of the week.

Bronius and Ema were very happy together. Only one thing disturbed them. That had been Alfa who kept constantly picking on Ema. Just like at the collective farm, he would not leave her alone at the university, too.

Both Ema and Bronius avoided him in order to escape any troubles. They had known his rotten moral character by now, and they had been aware what to expect from him, as well. Finally, both of them had come to an agreement that the best thing for them would be to wait without advertising their friendship for seven more months, until Alfa finished Vilnius University. They both realized there would not be any opportunities meeting him in the corridors of the university.

Neither Bronius nor Ema expected that soon their peaceful relationship could be disturbed by another unexpected incident. One day Bronius received summons to present himself to the Military Registration and Enlistment Office.

Not having any misgivings, he took his passport together with a military card and went to that institution. He walked from one office to another showing the summons to every official he met on his way. However, each and every one of them told Bronius the same thing that nobody had invited him to come here. The military officers kept further driving him back and forth, but the only thing Bronius was sure of at the moment was the fact that, in his hand, he was holding the summons.

Being sent from one cabinet to another, Bronius Adomaitis became completely lost, and he was already determined to leave the building. While he was looking for the way out of labyrinth of corridors, a man about forty years old came up to him. He was dressed in civilian clothes. The man asked, "What cabinet are you looking for?"

Bronius looked with suspicion at this thickset human figure growing a little bald on the back of his head. For some reason, Bronius's feeling prompted to him that this man was somewhat shady. However, after being caught so unexpectedly, he embarrassed began mumbling and stammering, "I've the summons... which indicates... that I must come to your institution. I can't understand why everybody around... maintains no one had asked me to come here. It seems very strange..."

"Show me the summons."

Adomaitis again distrustfully glanced at the strange man. Then, he pulled a folded document out of a pocket of his pants and handed it to the official. After quickly skimming with his eyes the oblong in shape paper, the man commanded, "Follow me, please. I was the one who had summoned you to come to our office."

He was the first to turn around and walk along the narrow dark corridor. Bronius followed him. Both of the men walked into a spacious cabinet, in the corner of which there was standing a big writing desk. There were two soft armchairs in front of it. They appeared to be too nice in comparison to the rest of the furniture in this rather gloomy room.

"Sit down, please," he pointed with his short thick finger at one of the armchairs and sank himself into a tall chair at his table.

"If I am not mistaken, your name is Bronius Adomaitis."

"Yes, it is," Bronius answered quite firmly.

"Namely with you, I wanted to become acquainted. I hope you won't have anything against if I, right away, without circling around, get down to business. I'll tell you upfront that I have no desire hiding anything from you. Hopefully, you will also be open with me."

"Of course," responded Adomaitis in a slightly quivering voice wondering what this stranger wants from him.

"I like your attitude. Probably I will not be mistaken by saying that you are a righteous person. I hope you are well disposed to the Socialist System implemented in the county, aren't you?" The functionary went with his eyes right through an entire body of Adomaitis collapsed in the armchair.

Bronius started feeling very uneasy in his fancy chair. However, he did not have another choice but to sit meekly and listen to the demagogic phrases of this strict man and, then, assent to them, too.

"It goes without saying this is my civic duty to be the righteous person. One thing I can assure you of is that I have no slightest grounds to be against the thriving Socialism."

"I'm glad to hear that! I am sure if the treason threatened our socialist system, you would inform the organs of government without hesitation, wouldn't you?"

"Of course, I would report such a thing. It is the duty of every Soviet citizen. Now, I myself am one of those citizens…"

"I like your point of view. Now, please sign this declaration that you will inform us of all the cases that you discover going against the Soviet Union, including reporting any suspicious individuals and any probable preparations for a diversion. Go ahead, write the statement," and the official handed to Bronius the sheet of paper and a penholder.

Suddenly, Bronius broke in to cold sweat. He was totally lost and did not know what to do, but there was no time to weigh. He had only a split second to make a decision.

Various thoughts started swimming in his head. Bronius was still hesitating. He was afraid that if he refused to comply, then it would reveal his hatred for the new Soviet order with all its violence. Even his forehead turned damp out of tension, and his shirt started sticking to his body. There was ringing in his ears. For a minute, it appeared to him that the floor under his feet started swaying and he could not find a fulcrum. It seemed as if he was going to fall out of this damned armchair. Sitting in it, he felt like being in some hell's boiling copper of tar.

"Have you already started having any doubts in our government? Maybe you are one of those people who are still waiting for the American way of life... Are you with us or against us?!"

"I have never thought about living the American way. My homeland is plenty for me... It is precious to me just the way it is, and I am against all kinds of intruders!"

"What do you mean?"

"I mean, if Americans invaded my county, I would look upon them the way I look at the German fascists. The same applies to any other county, meaning that if it happened to invade my native country with the aggressive purposes... I would consider that country to be the occupant. No one likes occupants. I hope, now, you have understood what I meant... I'm sorry, but I really don't know what I must write here."

"I will tell you what to write."

Adomaitis with a trembling hand wrote words to the official's dictation. Then, he was incited by him to sign the document, too.

He did not remember how he ended up back in the street; this moral coercion affected him so strongly.

When Bronius returned home, he fell onto a bed and buried his head in a pillow. He wished he could have a good cry, but the tears only squeezed his throat, and it seemed as if they were just stuck there. Not even one tear come out to help relieve his tension. A painful groan escaped his chest, and Bronius sorrowfully whispered to himself, "Oh, my Lord, what have I done to deserve this? Why are you tormenting me so grievously?"

"Bronius, what has happened to you now? Have you got sick?" the landlady asked him when passing by the opened door of his room.

Bronius with difficulty lifted his head off the pillow. He sat down on the edge of the bed and sat there for a few seconds his eyes looking down at the floor.

"Yes, I am sick, aunty. I'm in pain..."

"What is hurting to you?"

Bronius heavily lifted his eyes to the old woman and uttered in an oppressed voice, "I don't know what one blackmailer wanted from me today. It must be some curse placed on me by the Universe itself... All the time, I keep meeting people, who would not let me live in peace. They continually rummage in my old wounds. Today, one of that kind of people managed to even open a new wound right in my heart... This morning, I was literally forced to sign a document ordering me to do something I don't want and I don't agree to do. After the conversation with the officer at the Military Registration and Enlistment Office, I feel like some Sancho Panza. Now, I am having pangs of conscience for some sin that I have never committed. Nothing new under the sun. The author Cervantes had created the perfect picture of this character. Even though four centuries have passed, the same idea could be applied nowadays as well. Looks like people have not changed much, in spite of living in another system under the red Soviet government's regime. People are literally forced to exalt and idolize their foreign Soviet government and its new system."

"The impression I'm getting just by listening to you, Bronius, is that the Soviet government officials have started picking on you for some reason..."

"If that only was the truth, then this wouldn't be so difficult to tolerate. However, it seems that the matter is turning for the worst. It could had been not just some faultfinding act this morning, but it might have been a blackmail instigation against me. I have no strength left to handle one more blow to my life. Lately, I've started to get accustomed to an idea that my father has been gone forever out of my life. For a little while, it seemed things had started getting better, since I had been allowed to attend the classes at the university again. But today, I have been hit by the new blow..."

"Bronius, as far as I understand, you are going through another turning point in your life that gives you no rest, and it seems to you that talking about that with the loved ones could alleviate your pain and make things better for you. Sometimes, indeed, we feel better after revealing our secrets to others. However, in your case, I wouldn't advise you to resort to this way of dealing with your problem. I don't think you should disclose anything related to the new government to anyone, not even to your family members, of course, if you care about them... By telling this to others, you could ruin your own life as well as life of your family members. Therefore, you should not tell to anyone what happened to you this morning. The times have come when all of us will have to adapt to this new order..."

"Auntie, according to you, I have to keep silent and suffer this injustice?"

"Yes, you have to be silent if you don't wish to hurt yourself or your loved ones. If you keep this incident a secret, then maybe the Soviets won't hurt you. But if you'll start telling everyone about this morning's conversation at the Military Enlistment Office, then, eventually, the Russian officials will find out about that. The further troubles would definitely follow as a result of vengeance from their side. And your family would have to suffer along with you. Therefore, you must self determine to keep it a secret. You can get used to your new lifestyle, and you'll see for yourself that by acting this way you will come out a winner..."

Bronius experienced the past incident with the Russian officer so painfully, that he did not even go to work next day, and he missed his lectures at the university, too. Instead, Bronius shut himself in the room for the whole day. He did not go to the Gediminas Hill that evening either, even though Ema and him had arranged their meeting there.

In general, after the incident, he closed himself in his own shell. At some moments, he was afraid even of his own shadow.

He took in consideration the landlady's advice and kept his secret to himself that felt now like a heavy rock constantly and precariously weighing on him. He tried hard to not let the black cat out of the bag... and he just suffered home alone.

Next day after classes, Ema caught up with Bronius right when he was leaving Vilnius University. Not surprisingly, she asked why he had missed the lectures yesterday and had not come to their meeting at the designated place in the city. Bronius tried justifying himself, and he even lied to her making up a reason.

He understood there was no way he could tell her about the document he had to sign recently. Therefore, Bronius only calmed down Ema a bit, after what he himself started feeling better.

However, a big change could be felt in the air. He started seeing her less. Sometimes Bronius would not come to their meetings at all. Especially he avoided seeing her on Sundays, even though it was their only free day during a week.

In the beginning, he felt uncomfortable to refuse Ema the date on Sunday, because they always used to spend this day together. However, as time went by, Bronius more and more often became "busy" on Sundays.

At last, Ema realized that he had been avoiding her. She even started having doubts he was still in love with her. Being overwhelmed with fear, she kept asking him more and more questions about his feelings toward her.

There were days when Ema tried to quiet herself reasoning that maybe Bronius really had no time for her anymore. She grounded her arguments on facts that he had to go to work after the lectures at the university. In addition, there was a lot of homework to do after the school. That alone could take away all the leisure from any student.

Thus, she convinced and composed herself a little bit. A past summer turned just into a beautiful, distant memory now, and a cold and gloomy autumn reigned all around. It rained heavily almost every day.

Soon, All Saints' Day came when people in Lithuania commemorated their deceased loved ones. On this day of November 1st, folks massively made their way to cemeteries. In remembrance of their dead family members and other significant people, they would light candles on their graves. Many would say a prayer for their souls, also.

Ema insisted Bronius going with her to visit her family's graves. However, he categorically refused to do that. He said that he had to be at work and apologized to her for not being able to be there for her.

That day, he could not go visit his own family graves, because he had a meeting set at seven o'clock at night with the same official, who had made him to sign the ill-fated statement. Adomaitis had to meet with him and report about incidents aimed against the Soviet government's politics.

During their first meeting, Bronius also had to present information he had supposed to gather before the meeting.

Bronius was nervous because he had not collected any facts and, therefore, he had nothing to present to the Russian official. A thought flashed through Bronius's mind that even if he had noticed something the official had been after, he would not tell him about it.

Besides, during last few days, he had not left his flat even for a short while in order to search for an opportunity to obtain the information that could be beneficial to the Soviet government.

Sometimes, he would catch himself avoiding different kinds of people gatherings all together. Moreover, if accidentally he happened to hear somebody talking against the Soviet system, Bronius intentionally walked away.

Such peculiar restraint of freedom weighed down badly on Bronius, since he had promised in writing to supply the official with certain information. However, every time he met with this agent from the Military Enlistment Office, he had nothing to report. Therefore, every time Adomaitis saw this officer, his legs started trembling out of fear, but at the same time, his heart would fill with hatred for this spy of the government of the occupants.

Again, Bronius always came back home with new instructions and feeling like a squeezed out lemon after hours of this Russian official's "counseling".

In addition, Bronius started receiving new tasks. He was asked to attend dances at the university in order to associate with students and make as many new acquaintances as he possibly could.

Few times, his agent even offered him some money, so that Bronius could take the students to a restaurant. His goal was supposed to be to get into close relationship with those students.

However, Adomaitis always refused the money from the official knowing it had been offered to him in attempts to attain dirty moral objectives. In those instances, he would tell to the Russian officer that he had been receiving a stipend form the university and, in addition to that, he had been paid salary at his employment place.

Finally, Bronius managed to reassure his agent that he had enough money for living. He said that even if he had to swing by the restaurant with his friends, he could manage to pay for drinks and food there himself.

This All Saints Day holiday, at seven o'clock sharp in the evening, Adomaitis showed up for his meeting with the Russian agent by the Casino Cinema. There, he found the agent already anxiously walking back and forth.

Bronius was surprised that for the first time this red spawn of hell did not inquire about the information Bronius was supposed to deliver him. The official briefly greeted him and, right away, ordered to go to Rasos Cemetery.

Bronius had no doubts that this time, too, the agent had something dirty on his mind. However, Bronius did not know what exactly to expect which made him extremely nervous.

He was afraid to repudiate, and he just obediently walked next to the spy. In his mind, Bronius secretly called this refractory man, firmly walking next to him, a 'NKVD flunky'.

During their every meeting, the agent reminded Bronius to be in the places dense with people. His task was supposed to be to keep a conversation going with individual people in the crowd. One of the tactics he had to use was the approval of anything said even in those cases when their talk would be directed against the Soviet system itself. According to Bronius's agent, it was not wise to overdo it so that their conversation would not appear like some kind of propaganda. Bronius was supposed to guard against arousal of the interlocutor's suspicion.

This time, too, the secret agent taught Adomaitis to observe the mood of the people and be present mainly at those places where they had an opportunity to manifest themselves the most. He was advised not to stand in one place, but to observe the entire crowd together with all the environment around.

Listening to those commentaries, Adomaitis with the agent came to the Rasos Cemetery. Since visiting the graves of the departed people every year on November 1st had been very important ritual in Lithuanian culture, there were many people already gathered here. However, one place was especially dense with the folks. Therefore, the agent headed there first.

Soon, both of them found themselves next to a tall monument, on the top of which a big sculpture of an angel had been erected. Standing in the dark, Bronius caught himself complaining to this watch-angel. In his mind, he told the angel how much he dreaded being here with a stranger who had been serving the occupants of the country. Bronius wished he would rather stay at home, even though at this hour the entire county was serving its respect to the deceased Lithuanians.

Another thought that crossed his mind was about an odd coincidence. Namely, he was thinking that he had to refuse going with Ema to the cemetery. This had been an act that he had to resort to against his will. However, again against his will, he was standing in the cemetery anyway!

Bronius and the agent stood for a while there, and walked to another side of the cemetery where people mostly of Polish descent had been buried.

There, next to the grave of the Chief of the State of the Second Republic of Poland Jozef Pilsudski, the biggest crowd had been assembled. Here, only his heart had been buried. His entire body had been buried in Wawel Cathedral located in Poland, next to the tombs of the kings and queens and the most distinguished personalities of Poland. In accordance with his will, only his heart had been enclosed in a silver urn and interred in his mother's grave at the Rasos Cemetery in Lithuania.

It was almost impossible to come close to his gravestone at that moment. On the ground, there were many little candles burning and a mountain of bouquets of flowers had already been piled next to the monument. In every corner of the grave, four teenage boys dressed in Polish uniforms were standing at attention.

As a wind kept blowing, some of the candles would go out, and an elderly man standing by would light them again. The sea of the candles endlessly kept flickering until they burned down. Then, the new candles flared up on the grave. A thin elderly fellow had been taking care of them by continuously replacing the candles and managing the guards of honor, since they needed to be switched every half an hour. He also accepted newly brought flowers and put them onto the already existing pile of them. The old fellow did this mechanically without paying attention to anything else around but doing his task.

Most likely he had been disposed very patriotically, and he did not care what would be consequences of his activities. People standing in a big circle around the grave of the Chief of the State of Poland continued singing hymns and religious gospel songs. As soon as the song ended, there was always a moment of silence. Then the whispering could be heard in the air, and someone from the crowd would start a new holy song. Soon after, all around would join the singing. Thus, the beautiful song was spreading far away in the somber darkness of the late autumn.

Both of them stood by the grave of Jozef Pilsudski for a good half an hour. Then, the agent ordered to leave the crowd, and they walked to the central gates located by the entrance to the cemetery. There, on both sides of the gates, next to a tall stone fence, a couple of dozen of women had been selling candles and flowers. Here, the same profitable business always boiled over during ordinary days of a year as well.

Bronius with his agent turned onto a steep narrow cobble road that led to the top of the hill, where a central chapel had been situated. As they slowly walked up the road, Bronius noticed Ema.

Unexpectedly seeing Bronius, her face instantly started radiating with joy. She tried to say something to him, but the agent gave a hard jab with his elbow at Bronius's side giving him the sign not to fall behind.

Frustrated Bronius reluctantly had to leave the girl without getting a chance to say her word. A strange feeling crossed his heart that he was being escorted by his own red "watch-angel".

Soon, both of them were standing by a grave of a proponent of the Lithuanian National Revival Jonas Basanavicius, where also an unusually big crowd had gathered.

His small monument had been covered with little twinkling candles, and it looked like mysterious alien ship in the dark of the night.

After the unlucky encounter with Ema, Bronius was standing his head down; he was not interested in anything happening around anymore. He did not hear a beautiful song, too, that the patriotic crowd had been enthusiastically singing. He only felt cold drops of sweat on his forehead. His heart was bleeding out of sorrow, and a moan captured inside was tearing his chest apart. For a few seconds, he even came short of breath. It seemed to him that he could suffocate on the spot, no matter that the air was so cool and pure around him.

Therefore, Bronius, time from time, kept drawing the night air deep into his lungs through his slightly opened mouth. However, the worst thing was that he was disgusted with himself for not being able to resist his new duty.

At the moment, he just wished for the ground to open up and swallow him burying him together with all the rest of the dead in this cemetery. It seemed to him this was better way out of the situation than to continue serving as a worthless traitor of his nation.

Bronius remembered a look on Ema's face right before they had separated this evening, and it appeared there was a slight shadow of disgust in her eyes. Just remembering that one split moment, he no longer wanted to live.

For a while, a feeling of emptiness, mixed together with wild pain, reigned in his soul. While standing in front of the grave of the Patriarch of the Nation, Bronius, in his mind, took an oath to never betray his fellow-countrymen despite the scope of suffering he would have to endure.

The agent with Bronius stayed in the cemetery until the crowd started breaking up. Only then, the Russian officer released him to go home.

Next morning, Bronius impatiently waited for an opportunity to meet with Ema at the university so that he could talk to her. He had already an entire scenario made up about what had happened at the cemetery.

However, to his biggest surprise, when he saw her in the street after the classes, she demonstratively came up to Alfa, took his arm, and walked away with him. Bronius remained standing in astonishment.

He still tried to see her, though, but he either was unable to catch her, or an opportunity to meet her simply did not come along. And when he finally saw Ema, she was together with Alfa again.

Distressed Bronius had been waiting when, at last, he would be able to see her alone. Finally, one day he ran into her in a hallway of the university. He came up to the girl and asked her in a trembling voice, "Ema, I want you to hear me out. Let me explain what happened during the All Saints' Day at the cemetery."

"I don't want to hear anything. You lied to me. I'd felt before, too, that you had tried making a fool of me. Thanks to God, I have begun to see things clearly on time... Now, I understand your malicious intent. To tell the truth, I have never really loved you, but I always liked Alfa. As about our relationship while I'd worked at the collective farm, I had just tried to make him jealous. Therefore, I used to run away from him. Girls do that to their dates..."

"This is not true. Don't lie at least to yourself, Ema. Why did you kiss me, then?"

"It's better to lie to myself than to be cheated on… I had simply tried to choose the best cavalier for myself… Any girl should date at least two boys in order to discover which one of them is better… I made my choice! Here he is… to pick me up. Good bye!"

As soon as Ema saw Alfa in the hallway, she cried out, "Alfa, let's go to see a movie! There is a great new foreign movie at the Adrija Cinema."

"You know, Ema, that I don't really like foreign movies. Let's better go to see some movie of our domestic production."

"Ok, let's go. We'll discuss this on the way."

"Ema, wait! We need to talk…" Adomaitis babbled while turning red on his face.

"There is nothing left for us to talk about. Don't come near me anymore. I will not tolerate that!"

After harshly cutting Bronius off, she turned away from him and walked arm-in-arm with Alfa. However, it was not easy for her to act this way, since she had not been accustomed to this kind of unrestricted behavior. Nevertheless, compelled by the situation, she performed this clever stroke in a masterly fashion trying to stir up Bronius's jealousy. It sure worked.

Bronius his heart aching went home and left for work after lunch, even though he did not have to leave so early.

A week and a half passed by after the hapless All Saints' Day evening. During that period of time, he had not seen Ema. In the beginning, their classes did not concur for about three days. Later, he himself would delay to leave a lecture room after his classes had been over, since he no longer wished seeing Ema together with Alfa. Their radiating with joy faces drove him insane.

However, Bronius had no idea how badly mistaken he had been. In reality, Ema had stopped seeing Alfa, too. In fact, she even had not gone to the movie with him after all. On the way to the cinema, she had found a good reason to refuse watching a movie. It had not been difficult for her to do so, since Alfa had said earlier that he did not like foreign movies. Therefore, she'd used this as an excuse. Even though Alfa had tried to remedy the situation by telling her that he was ready to watch any film with her, Ema did not submit to him.

One beautiful day, the sun shining brightly, Adomaitis was walking along a slope of Gediminas Hill after his classes at the university. He liked sitting on a bench in one cozy place in the park there.

This time too, he sat down on the same bench. For a while, Bronius, his head up, was gazing through bare treetops at the clear, blue autumn sky. He was overwhelmed with tender longing while thinking of his home country. He also remembered when he and Ema used to sit on the same bench in this park. How happy they had been then. They had cherished most beautiful hopes for the future.

Nevertheless, his wonderful memories were suddenly disturbed by a single thought about the Soviet blackmailer who had seemingly come from nowhere, had abruptly intruded into his life, and with one stroke had ruined his love and his bright future.

Immersed in his pain, he was sitting on the bench. Not far away, a few noisy children were playing pranks, and a couple of pigeons were walking right next to his feet looking for some crumbs to peck on. The birds, time from time, kept turning their little heads sideways and looking at him with their tiny, round eyes. Apparently, the birdies were waiting when, at last, this stagnant person on the bench would come to life and strew some food to them.

However, Bronius was not paying any attention to anything that was going on around him. He had not moved even when Ema walked up to him.

Frightened pigeons loudly rose into the air and flied away. He noticed her only when she sat down next to him on the bench.

"Ema..." surprised Bronius uttered the name that had been so precious to him. "How did you end up here?"

"What do you care? I made a date here," agitated girl lied in a quivering voice.

"Ema, but what about me?.. You don't love me anymore? And I'd believed your every word..."

"Was it the real love? You better, Bronius, leave... Alfa can show up any minute now."

For some reason, Ema burst out laughing. Her laugh, Bronius, however, found to be fake and even painful as if she had forced herself to laugh.

Bronius could not believe this was the same Ema, and that this sarcastic laugh was coming out of her beautiful mouth that he had kissed passionately not so long ago.

Not being able to bear the humiliation, he got up with difficulty like some old man under a burden of the hundred years and walked away the direction of the Cathedral.

However, he did not get very far, since Ema again shot up right in front of him. She blocked his way. Now, she was standing and looking straight into his eyes. She did not step aside. Bronius saw that her eyes had been filled with tears. In a minute, they started rolling down her pale cheeks.

"Bronius, wait. Can't you see what you are doing to me?" she said.

Bronius was standing totally lost. He could not understand what was happening, and if this wasn't some mockery of his feelings again.

"Why are you crying, Ema?" he could hardly talk.

"Because it's so difficult on me... Can we go back and sit down on the bench? Please... You wanted to tell me why you had treated me so badly at the cemetery. Remember?"

"Ema, forgive me, please. Maybe it's for the better; maybe it had been fated that we didn't get an opportunity to talk then. I'll tell you the truth - circumstances had forced me to lie to you. Now, too, I had an entire storey made up to tell you... However, at this moment, I no longer have the strength to mislead you. But I can't tell you the whole truth either..." Bronius with his thumb wiped away a wet spot right next to the outer corner of his eye and cast his gaze down on the ground.

"Bronius, the best thing is always to tell the truth. I wouldn't want you to keep any secrets from me. You already know how crazy I am about you. Maybe there still is some hope to save our love... Let's go back, sit down on our bench, and talk it over. I promise to listen to you and not reproach you with anything no matter how bitter the truth would be."

"I can't tell you the truth, Ema, and I don't want to lie to you, either."

"Bronius, you love somebody else..."

Bronius kept silent. Then, Ema all agitated asked, "Are you married?"

Not getting any answer again, she turned away from him and walked to the bench. There, she crouched on it, buried her face in her hands, and started crying bitterly.

There were no passers-by. Therefore, nobody could see the love drama taking place. Bronius walked up to Ema and sat down on the bench next to her. For a few minutes, he was sitting quietly and waiting until she calmed down a little bit so that he could explain the situation.

However, Ema uttered first, "Bronius, why did you do this to me? Why did you let me fall in love with you? What's going to happen now? Oh God, how unfortunate I am!"

"Ema, calm down and listen to me carefully. I will try to do my best to cast new light on this problem."

"You frighten me. However, I should listen to you, even if I really don't care anymore... my life has been shattered into pieces, and I would not be able to put it back together."

"Ema, believe me, you are tormenting yourself for no purpose. I am not married, and I have not loved any other girl, except you. Whatever happened on the All Saints' Day has nothing to do with you, either. I didn't want to lie to you. It just had happened that I had become tangled up in the web of some political intrigues. Now, I even don't know when I would be able to free myself of it and, in general, if I would even be able to get out of it alive... Please don't ask me any questions about that. The time should come when I would be able to tell you everything myself. However, for now, we have to forget about this subject, and let's not touch this matter anymore. It is dangerous to discuss that. We can't blow against the wind... Every imprudently uttered word could ruin not only my life, but it could also cause problems to you and your family. Simply put, we can't discuss this subject. Do you understand?"

"I understand, and I'm very happy to hear that you still love me. I had begun to think all kinds of thoughts..."

Bronius and Ema were talking at the foot of the Gediminas's Hill until it started getting dark. Not having any time left to swing by his flat, Bronius went straight to work, but he was still late. Luckily for him, he had a job where he did not have to report to an immediate supervisor. The doctor who worked with him in the same office used to come and go whenever he pleased himself. Therefore, even if Bronius did not come to work at all for a day or two, nobody would probably notice that. At his work place, accidents on a big scale almost never happened. Even when some worker cut his finger or got some other minor injury, he usually managed to put a bandage on it himself, since medicine kits had been displayed in every department.

Ema settled down a little bit when she had learned about Bronius's situation. Now, she knew that she could trust him and there would be no surprises. However, she was still worried about him, only this time, for another reason. Now, she took it to heart every time he broke a date. She was worried that something bad might had happened to him.

She could not understand how he had managed to get involved in some political affairs, but after their conversation in the park, she did not dare asking any more questions about it, either. When Ema could not handle uncertainty, however, she called Bronius on the phone at work. Upon hearing his voice on the other end of the receiver, she always became happy knowing that he was safe.

One day, when Bronius did not show up at their designated place in the park, Ema called him at work again. This time, he only excused himself and told her he could not talk. She was fretting all evening long, and only the next day at the university, Bronius told her they had had an accident at his work.

Knowing the situation, calmed Ema a little bit, but she still upbraided Bronius for frightening her. Bronius realized that Ema, after finding out about his circumstances, was very sensitive to every little thing that could affect him. Therefore, he tried hard to keep her at peace by making her less aware of his meetings with the Russian agent.

Living in uncertainty and tension, the winter and spring passed by, and came the beautiful summer. Bronius decided to take three months of unpaid vacation and spend it in his homeland again, even though he did not want to part with Ema. He figured that it would serve him as an escape from his new dreadful duties that Russian authorities had forced on him. If not for that, he would had never taken such long time off work. Tired of constant meetings with the agent, who had dared to call him even at his work, Bronius finally decided to leave the city for a while.

Ema also assented to his determination. She was even glad to know that now, at last, he would be able to take a break from those problems shrouded in secret. She also knew that she won't have to distress over him, since he would be staying in the safe place.

After coming to his mother's homestead, Bronius missed Ema a lot, but at the same time, he felt huge relief because he no longer needed to go to the meetings with the Russian officer twice per week.

This year, he no longer had to help his mother with the harvest since she had already been working at the collective farm. Russians took away their land, just what they had done to other local farmers. Therefore, the mother had been left with sixty ares of land only. There was nothing to do in such a tiny plot of land.

Therefore, Bronius had been spending his time in the country half way loafing around. Only in the early mornings and late evenings, he often sat with his fishing rod at the riverside.

During heat of the midday, he liked to take a nap. Having so much time, Bronius had been intensely working on the chronicle that his grandfather had started writing almost one hundred years ago. In addition, he set himself a task to finish writing his story, which he had given up due to all his problems while living in the city. Thus, setting his daily schedule to work on his goals, he had been quite productively spending his time out in the country.

Sometimes, he felt a little bored being alone in the house. He remembered when this house used to be full of sounds, smells, and life since there had been more people living in it. Now, it appeared to be dead with just him alone left there.

The mother worked at the collective farm, and she had only one day off per week on Sundays. She had not hired a cowboy to help her with the animals. Almost all their livestock had been taken away along with their land. Therefore, the shepherd was no longer needed.

Bronius's grandmother had already been so weak that she was no longer able to get out of bed. She could barely recognize people anymore, and her life had been going out right in front of his and the mother's eyes.

Bronius had difficulty watching her growing weaker every day. The mother had never notified Bronius that grandmother's days on this earth had been almost over, and it was unexpected to him seeing her in this condition.

Bronius would often sit down on a chair next to her bed and sit there for a while. He looked at her eyes that had become almost colorless over the decades of her life. His heart was aching every time he saw her idle stare directed at the ceiling.

The other times, when Bronius came to her bed, Grannies eyes were closed. Only her chest kept intermittently moving up and down. Then, he looked at her long and attentively trying to convince himself that she was still alive.

During the last few days, the mother was coming out of the field a couple times per day to check on Grandma at home.

This time sitting next to her, Bronius noticed the old woman open her eyes. She stretched out her entire body as if she was trying to get comfortable in bed. Such an unexpected and sudden movement frightened Bronius. In a few minutes, he heard some strange wheezing coming out of her mouth. It appeared as if she was trying to say something, but Bronius being very agitated could not understand a word.

He bent down closer to her. Grandmother again snorted out some strange sounds along with words. A few of them Bronius was able to understand. She asked, "Grandson... light up a candle..."

He could not hear well the other words. However, he right away ran to the next room, found there a little candle with a box of matches, and placed it into a candleholder. Then he lit the whitish yellow candle up and showed it to the grandma. He sat the candle onto the chair that was standing by her bed.

The grandmother was lying stretched all the way on her back. She continued wheezing and saying some incomprehensible words with Bronius standing by her bed. He no longer could understand what she was saying. Bronius only noticed that her hand that was laying by her side gave a slight stir. He lifted grandma's bony hand and placed it onto her chest, but he still was holding it in his palm. For a second, it seemed that he felt a weak squeeze, and the grandma became calm.

Her eyes widened, and the pupils disappeared under upper lids. Then, her entire body became limp. Bronius continued holding his granny's hand. Soon, he felt unpleasant cold coming out of it, and he understood that she had left to her eternal resting place. Thanks be to God, grandma was in time to say goodbye to him.

Frightened Bronius pulled his hand out of her pale hand and walked a few steps backwards. He was overwhelmed with pity mixed together with fear. For some reason, he felt like in a morgue, where he had already been a few times and even had dissected corpses.

Bronius's hands were shaking, and his entire body was trembling. He still could not comprehend what was happening to him. Collecting himself once more, he quietly walked backwards on his tiptoes out of the room as if being afraid to wake the granny up from her eternal sleep.

When Bronius found himself in the yard, he broke into run through the fields. On the way, neighbors saw him running. Bronius had not known many of them, but everybody in the village knew him. Now, they took their hats off their heads showing respect to him, the only educated person in the vicinity.

However, Bronius did not notice anybody while running out of breath straight through the fields the direction where his mother was supposed to be working. He knew where to find her.

Some locals were looking at him running his hair blowing about in the wind, and they understood at once why and where he was hastening. Everybody in the village knew that the grandmother had been very weak.

Before he even reached the place where his mother had been working, she already noticed Bronius running from far away, and she understood what had happened.

The woman dropped everything she was doing and burst into run toward Bronius. When they came close to each other, Bronius, not being able to take a breath, uttered only one word, "Grandma..."

After falling into each other's arms, they cried bitterly. For a while, neither one of them could say a word. Then, the mother tried to do her best in order to calm her son down while suppressing the pain in her own heart.

When they came home, Mother sat down onto the edge of the bed next to the grandmother. Pain stricken, she cried and cried.

Bronius for the first time in his life saw his mother crying. She had always been the person of a very strong will, but this time, grief broke her down.

It had become simply unbearable being at home after the grandmother was buried. Bronius now felt even more alone here. Before, he at least knew that in another room, in bed lay his grandma.

However, now, it appeared as if she was still in bed, but only dead. This thought gave him creeps all the time. If only his mother were at home with him, then it would definitely feel a little livelier in the house. Only on Sundays, when the mother did not have to go to work at the collective farm, Bronius diverted and felt more cheerful.

On the other days of the week, though, he kept leaving the house. Most of the time, he went by the river, and he would not return home until the mother came back from work. This way he had been spending his remaining days in the village.

His vacation was nearing to an end. The day was approaching fast when he had to go back to Vilnius, where Ema had already been impatiently waiting for him.

His last Sunday at home, Bronius brought himself to talk openly with his mother. He had been preparing himself for this conversation for a while now, and he only couldn't find a right opportunity to do that.

Bronius understood well that, now, after the grandma had passed away, the mother was left alone with a burden of the entire household on her shoulders. Therefore, he wanted to find out how she felt about her situation and what was her outlook on the future.

During their lunch he said, "Mama, I'm going back to the city very soon, and you'll remain here all alone. Will you be sad?"

"Of course, I will be sad. Before, at least, I had the grandma to talk to. My new life certainly is not going to be very pleasant. However, what can I do about that? I will just have to put up with it."

"In two years, I will have finished the university, and I will be independent. Mom, I would like to offer you moving in to live with me in the city. What do you think about that?"

"Of course, it would be nice. However, what would happen with our homestead, then? On one hand, if I sold it, then some strangers would get to enjoy our beautiful place. On the other hand, if I just left it empty, my heart would be aching, since I have been the happiest person in the entire world living here. Here, I had my beloved husband; here, I had given birth to you. I think I would remain conscience-stricken until the rest of my life if I gave away my memories to the other people or if I abandoned my property in any other way. No, Bronius, I will never bring myself to do something like that. I'll better continue staying here and looking after our property that is so dear and needed for us both. Our family had organized it nicely over the years. I don't think you yourself would want to lose our homestead forever. This home should evoke many wonderful memories to you as well. This is your birthplace, son, where you had seen daylight for the first time making me an exceedingly happy mother. Therefore, I have to preserve this place not only for myself, but also for you and your future children, my grandchildren. Therefore, sonny, don't worry about me; go back to Vilnius and finish the school. Few more years, and you will be a very educated young man who is going to make me very proud. I will be telling to everybody, "That is my son!" I think you should marry Ema. She is a very modest girl, and you both will have a nice life together. And when you have your children, I will be impatiently waiting for them to come for a visit. You could leave your kids to me for the whole summer. Then, son, I won't feel alone anymore. I think we'll never leave this place that your father had loved so much as well, and I will continue taking care of the homestead, so that we all together could enjoy it for the years to come."

"Okay, mom. I only regret you alone would torment yourself by doing all the hard work here."

"Bronius, people do not torment themselves by laboring, but rather live because of the labor. We stay alive as long as there is some kind of moving power that governs us. Work is life, and living is working..."

After having such a hearty conversation, Bronius made peace with the new situation at home and left to Vilnius feeling relieved."

At the train station in Vilnius, Ema met him again. Many nice words were said then. They both could not separate. Therefore, Bronius and Ema had to say good-bye to each other a few times.

As soon as Bronius came back to work, he was informed that the same day he had gone on vacation, some man called many times trying to find him. Finally, he gave up calling and asked the staff to convey it to Adomaitis that he must call him back as soon as he returned to work.

Bronius knew very well who that person was... He did not know what he was going to say to the Russian agent during their upcoming meeting, and he waited for it in fear. Being scared to death, he only after three days finally brought himself to call the agent.

Right away, an appointment had been set for Bronius. When they met, the agent kept questioning him about moods prevailing even in Bronius's native village. Not being able to receive from him any information, the Russian officer expressed his dissatisfaction with Bronius's inactivity.

Bronius, his teeth clenched, did not say anything; he just stood beside the agent all trembling inside. Soon after, both of them separated.

It was obvious the agent had been terribly angry with Bronius because of their numerous fruitless meetings.

The official contacted Bronius again next day and set another appointment. However, both of them did not walk in the city streets together as they used to do all the other times before.

This time, Bronius and the agent met in front of the Railroaders' Administration Office that had been located in Mindaugas Street.

Inside of the building, they stopped when they were passing a guard in the watch booth. Russian agent gave a short order to the guard, "Let this individual in."

"Major, I was asked to let you know that the meeting has been scheduled in the room seventeen," reported another man on duty standing in the same watch-box covered with big glass windows all around it.

Thus, unexpectedly, Bronius learned a military rank of his "watch-angel"... He had long felt that his agent was the military officer working for the Russian government's Secret Police Organization.

Both of them passed a long, narrow darkish corridor that had been lit up only by one dim electric light bulb. Then, they crossed a small sullen courtyard cobbled with the stones and found themselves in another similar dark corridor. Bronius followed the officer when he turned left. There was a narrow staircase in front of them that led downstairs. It was even darker here, since no light bulb at all had been fixed onto the ceiling. The scarce light was coming only from the corridor behind their backs. The steep stairs were leading into the basement. They walked down the stairs and found themselves at a door upholstered with metal.

The major knocked hard. The door did not open at once, and a person's eye appeared first in the hole placed on the upper part of it. After that, a click of the lock was heard, and the heavy door opened up making a creaking sound.

Bronius, his blood freezing out of fear, followed the major through the door. There was felt a strong smell of mould on the other side of it. The air was so stuffy and so saturated with dust down there that it even squeezed Bronius's throat every time he breathed it in.

It appeared they were in the underground corridor. Passing by a few doors located on both sides of the corridor, all three of them stopped at the last door. The man who had let them into the underground area took another key out of his pocket and turned it a couple of times in the big metal lock. The door squeaked and opened up.

Adomaitis was let the first to walk into the room that had no windows. There, to his big surprise, a big bright lamp was spreading light into every corner of the room. The room itself was about twenty square meters in size. There stood a simple table and a couple of chairs in the corner. On the table, there was nothing else but a carafe with water and an empty glass.

Bronius was ordered to sit down, and he obeyed. The Major who had been silent all this time, uttered in a stern voice, "We need to have a serious conversation."

Bronius was quiet. Frightened, he waited to see what will happen next. However, the Major did not say another word and left the room. Now, it became totally clear to Bronius that without the Major's help he would not be able to get out of this hole.

All the time anxiety was tormenting Bronius while he alone was sitting in this room not knowing what to expect. Thus, he sat for about half an hour.

When Major came back, he started his "serious conversation" with Bronius which rather resembled the interrogation. After about five minutes, a muffled scream was heard behind the thick stonewall of the room. At first, Bronius thought he just seemed to hear something.

However, soon, another strange knocking sound mixed with yelling was heard. Bronius fixed his eyes onto the wall as if trying to see through it. Then, the Major told him, "Don't worry, they are just trying to have the conversation with him…"

Bronius broke into sweat. Now, he knew for sure that all this had not been happening just in his imagination, since the shrieks behind the wall kept reiterating. In addition, they kept becoming louder and more severe. After a while, the cries ceased, but the hollow moaning could be heard instead. Soon, the Major's conversation with him was over. However, Bronius knew he would never be able to forget it.

When Bronius returned home, he noticed there was still half an hour left until his meeting with Ema. However, he felt so tired and was so frightened that he did not even go there at all.

Bronius also refused to have his meal when the auntie knocked on the door of his room. He was lying in bed and staring at the ceiling. He lay there for about an hour, and then he finally got up with difficulty.

When he went outside, there was Ema in his yard. However, he almost passed her by casting only an indifferent glance at her as if she had been some unfamiliar girl. The last meeting with the Russian agent made him totally indifferent to an outside world. Only after Ema herself started talking, he stopped.

"Bronius, have you met with those people again?"

"Be quiet, don't talk so loud," he hushed Ema and looked around startled, even though she spoke in a low voice, and there was no one around. However, it appeared to Bronius that some invisible spy could be listening to them talking.

"Ema, go home. I'm leaving for work, and I am late already."

Ema sensed some inner pain that had been tormenting him. She was frustrated not knowing how to alleviate his state. She asked, "Bronius, when are we going to meet now? Tomorrow, our lectures at the university don't coincide. Therefore, I will not be able to see you. And after tomorrow, it will be Sunday."

"I don't know. I'm not sure about that right at this minute," he answered apathetically.

"Aren't we going to meet on Sunday?"

"Forgive me, please... sweetheart, I don't feel good. Sometimes, I don't even know what's happening to me. If you only knew everything..."

"Bronius, I can only guess... Okay, I will go now. But before I leave, can you tell me when we are going to meet?"

"I don't know yet, Ema."

"Oh, my God... What has happened to you? You seem so lost."

"For God's sake, Ema, please don't talk like this. So far, I'm free. I have to go now. We can see each other on Sunday, only I don't know where we should meet. But please don't worry about me... You are my only consolation at this difficult time in my life. Forgive me please for my rudeness. Now, I have to hurry, but on Sunday, I will certainly come to your home to pick you up myself. We could go see some movie or, maybe better, some show at the theatre. We need to have some fun. Lately, I've made you suffer so much because of my sluggishness. I'm sorry..."

Bronius went to work. Ema was walking home feeling sad, but at the same time she also cheered up. She was very glad to hear that Bronius was coming to pick her up on Sunday. She figured this would be a great opportunity to introduce him to her parents. She had always wanted to do this, only such an opportunity had not come along before.

Therefore, upon coming home, she with joy announced to her mom and dad that Bronius was coming on Sunday.

How much trouble the entire family went through because of this visit! Even the mother with the father started intensely preparing for it. They re-arranged some furniture, so that the room would look more tasteful.

Finally, the long waited Sunday came. However, when Ema's father asked what time Bronius was supposed to come, she did not know what to answer.

Now, for some reason, the worst thoughts started swimming in her head. The idea even struck her mind that he might not show up at all. She began thinking he had probably promised to come and pick her up only so that he could get rid of her sooner.

There had been so many arrangements made for this meeting. However, now, it seemed as if everything could come to nothing! Just thinking about that, Ema's eyes filled with tears.

When the mother saw her nearly crying, she tried to remedy the situation. She said, "Ema, don't torment yourself. If he is a real gentleman, then he did not fuss with the empty promises. He will come."

For some reason, those words uttered by the mother offended Ema's already sensitive soul even more. She kept walking lost from one room to another. Then, the father added to her heartbreak with his rebuke, "The lunch time has already gone by, and he still hasn't showed up!"

He took out of a buffet a bottle of cognac that had been bought before the World War II. While reading the label on the bottle, the father grumbled under his nose something about Bronius not having a sense of punctuality.

Those words were cutting Ema's heart like a knife, and she yelled to the mother toiling in the kitchen, "Mom, serve daddy lunch. Bronius probably will not come soon."

"Why?! We are going to wait until he comes, and then we'll sit down at the table all together," the father stated.

"He had never said what time exactly he was going to come here. He might not come at all... That's my own fault; maybe I had understood something the wrong way. I'm to blame here for everything; don't get mad at me, please."

Not being able to handle the pain, she left the room, so that nobody could see the tears in her eyes. Being alone, she started crying. Soon, the mother came after her. She was stroking Ema's shoulders trying to soother her.

"Ema, dear, don't cry. It's not worth to get so worried if he is such a person..."

"Mother, for God's sake, stop accusing Bronius!" Ema lifted her eyes red with weeping and snapped at her mother. "He has done nothing wrong. If you only knew him, you would have different opinion about him. He has suffered so many pains in his life. His father had been arrested practically for nothing. Then, Bronius himself was unjustly expelled from the university. Even now, there are some people who constantly are looking for a reason to exclude him from school again. As if it was not enough, he has got tangled up in some political blackmail affair lately. It's way too much for one person to handle… In addition, I, too, importuned him insisting to meet with me this Sunday. He seemed so broken-hearted then… He probably agreed without even thinking. Now, that you and daddy know everything, please don't blame him for this. Most likely, I myself understood something the wrong way as far as his visit goes. I just figured we always used to meet on Sundays after lunch. You don't need to wait for him. Mom, please have lunch with dad now."

"Then maybe he will come here after lunch?"

"I doubt it. I probably just rammed it into my head without having fully understood his words."

Thus, Ema succeeded convincing both parents that Bronius most likely would not show up, and they ceased waiting for him. All three of them sat down at the dining table. At that moment, suddenly, the doorbell was heard. Father got up the first to open it. After him, Ema followed wiping her tears.

Seeing Bronius all dressed up, she loudly slapped her palms out of joy and yelled fascinated, "Bronius!"

Before father had a chance to say anything, Bronius uttered, "Good afternoon."

"Hello hello, come in, please," the father invited him.

Ema introduced Bronius to her mother and father. She was all shining with happiness, but her eyes, red with weeping, called for Bronius's attention.

"What happened? It looks as if you have been crying, or your eyes are simply red for no reason?"

"Yes, I was cleaning onions in the kitchen. The onions made my cry," lied Ema.

Bronius looked unusually handsome, not like on any other ordinary day. Ema just wanted to hug and kiss him. But especially she triumphed over his joyful demeanor today. There was not a trace of his recent melancholy and absentmindedness.

After having a second glass of liqueur and a big piece of turkey, the father started a conversation about culture and its future prospects in the capital.

"You, Bronius, are a person of a new generation. The future is in hands of the people like you. You will create a new culture. Therefore, I would like to know your opinion about the up to date cultural life in Vilnius. To tell the truth,

I personally find the contemporary art to be worthless. It seems somewhat restrained. Moreover, it feels like it's slipping away. I would even dare to say that our culture today is below the standards of what it ought to be. Lately, I have not stumbled on even one interesting book, which I would want to recommend reading to others. Or, let's take for example modern movies. Most of the time, they are penetrated with such false idealism that by the time you come home from the movie theatre, you already have forgotten the content. Similar situation is with our dramaturgy as well. After seeing some performances, you don't want to go to the playhouse anymore. In general, I've got an impression that only some Russian propaganda is happening around us. Only constant lack of confidence in people and government hovers in the air. Many people have reached the point where they spy on their own brothers and sisters so that they could only ruin each other's lives when the opportunity came along. The times have come when people don't trust each other, when everybody is afraid of everybody and is cautious of not 'letting the cat out of the bag', even though they aren't really doing anything wrong. People just try to drown each other. Practically any person can be led to perdition just because of carelessly uttered words... The times are so horrible now when the Russians are in power. Everywhere reigns despotism and hatred to one another. It is difficult to believe that those kinds of things are happening in the middle of the twentieth century when the world has achieved the greatest loftiness of the technology! Nevertheless, it seems that people keep being buried into some kind of quagmire. We have come to be afraid not only of strangers, but even of our close friends! You would think we had grown up together, we got along nicely, and now, we have to hold ourselves aloof with an invisible wall of the suspicion and mistrust. Every incautious word can ruin not only life of the person talking, but the life of his entire family as well..."

"Daddy, could you please talk about something different? Better tell us something more interesting."

"I want to have an open talk with the people I trust. I am tired of the fear and hypocrisy. At least, we don't have to be afraid of anyone at this table... Don't I have the right to express my opinion?"

Listening to Ema's father, Bronius was blushing, sweating, and trembling. Few times, he even fancied he saw himself sitting not just with this loving family; it appeared to him that there were the invisible spies hiding all around them. They were sitting in the adjacent room, in the corridor, behind the front door, and even under the table.

Ema with her mother were listening and soaking up the words being uttered by the father that were making Bronius shake inside. Blood gushed into his head. Feeling helpless, he took an involuntary deep breath and started having a fit of cough.

Ema noticed that her father's speech affected Bronius poorly. Therefore, she brought herself to turn the conversation flowing another direction.

However, the father got offended because of such his daughter's tactless behavior. Therefore, he even more zealously began expressing his outlook on the oppression and the blackmailing of the people in this new system. Ema's father said he could not see how under those circumstances Russian government could promise to transition peoples' lives into some bright Communist tomorrow. Finally, he got so agitated that his talk turned almost into an entire lecture on the subject of politics; he even started backing it up with various facts.

Bronius only politely and quietly listened to him. However, he no longer touched anything out of the abundance of the beautifully displayed hors d'oeuvres on the table. Seeing this, the hostess was not happy. She interrupted the main talker at the table, "Father, you have occupied everybody too much with your preaching. I think we should try some more food before it gets too cold."

The lunch lasted almost a couple of hours. There were a few of other topics discussed, at the table. At the end, though, everyone got up from the table in good spirits.

Soon after, Bronius cordially thanked Ema's family for the warm welcome, and they invited him to visit again.

That evening, Bronius with Ema went to the Opera House to watch the opera Eugene Onegin. After the show, he saw Ema home. Then, they lingered about an hour talking.

When he came back to his flat, it was already after midnight. However, even then, he did not get asleep right away. He remembered the past evening with all its details. Bronius did not want to think about tomorrow's day awaiting him.

Bronius understood well that namely such people like Ema's father should interest his agent the most. Now, Bronius had no doubts whom his agent faithfully served, and he knew that he never could betray Ema or her family. With that thought, he finally got asleep.

For the rest of the week, Bronius continued meeting with his secret militia agent every day. Most of all, these meetings took place at night.

Sometimes Bronius and the agent walked along the streets of the city for a few hours straight and observed passersby, or they sat at some restaurant having a big glass of beer each. The other times, they dropped in at an administrative office or the cabined of the Director feeling themselves like at home. Guards neither asked the two men what they needed there in the middle of the night nor stopping to search them. Often Bronius with the agent just observed through the window of the office what was happening outside. Bronius used to come home after midnight feeling completely drained and out of strength. Being immensely tired, he used to fall on bed with all his clothes and sleep like a log.

Soon, he started performing poorly ant the university, since he had never had enough time to do his homework. He abandoned everything that had been so important and dear to him, and there was nobody to complain to about it, either. He could not mention anything about his personal life to the Major who only needed the information about the attitudes and the opinions of the students and the other countrymen of Bronius. He figured the Major would probably love it if Bronius delivered the required information in the darkest colors possible. However, he did not get out of Bronius anything worthy neither about his school friends nor about any other people.

At last, the agent himself got tired of the fruitless meetings with Bronius. One day, unexpectedly, Bronius was entrusted to be under wardship of another agent. The new agent was a head of human relations' department of one of the city ministries'. The official also kept meeting with Bronius for a period of a couple of months, and he, too, passed Bronius on to one more official who also was unable to wring the required information out of Bronius.

Spring was approaching. Exhausted from meeting with different agents and lost his hope to make any progress at school, Bronius had been walking with his head down, feeling depressed and sad. He even made himself to believe his studies had been coming to an end, because there was no way he could pass his exams. Even during those rare occasions when he had a little free time to prepare his homework, he still could not concentrate on doing it.

Bronius began suffering from nerves. Sometimes he even acted like an ailing person. He became scared of people, and it seemed to him that others were after him. He was overwhelmed with paranoia that someone could find out about his vile employment at the Russian Peoples' Commissariat for Internal Affairs.

Bronius, shrunk to himself, suffered and delayed revealing his problems that seemed to weigh on him harder and harder every day. He was afraid to tell the unvarnished truth to Ema whose family so strongly opposed the new government system. Bronius with fear waited for his exams at the university, also, having lost all hope to pass them.

Soon, unexpectedly, he found a summons in his mailbox. Adomaitis instantly remembered the time when, two years ago, he had also received the summons ordering him to come in and see his agent. This time, too, his heart was struck with fear.

He opened the envelope with the trembling hands. It was again another order to come to the Military Commissariat on a certain day and time. Bronius had been so badly overworked with endless tension and stress, that he almost stopped caring about his own destiny.

When he came to the Commissariat at the indicated time, the officer on duty sitting in the watch-box in the front hall of the building got in touch with somebody by phone. He informed Bronius that he had to go to the office of the Commissar himself.

There, he again met his very first agent. The Major looking at Bronius with his sharp eagle eyes, made his heart tremble again.

The Military Commissar whom Bronius had known only by sight was sitting at the big table with the Major standing next to him. This time, too, the Major approached this matter without any further formalities.

For a while, Bronius was listening to his rebukes. Then, the Military Commissar announced that he was being relieved from his duties. This time, too, the Major dictated to Bronius what to write in the statement, after what he had to sign it along with another document promising to keep his service at the Russian Military Commissariat confidential.

For the first time during the past two years of nothing but mental suffering Bronius felt finally free! He returned home and went to sleep. For the first time in last few weeks he had a peaceful sleep. He slept long and almost missed his time to go to work.

It turned out that, finally, after this long-lasing and strenuous battle, Bronius came out a conqueror. This fight had required of him much energy and willpower. Even though he had experienced enormous amount of stress and many losses in his personal life, he managed to free himself!

Now, he was overjoyed! Life, for a while, turned into a true celebration, and his heart had been singing out of happiness. He, also, had hope to put back on track his studies at the university, especially because exams had been approaching.

Bronius studied day and night with all his might. He devoted all his spare time just for that. Therefore, he spent every free minute reading the schoolbooks and notes of the lessons trying to derive from there so needed knowledge. He no longer had time to meet with Ema, but she herself had been intensely preparing for her exams, too.

They saw each other only on the way home from their lectures. Also, they went to see movies a couple of times on Sunday. However, they did not spend much time talking afterwards as they had been doing before.

After studying long and hard, Bronius managed to stay at the university, even though he did not reach a level of knowledge that he had desired to attain. He still was satisfied with his situation at school, however, because he managed to pass the exams which enabled him to roll over to his forth course. Bronius considered it to be a huge achievement.

It was obvious to him that the blackmail, which he had been put through for the last two years, almost killed his studies together with his dreams for the future.

Bronius rejoiced at being able to pass his exams. Now, the time came for an honestly earned vacation. He waited after the school year was over and then longer, since he did not want to separate with Ema. However, she was the first to leave to Palanga resort to spend a big part of her summer vacation by the Baltic Sea. Left alone, he decided it was right time to visit his mother.

When having his vacation in the homeland, Bronius kept regularly receiving letters from Ema once a week. She wrote how lively and pleasantly she had been spending time in Palanga.

Bronius had never seen the sea. In spite of that, he was very happy for Ema because she was having such a great time there.

However, he also had a good time out in the country. The only thing he missed was Ema. He was entirely separated from people, but in a way he had better living conditions at his mother's than Ema had in the resort town. One of the best things the country life had to offer was an opportunity to eat healthy. Bronius consumed fresh eggs and drank milk right from under a cow every single day. His mother had accumulated a lot of grains and meat during the past few years living on the farm. One could say, there was no lack of anything in their homestead but the "bird's milk".

Ema spent an entire month in Palanga and came home with a beautiful suntan. During that time, Bronius still had been enjoying the nature of his homeland and was not planning to go back to the city, even though his heart had been longing to see Ema.

Up until she returned to Vilnius, he had not remembered his beloved city even once. He had wished to be with Ema in Palanga resort by the blue sea that he had not seen in his entire life. However, as soon as Bronius received Ema's letter from Vilnius, he instantly began to feel longing for uproar of the capital.

Bronius was tired of waiting to be with Ema, but he decided to stay at his mother's for one more month. He could not make up his mind to leave his mother just yet. She, had been left alone in the homestead, lived only because of him, cherishing most beautiful hopes about his future.

While staying at his homeland, Bronius did not idle but planned his daily regime and diligently stuck to it. He liked getting up early in the morning and going fishing. After breakfast, he usually returned to the riverside where he sunbathed and, at the same time, kept writing a new story that he had started during this vacation. Most of his time he spent working on the book since there was no need to do any work in the fields.

Thus, his book kept getting thicker and thicker with each week. During midday heat, he used to take about two hours nap at the storeroom in order to make up for the time of sleep that he had cut short early in the morning. In the evenings, sun already going down, he went swimming in the river which served him as his biggest treat. He always had difficulty getting out of the warm water.

Bronius had promised his mother to stay with her for two months, and he kept his word. At the end of his stay, Mother was happy to see him off back to Vilnius well rested, in excellent health, and in good spirits.

When Bronius returned to Vilnius, he no longer had a chance to go fishing. However, he still was glad to be able to live in the city that he loved so much. Here, he also did his best trying to spend his time meaningfully. He and Ema often went to Verkiai Park by a steamboat on the Neris River. They would stay half of a day in this magnificent park. The two of them also visited Trakai resort town, where they admired the scenery there to their hearts' content. Bronius told Ema history about this part of the country. She was fascinated to learn that Trakai had been the first capital of Lithuania five hundred years ago, when Lithuania had been the biggest country of Europe. Of course, they visited Trakai Castle – the residence of the Duke of the Land Vytautas the Great during those days of glory. Every time after a trip like that, both Bronius and Ema returned home happy and full of great impressions. Again, they had difficulty parting with each other like in good old days.

However, those happy times soon ended, since Bronius started working two weeks earlier before the school year was starting. He could see Ema less, since he had to work late shifts all the time. Now, they had only Sundays when they could go to the movies.

Bronius and Ema especially enjoyed walking in Bernardinai Park that had been cleaned nicely after the World War II. When Russians came into power, the park's name was changed to the Garden of Youth. The name seemed felicitous enough, since the park had been frequently visited by the youth of the city.

Thus, carefree and happy, both of them were spending their leisure until one ill-fated day, right before the school year was starting. Working his evening shift, Bronius as usually had little to do at the office. Therefore, he started reading his book of medical science. The information had helped him not only to pass the exams, but it also had been very useful at his work. He needed all the knowledge he could get in case if some industrial trauma happened or somebody got hurt.

A secretary came into the dispensary and informed Bronius that he had to go to the Director's office. Not foreboding anything bad, Bronius went to see him. Before entering his cabinet, he stopped and listened at the tall, fancy door. Just like in the corridor, so as behind the door, silence reigned.

Bronius thought that Director most likely was alone in his office reading some documents.

He composed himself and rather loudly knocked on the door. Right away, he heard hollow, barely audible voice, "Come in."

Having no worries, Bronius opened the door widely and instantly got rooted to the spot. A Commissar of the Militia, his previous secret agent, was sitting behind the Director's writing- table!

Thoughts started swimming fast in Bronius's head. His astonishment in a flash grew into fear. At the same time, he was so confused that he even forgot to greet the man.

However, the Commissar saved Bronius from this puzzled situation by greeting him first. Then, he rather politely inquired after his health and, as usually, he got straight down to business. He wanted to know how Bronius spent his vacation, whom he met in the country, and what they talked about. The most he was interested in, though, was moods of the people there, namely, what was the folks' outlook on the entire Soviet system. Just like the times before, getting nothing for his pains, unhappy officer separated with Bronius. This time, however, he didn't even set a date for their next meeting.

After this unexpected meeting with the Major, Bronius became overwhelmed with uncertainty. Again, constant anxiety began to haunt him threatening that Russian Secret Militia would try to blackmail him anew.

Just now, a thought suddenly struck Bronius's mind what kind of secret document at the dictation of the officer he had signed the last time. According to that document, he had been prohibited to disclose Russian government's espionage of common Lithuanian people, and the officer had mentioned about Bronius's dismissal from the spy's duties only by his mere words.

Even though the secret agent had not been trying to contact him for quite a while, Bronius was still worried. In fact, he had buried all his hope that he would ever be left in peace.

Therefore, every time someone telephoned Bronius at work or he was called to come to Director's office, the first thought that came to his mind was always the same… this must be again the blackmailer.

Bronius had finished Vilnius university, but he still hadn't received a single call from the agent. Another good thing was that Ema had been free from Alfa, since he had long been done with his studies. Therefore, she no longer had to fear his continuous propaganda and pressure to join the Komsomol. Now, Bronius and Ema were able to openly date each other.

Years kept passing by, but the secret agent had vanished into thin air. Bad memories, however, remained. Bronius in no way could wipe them out of his mind.

He started working as a surgeon at the hospital in Vilnius. Bronius continued perfecting himself further in medical field by going to various seminars and on numerous business trips to far away cities, such as Moscow and Leningrad.

During his free time from work, Bronius proceeded with writing the chronicle that his grandfather had started decades ago. Moreover, he had already written a few of his own novels and a collection of stories.

His mother and other people in the village had somewhat got used to the system of the collective farms. Wounds of the dreadful regime started healing.

Only scars remained in Bronius's sensitive soul, and vague pain as if through the fog flashed in his memory from time to time.

A decade of time passed, and all his efforts paid off over the full measure. Bronius Adomaitis had become a well-known surgeon in Lithuania. He had been commissioned to practice complex operations at the Antakalnis Hospital. Patients considered it an honor to be treated in his department. With no hesitation, they lay down on his operating table.

Unexpectedly, in one of the wards of the department led by the Doctor B. Adomaitis, his former secret agent ended up waiting for a treatment. Bronius got suddenly flooded with unpleasant memories that had been almost completely sunk into the past. Now, he remembered when his entire future had rested with this man. Both Bronius and the ex-agent had been aware of this. Today, however, it seemed as if all this suddenly changed head over heels. Now, the future of the agent seemed to be in the hands of Bronius.

Doctor Bronius Adomaitis thoroughly examined the Major and scanned through results of his various tests. Then, he reluctantly approached the feeble body of the Major lying in bed. He looked so different now - old, pale, and thin.

Bronius accosted him, "I don't understand why you have chosen namely me for the operation. Years ago, my future had been at your mercy; today, you entrusted your life to my care... I think it might be better if some other surgeon operated on you. We have quite a few good surgeons in our hospital. They can perform the operation just as good. However, maybe you didn't know I was the same person whom you had made to sign the agreement to work for you many years ago? Then, you still have some time to change your decision... You have right to choose another doctor and, thus, give your fate into the other hands."

"Doctor Adomaitis, this is not a coincidence. I have chosen you myself to be my doctor... You are a popular surgeon not only in this clinic but in the entire country of Lithuania as well. I have observed the growth of your career for a few years now. Yes, I trust you will do the right thing! I have no doubt you have remained the same stubborn... and decent person. Therefore, I believe you'll follow principles of humanism and not seek revenge..."

"That is my calling and my duty as a citizen to cure people. Therefore, settling the score with anybody is out of the question... I try to do my best for all my patients and not disappoint their hopes. Don't bother yourself thinking

Violeta Treciokaite "Blackmail"

about what had happened in the past. At this time, you can't afford to waste your strength. Save it for healing…"

The meeting with the ex-secret agent made Adomaitis to remember his past, and gloomy thoughts oppressed him for a while.

Another year passed, and one more familiar to Bronius person came to hospital seeking his help. This time, it was the Director. Bronius had worked under his supervision while still studying at Vilnius University.

The man also needed an urgent operation. This time, however, Adomaitis's memories about the past were different. Bronius could not remember anything other but pleasant things in relation to him, since this man had done so much good for Bronius.

Doctor Adomaitis was amazed how life sometimes could play tricks by bringing the people from the past together with the old memories. Who would had thought that two pivotal people in Bronius's life, who had had tremendous impact on his future as well as on development of his character, would surface again after so many years?

Continuous caring of Bronius Adomaitis contributed to snatching both men out of clutches of death and putting them into hands of life…

Success accompanied Bronius not only at work, but in his personal life as well. Every evening, Ema with three children waited for him to come home. The oldest one, Edvardas, was already sixteen. He got his name in honor of his grandfather, Bronius's father. For his daughter, Bronius picked a name himself, and Ema insisted on choosing the name for their youngest child, their newborn son.

For this child, Ema's mother and father spent long time trying to help select the name. They even had a few arguments over it and, only after the long debates between Ema and her parents, everybody arrived at a unified conclusion.

Ema was not mad at her husband for holding himself apart this time and letting Ema decide what should be their little one's name.

Bronius only made a helpless gesture with his hands and said, "Ema, the name of a person is not the most important thing in life… The character is… Therefore, I'm not too worried about what first name our son is going to have. To live is not to have, but to be… Our son will be a member of a new generation. The future is in hands of citizens of the new generation! Whether this country turns out to be happy or full of fear and destruction is up to them…"

Life in Lithuania during Stalin's era

This is a historical romance novel depicting life in Lithuania after World War II. During those years, NKVD (People's Commissariat of Internal Affairs) helped implement Stalin's plans to forcibly collectivize agriculture and deport wealthy peasants. The NKVD oversaw all aspects of internal and state security. It controlled the police, criminal investigation departments, internal troops, and prison guards.

As World War II wound down, the NKVD quickly moved into territory captured by the Red Army and set up operations. They appropriated the former Nazi concentration camp, just outside the ancient German city of Weimar. The camp had been liberated by the U.S. Army in April 1945. The NKVD renamed it Soviet Special Camp Number Two and began using it to imprison former Nazi functionaries and others the Soviets wanted to get out of the way. An estimated 7,000 people died under the Soviet administration of the camp before it was finally closed in 1950.

"Everything around you was injustice, not only in the camp but around the camp. Everywhere where there were Russians, there was injustice, so it was just a matter of trying to survive to get this thing over with. And then as I came out immediately with the American authorities I said I've got a lot to report," said John Noble, American imprisoned by the NKVD in Soviet Special Camp Number Two. Never charged with a crime, he was released in 1955 after serving nine years in Soviet detention.

As the Cold War began, secret police agents helped the Soviet Union strengthen its grip on Eastern Europe by working with local Communists to align each nation with Soviet ideals. The nations forged close economic ties with the USSR and underwent social upheaval in an attempt to emulate the Soviet Union. Communist parties in the countries quickly worked to indoctrinate their populations and, with the help of Soviet security forces, used show trials, arrests, and torture to quell adversity. Soviet military and security forces managed to subdue the nations' populaces, although anger and hostility toward the new political regimes remained rampant.

You can also order this book at the address:

Jurate Somerville
224304 E 421 PR SE
Kennewick, WA 99337
(509) 582-6403
Eagleview1@live.com

Cover page is created by using an image at http://freebigpictures.com

Printed in the United States of America

ISBN: 978-0-692-02097-5
Library of Congress Control Number :   2014933713

Violeta Treciokaite "Blackmail"

www.ingramcontent.com/pod-product-compliance
Lightning Source LLC
LaVergne TN
LVHW011321080426
835513LV00006B/142